Oxf

Shakespeare's

OXFORD SHAKESPEARE TOPICS

Published and Forthcoming Titles Include:

Oxford Shakespeare Topics

GENERAL EDITORS: PETER HOLLAND AND STANLEY WELLS

Shakespeare's Reading

ROBERT S. MIOLA

OXFORD

UNIVERSITY PRESS

OXFORD
UNIVERSITY PRESS

Great Clarendon Street, Oxford OX2 6DP
Oxford University Press is a department of the University of Oxford.
It furthers the University's objective of excellence in research, scholarship,
and education by publishing worldwide in

Oxford New York

Athens Auckland Bangkok Bogotá Buenos Aires Calcutta
Cape Town Chennai Dar es Salaam Delhi Florence Hong Kong Istanbul
Karachi Kuala Lumpur Madrid Melbourne Mexico City Mumbai
Nairobi Paris São Paulo Singapore Taipei Tokyo Toronto Warsaw

and associated companies in Berlin Ibadan

Oxford is a registered trade mark of Oxford University Press
in the UK and certain other countries

Published in the United States
by Oxford University Press Inc., New York

British Library Cataloguing in Publication Data

Data available

Library of Congress Cataloging in Publication Data

Miola, Robert S.
  Shakespeare's reading/Robert S. Miola.
    p. cm.
  Includes bibliographical references (p.) and index.
  1. Shakespeare, William, 1564–1616—Books and reading. 2. Books and reading—England—
History—16th century. 3. Books and reading—England—History—17th century. 1. Title
PR3069.B6 M56 2000 822'.3'3—dc21 00–024417
ISBN 0–19–871168–9
ISBN 0–19–871169–7 (pbk.)

10 9 8 7 6 5 4 3 2 1

Typeset by Kolam Information Services Pvt Ltd, Pondicherry, India
Printed in Great Britain
on acid-free paper by
Biddles Ltd,
Guildford and King's Lynn

For Karen, 'pattern of all those'

Acknowledgements

Peter Holland and Stanley Wells invited this contribution to the Oxford Shakespeare Topics series and read the entire manuscript promptly, carefully, and helpfully. The National Endowment for the Humanities and the Folger Shakespeare Library provided an opportunity to formulate ideas in a lively summer seminar, 'Habits of Reading in Early Modern England', 1997. In 1998 Michele Marrapodi arranged for my lectures on the material at the University of Palermo, where the faculty and students were gracious and stimulating. As ever, colleagues at the Shakespeare Association of America meeting and at the biennial International Shakespeare Conference talked and listened instructively. Laurie Maguire and Alexander Leggatt suggested improvements minor and major to individual chapters. Two representatives of the intended audience, Daniel Miola (Villanova Univ.) and Christine Miola (Columbia Univ.), read sections critically to note unclarities and test style. The Center for the Humanities at Loyola College, Dean John Hollwitz, the students, my daughters Rachel and Rose, members of the Ricciardi family, the Fuoco family, and the Club del Fratino, provided other kinds of professional and personal support. Karen Sams consoled and inspired. I am grateful to these institutions, scholars, readers, and friends.

Contents

Illustrations

All illustrations are reprinted by permission of the Folger Shakespeare Library.

Note on Texts and Abbreviations

All references to Shakespeare are to *The Complete Works*, ed. Stanley Wells, Gary Taylor, *et al.* (Oxford: Clarendon Press, 1986) and to their accompanying *William Shakespeare: A Textual Companion* (Oxford: Clarendon Press, 1987). I have referred to sources as conveniently reprinted in the collection of Geoffrey Bullough (ed.), *Narrative and Dramatic Sources of Shakespeare*, 8 vols. (London: Routledge & Kegan Paul, 1957–75) (abbreviated as Bullough); and to early critics and editors of Shakespeare in the collection of Brian Vickers (ed.), *Shakespeare: The Critical Heritage*, 6 vols. (London: Routledge & Kegan Paul, 1974–81) (abbreviated as Vickers). Throughout I have silently modernized the spelling and punctuation of quoted texts.

Elizabethan Reading

The temptation has proven irresistible: people have always imagined that Shakespeare's poetry and drama arose not from his reading but from his life. The sonnets, accordingly, recount actual passions and aspirations; the tragedies reflect some personal catastrophe, perhaps the death of Shakespeare's only son Hamnet in 1596 at the age of 11. This desire to see the life behind the art motivates the recent film, *Shakespeare in Love*, wherein Gwyneth Paltrow's captivating Viola de Lesseps inspires the smitten poet to write *Romeo and Juliet*, and then, as she sails out of his life, *Twelfth Night*. Revealing more about their inventors and audiences than about Shakespeare, such delightful fantasies have no basis in fact.[1] No record of Shakespeare's affections survives except, presumably, those pertaining to his wife Anne Hathaway (the issue of a marriage licence and the will) and to his patron, the Earl of Southampton (dedications to several poems). We can only guess at his grief over the death of Hamnet, apparently named for a Stratford neighbour and baker, by the way, not the legendary Danish prince. Shakespeare's personal life, unfortunately, remains largely lost in the 'dark backward and abyss of time' (*The Tempest*, 1. 2. 50).

The surviving work itself, however, gives more reliable witness to its genesis and origins. Shakespeare created much of his art from his reading. At first, the idea of Shakespeare as reader may shock and disturb. We prefer to romanticize him as the 'Bard', i.e. a divinely inspired singer, or as a natural genius, 'Fancy's child' warbling 'native wood-notes wild' (John Milton, *L'Allegro*, 133–4). Such myths only obscure the reality of Shakespeare's work and achievement. To fashion his poems and plays Shakespeare read all sorts of books—classics like

Plutarch's *Lives*, Vergil's *Aeneid*, and Ovid's *Metamorphoses*, medieval works like Geoffrey Chaucer's *The Canterbury Tales* and John Gower's *Confessio Amantis*, histories like Raphael Holinshed's *Chronicles*, Italian and English prose romances, miscellaneous poems, and plays. G. B. Shaw wryly praised Shakespeare's 'gift of telling a story (provided someone else told it to him first)'.[2] He freely borrowed characters, plots, and ideas from other writers and just as freely ignored or contradicted them when it suited. He often used several sources simultaneously, collecting varying accounts of a character or incident. Heirs to later ideas about originality, modern readers sometimes confuse this creative method with plagiarism, the stealing of someone else's work. But our notion of plagiarism is foreign to Renaissance poetic theory and practice, which stressed the importance of *imitatio*, the creative imitation of others.[3] According to this theory, a poet demonstrated originality not by inventing new stories but by adapting extant, particularly classical, ones. The genius lay not in the invention but in the transformation.

Reading Practices

Like other schoolboys in Stratford-upon-Avon, young William Shakespeare learned to read in an elementary or 'petty' school.[4] There he practised on a hornbook, a leaf of paper on a wooden tablet covered with a sheet of translucent horn, which featured the alphabet, numbers, and the 'Our Father'. After acquiring the rudiments of literacy from a primer and catechism, students passed on to the grammar school, where the great Dutch scholar Erasmus and the first wave of English humanist reformers had forged for Europe a philological curriculum and a rigorous method of study.[5] Students like Shakespeare received extensive training in Latin and rhetoric. For ten or eleven years they spent the best part of six days a week reading, translating, and writing Latin, composing poems, essays, and arguments. They learned to value ancient authors—Greek and Roman—as models in the arts and sciences and also as valuable guides to practical problems.

Such training fostered certain habits of reading, thinking, and writing. Students acquired extraordinary sensitivity to language, especially to its sound. The practice of reading aloud and of reciting verse developed acute inner ears that could appreciate sonic effects which are lost on moderns. The declamatory rhetoric of Seneca's Latin, for example, thrilled Elizabethan auditors, who adopted him as their model for tragedy. Only specialists today read Senecan tragedy, silently, alone, usually in translation and out of obligation. Elizabethans appreciated sound effects such as shifts between verse forms and between verse and prose. For such attuned audiences Shakespeare gave to the witches in *Macbeth* that eerie chant in trochaic tetrameter ('Double, double, toil and trouble, | Fire burn, and cauldron bubble', 4. 1. 10–11) and to Hamlet those searching, blank-verse soliloquies. Elizabethan aural sensitivity led to delight in wordplay of all kinds, repartee, *double entendre*, puns, and quibbles. In the eighteenth century the sober and serious editor, Samuel Johnson, commented disapprovingly:

A quibble is the golden apple for which he [Shakespeare] will always turn aside from his career, or stoop from his elevation. A quibble, poor and barren as it is, gave him such delight that he was content to purchase it by the sacrifice of reason, propriety, and truth. A quibble was to him the fatal Cleopatra for which he lost the world, and was content to lose it. (Vickers, v. 68)

Today Shakespeare's quibbles, often cut in production, may seem trivial and tedious; but to contemporaries such wordplay exploited the energies of language and intellect in entertaining display.

The emphasis on memory in Elizabethan grammar schools also conditioned readers and writers. Students memorized hundreds, perhaps thousands, of Latin lines and constructions. The extensive cultivation of memory created a literary culture of quotation and allusion, wherein the classics and the Bible served as a common repository of significant reference. Niobe stood as an example of grief, Hercules as a type of courage and strength. Shylock alludes to the story of Jacob and Laban's sheep in Genesis (*Merchant of Venice*, 1. 3. 70 ff.); Hamlet, to the tale of Jephthah and his daughter in Judges (2. 2. 403 ff.).[6] Later, differently trained readers misunderstood this culture and Shakespeare's allusions. Such learning, they concluded, signalled a university education and, hence, an author for the plays other than the man from Stratford, William Shakespeare. In 1944 T. W. Baldwin demolished such arguments by demonstrating (in two thick volumes numbering 1,525 pages) that the great majority of Shakespeare's quotations, allusions, and references derive from the standard books and curriculum of an Elizabethan grammar school. Shakespeare can be inaccurate and imprecise, of course, and pernickety types, beginning in 1767 with the Cambridge don Richard Farmer, have always enjoyed pouncing on his errors of recollection.[7] But the Elizabethan exercise of memory added depth and scope to writing and enabled readers to perceive significant connections with the past.

A reading practice centred on memorization naturally fostered the impulse to collect. Readers routinely kept commonplace books into which they copied striking thoughts or expressions.[8] Erasmus gathered proverbs and wrote voluminous commentary. Enterprising authors like William Baldwin published *sententiae*, or 'wise sayings'; his popular *Treatise of Moral Philosophy* arranged snippets from Plato, Aristotle, Plutarch, Seneca, and other ancients under rubrics like 'Of Patience', 'Of Gluttony', and 'Of Death Not to be Feared'. Some picked fruits, others picked flowers. Octavianus Mirandula displayed poetical posies from various Latin authors in his 1566 collection, *Illustrium poetarum flores* ('Flowers of the famous poets'). Writers such as Thomas North, William Painter, and George Pettie served up in English anthologies hundreds of classical and contemporary stories. Nobody seemed to mind much the fragmentation, the wrenching of text out of context. Like readers today who surf the internet, clicking on hot links, superimposing image on image, Elizabethans moved rapidly, eclectically, and associatively from text to text looking for connections, following impulses, working and playing. Their reading machine was not the computer but the 'reading wheel', an upright mini-ferris wheel with books arranged on consecutive stations to enable simultaneous, synchronic reading and search operations [Fig. 1]. The contraption could not have enjoyed wide use but, nevertheless, stands as a metaphor for a kind of reading that subsists on the cross-reference. Editions of classical authors routinely glossed passages with citations of parallels from other works. Elizabethan readers generally valued abundance, or *copia*, over accuracy, individual texts and pieces of texts over contexts, multiplicity over coherence. They read analogically, i.e. across texts, as well as logically.

The impulse to read analogically and collect parallels everywhere shows itself in Shakespeare's work. Menenius' fable of the belly in *Coriolanus* (1. 1. 94 ff.), for example, draws from five separate accounts —those of Plutarch, Livy, Sidney, Camden, and Averell. Jaques' tale of

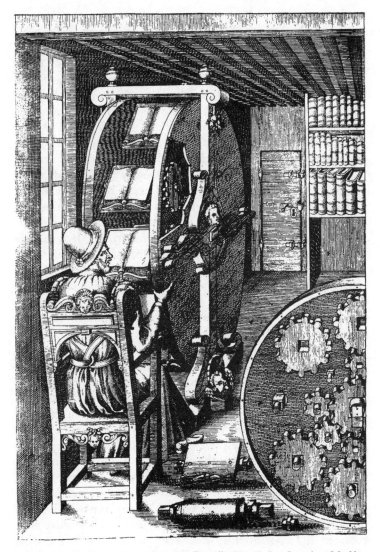

1. The Reading Wheel, from Agostino Ramelli, *The Various Ingenious Machines* (1588), 317. The machine, enabling the consultation of many books simultaneously, suggests the kind of associative and eclectic reading the Elizabethans regularly enjoyed.

man's seven ages in *As You Like It* (2. 7. 139–66) likewise owes details to many similar schemata. As in small things, so in large. Shakespeare often gathers several competing accounts of incident and action to furnish his plots. The cannibalistic banquets of both Seneca's *Thyestes* and Ovid's *Metamorphoses* (Bk. 6) supply the horrific climax of *Titus Andronicus*, wherein a mother unwittingly eats the remains of her sons. The habit of analogical thinking, moreover, leads always to the mixing of disparate stories and texts. Shakespeare, for example, constructs *Macbeth* out of contemporary history, classical tragedy, and the medieval mystery play. Several different stories in Holinshed's *Chronicles* (1587) provide the basic plot (assassination and usurpation) and the cast of characters, Duncan, Macbeth, Lady Macbeth, Banquo, and others. Following the powerful example of Senecan protagonists, Shakespeare transforms Holinshed's Macbeth into a bloody, soliloquizing, wilful, and tormented tyrant. Like these Senecan prototypes, Macbeth urges himself to *scelus*, or 'crime'. Finally, the gigantic shadow of Herod from the mystery play further darkens the action and protagonist. Slaughterer of the innocents, Herod serves as a model for the child-killer Macbeth. Collecting parallel stories, thinking analogically across texts, Shakespeare writes plays that combine selectively the plots, characters, and power of their constituents.

Elizabethans also read actively. Grammar-school training in rhetoric required readers to find in texts arguments concerning certain actions and propositions. Students, for example, 'would be trained to find arguments for and against Brutus' act [the murder of Caesar]: there was no question of coming down simple-mindedly on one side'.[9] Mature readers often carried on a dialogue with a book in the form of marginal notations. Shakespeare's friend and fellow playwright, Ben Jonson, routinely drew asterisks or pointing hands in the margins, underlined noteworthy passages, annotated texts with cross-references and commentary, sometimes disapproving [Fig. 2]. A Cambridge professor and polemicist, Gabriel Harvey, copiously adorned his books with commentary. Though Jonson and Harvey were more educated and bookish than the average reader (and considerably crankier), such active reading characterized the period. In his survey of 7,526 Renaissance books William H. Sherman has discovered marginalia in 1,531, or 20.3 per cent, with the highest concentrations appearing in books of religious debate, law, and medicine.[10] Moreover,

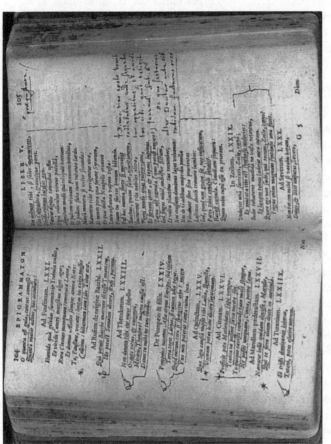

2. One of Ben Jonson's three editions of Martial, *Nova Editio*, ed. Petrus Scriverius (Leiden, 1619), 104–5. These pages, displaying Jonson's characteristic markings (his asterisks and pointing fingers) and his addition of a Latin cross-reference from Juvenal (*Satire* 6), show an active and engaged early modern reader talking back to his books.

people often read out loud and sometimes met in group sessions
for the Bible. These practices made reading a more public, social,
and participatory activity than it is today. Latin classics, the Bible,
the Book of Common Prayer, and Foxe's *Acts and Martyrs*, a sensational and popular account of Protestant martyrs, functioned as a
required core curriculum, the body of writing that constituted a shared
literary and intellectual heritage and provided common ground for
discussion.

Reading materials

A literate English citizen in the late sixteenth century could choose
among many and sundry reading materials. People in Elizabethan
England still circulated important material in manuscript. Professional copyists, called scribes or scriveners, produced an enormous
quantity of private, literary, educational, business, legal, and ecclesiastical documents written on parchment with quill. Manuscripts
appeared in various styles of handwriting, practised with the usual
idiosyncrasies and individual flourishes. Among these the secretary
and italic hands predominated. The workmanlike secretary hand, a
series of scratches and squiggles to the untrained eye, functioned as the
everyday hand of business, correspondence, and literary composition.
The graceful and sloping italic hand, imported from Italy for its
simplicity, beauty, and legibility, gradually displaced the secretary
hand at the close of the century. The surviving specimens of Shakespeare's handwriting, six autographs and a fragment from a play, *Sir
Thomas More*, appear in ordinary English secretary hand.[11]

Elizabethan readers also had at their disposal various printed materials. The advent of printing, beginning with Gutenberg's Bible, 1455,
transformed early modern culture in Europe and in England. Ballads,
or rhymed reports of newsworthy events, appeared on broadsides,
single sheets of paper. The government used broadsides for proclamations and admonitions. Chapbooks, usually no longer than twenty-
four pages, costing between one and three pence, flooded the market
with their longer cousins, pamphlets; both were cheap, topical, often
sensational. Broadsides and pamphlets reported the latest criminal
trial, natural disaster, sex scandal, travel experience, or fantastic
occurrence. Shakespeare makes several references to such ephemeral

reading materials. Threatening violence, the blustering Pistol asks rhetorically, 'Fear we broadsides?' (*2 Henry IV*, 2. 4. 179). A sharp conman, Autolycus (*The Winter's Tale*, 4. 3) hawks ballads on broadsides to gullible country bumpkins. Since many broadsides, chapbooks, and pamphlets have vanished, we can only guess at their specific importance for Shakespeare and his plays.

English readers also read books. The great Aldine press in Venice, and other Continental presses in Paris, Lyons, Antwerp, Frankfurt, and Basle, produced editions of classical texts and serious political and religious works in Latin.[12] Such books supplied the libraries of the wealthy and the learned. English presses produced some Latin works, but principally English Bibles, Books of Common Prayer, sermons and devotional books, school texts, translations, works of literature and history, and other miscellaneous materials. In 1600 some twenty-two printing houses and fifty-four licensed presses operated in London. There were also secret presses, especially Catholic ones, which published controversial or prohibited materials.

Accustomed to the size and plenitude of modern bookstores, a university student today would wonder at Elizabethan bookstalls, clustered at a few places in London, especially the yard at St Paul's cathedral. There the student would find manuscripts and printed materials, some used. Posted title-pages would advertise new merchandise. A single 'book' might exist in various forms—on unfolded or folded sheets of paper, unbound or bound. Sheets of paper folded once would produce a large folio, with pages measuring about 6 by 4 centimetres (15 by 10 inches), or a small one, 4.5 by 3 centimetres (12 by 8 inches). Sheets of paper folded twice would produce a quarto, with pages measuring approximately half the size of a large folio. The price of a text varied according to its format (folio, quarto, or smaller), state (bound or unbound), and condition of sale (wholesale or retail). An unbound quarto play requiring ten to twelve sheets (eighty to ninety pages) probably cost 5 or 6 old pence wholesale, 7 to 9 pence retail. The latter figure approximates to the average daily wage for a London journeyman of the 1580s; one penny then bought a one-pound loaf of bread. Peter Blayney has estimated that Shakespeare's First Folio, a collection of his works made in 1623 by fellow actors, probably sold wholesale, unbound for 10 shillings and retail, unbound for 15 shillings (12 pence = one shilling). Bindings varied in price according to quality and decoration; a plain calf binding for a folio cost about 3 or 4 shillings.[13]

Typing at computer screens and printing at a keystroke or mouse-click, a modern student would also marvel at the labour required to print a Renaissance book.[14] A worker called a compositor took copper letters and spaces from cases and placed them in a composing stick to spell out text, usually from manuscript, letter by letter, word by word, and line by line. When the compositor had set several pages of type (a *forme*) he locked them in an iron chase; a pressman applied a heavy, sticky ink to the letters and pressed wet paper down to form an impression. A corrector and/or author then or later read the printed sheet for errors and accidents like under- or over-inked letters. This process resulted in variation from copy to copy. Since printers sold uncorrected sheets along with corrected ones, books always differed from each other in small particulars. Sometimes the differences were large. The first issue of Shakespeare's First Folio in November 1623, for example, contained thirty-five plays; later issues of the book that year contained thirty-six plays because the editors added *Troilus and Cressida* to the collection during the print run.

Elizabethan reading materials present other surprises to the modern eye. The conventions of punctuation vary considerably from page to page and book to book. Since spelling did not become standardized until the eighteenth century and since writers and printers used abbreviations, many forms of the same word coexist. No two of the six surviving Shakespeare autographs are identical; the poet spelled his own last name in at least two different ways, 'Shakspere', and 'Shak-speare', neither of which coincides with our preferred spelling. More-over, many texts, including law books, chronicles, official documents, proclamations, jest-books, ballads, and elementary schooltexts, appear in a font called blackletter—thick, squat, and antiquarian. Though difficult for moderns to decipher, this font served the children and less-educated readers. And, finally, Elizabethans wrote, published, sold, bought, and read books in Latin, the language of educated discourse.

Renaissance books differ from modern ones, then, in format, construction, punctuation, spelling, typeface, and language. Moreover, a didactic impulse, political and moral, strongly conditions editing, writing, and reading in the period. Sermons, homilies, and devotional literature comprise a substantial portion of Elizabethan publication. Many literary and historical texts appear with polemical prefaces and notes to protect against misinterpretation and guide the reader in profitable instruction. Fulgentius, Landino, and Pontanus, for example, read Vergil allegorically, providing copious and influential commentary. Editions of the *Aeneid* routinely end with Maphaeus Vegius' conclusion, the thirteenth book that completes the hero's triumphant progress to heaven. Senecan drama, for another example, graphically illustrates the dangers of passion and the evils of tyranny, precisely according to Sidney's prescription, 'tragedy maketh kings fear to be tyrants'.[15] In the hands of Renaissance commentators even a bright and lively scene from comedy, from Plautus or Terence, illustrates any number of rhetorical devices and moral lessons. In what spirit readers took all the edifying lecturing is hard to say. Even if resisted, the sheer bulk and insistence of such commentary lent a seriousness to the act of reading and fostered sensitivity to moral issues. Alfred Harbage observed long ago that Shakespearian drama pervasively reflects moral concern: the lines of almost any page of text 'levy upon the vocabulary of ethics, or relate in some way to standards of conduct, to choices between right and wrong'.[16]

Like modern ones, Renaissance readers gathered books into collections.[17] At the beginning of the period, ecclesiastical institutions had substantial holdings in theology, law, medicine, and philosophy. When Henry VIII dissolved the monasteries and plundered church possessions (1538–9), however, most of these books passed into private and university hands. The subsequent expansion of the London book trade made available English and Continental imprints to later collectors like John Dee, John Donne, John Florio, and Ben Jonson. At the beginning of the seventeenth century Thomas Bodley undertook the restoration of the University Library at Oxford and the establishment of a new public collection, furnished with desks, bookcases, cupboards, locks, and chains. Bodley hunted after serious, i.e. Latin, books, notoriously excluding from his library such 'rife-raffe' and 'baggage' as English almanacs, proclamations, and plays. Of nearly 6,000 books in the Bodleian Library in 1605, only thirty-six were in English. Elsewhere, wealthy families built their own more eclectic collections, at first storing books in chests and trunks, and then, as the period went on, in closets (small rooms with one door) and studies. We don't know how many books a busy playwright like William Shake-speare owned or where he stored and read them. We can, however, trace some of his reading in his work.

Texts and Traditions

'The naming of cats is a difficult matter', says T. S. Eliot; so too, the naming of Shakespeare's books. Only one book with an alleged Shake-speare signature has surfaced, William Lambarde's *Archaionomia* (1568). He left us no library catalogue or probate inventory; he rarely tagged his poems and plays with revealing clues. To be sure, the Ovidian epigraph to *Venus and Adonis* steers us to the right author if not the right work; in *Titus Andronicus* Lavinia turns the pages of Ovid's *Metamorphoses*, a seminal work for that play; Mercutio mentions Petrarch, a deep presence in *Romeo and Juliet*; a character in *As You Like It* compares Duke Senior's woodland life to that of Robin Hood, thus evoking the underlying legends and folklore; Pericles brings on stage as a chorus John Gower, author of its source, *Confessio Amantis*; the Prologue to *The Two Noble Kinsmen* likewise pays tribute to Geoffrey Chaucer. But for the rest, Shakespeare's reading appears transformed in his writing; scholars scour the text for evidence, assemble patterns, draw inferences. Analysis of Shakespeare's reading has largely depended on verbal echo, on Shakespeare's repetition of words and phrases from other writers. Witness Enobarbus' description of Cleopatra:

> The barge she sat in, like a burnished throne
> Burned on the water. The poop was beaten gold;
> Purple the sails, and so perfumèd that
> The winds were love-sick with them. The oars were silver,
> Which to the tune of flutes kept stroke, and made
> The water which they beat to follow faster,
> As amorous of their strokes. For her own person,
> It beggared all description. She did lie
> In her pavilion—cloth of gold, of tissue—
> O'er-picturing that Venus where we see
> The fancy outwork nature. On each side her
> Stood pretty dimpled boys, like smiling Cupids,
> With divers-coloured fans whose wind did seem

To glow the delicate cheeks which they did cool,
And what they undid did.

(Antony and Cleopatra, 2. 2. 198–212)

Those who come upon the following description of Cleopatra's barge in Sir Thomas North's translation of Plutarch's *Lives* may well experience the thrill of discovery:

The poop [deck] whereof was of gold, the sails of purple, and the oars of silver, which kept stroke in rowing after the sound of the music of flutes, hautboys, citherns, viols, and such other instruments as they played upon in the barge. And now for the person of herself: she was laid under a pavilion of cloth of gold of tissue, apparelled and attired like the goddess Venus commonly drawn in picture; and hard by her, on either hand of her, pretty fair boys apparelled as painters do set forth god Cupid, with little fans in their hands, with the which they fanned wind upon her.   (Bullough, v. 274)

North's prose supplies Shakespeare's blank-verse magic, specifically, the gold poop, purple sails, silver oars, music, pavilion (cloth of gold of tissue), the idea of Cleopatra as Venus and the fanning boys as Cupids. Shakespeare, as ever, adapts his source: he creates an erotic fantasy in which Nature itself—the winds and the water—becomes animate and amorous; the boys' innocent fanning, both heating and cooling the queen, here suggests her paradoxical mystery: 'she makes hungry | Where most she satisfies' (2. 2. 243–4). Shakespeare's reading sometimes shows clearly in his writing. We can identify North's Plutarch as a book Shakespeare read, a book that functioned as a source for his play.

The evidence, alas, does not always prove to be so straightforward. Some plays (*Love's Labour's Lost*, *A Midsummer Night's Dream*, *The Merry Wives of Windsor*, *The Tempest*) echo no main source. Other plays, more typically, echo multiple texts simultaneously. Shakespeare fashions *King Lear*, for example, from an old play, a chronicle history, a prose romance, and numerous miscellaneous texts. Any complete list of Shakespeare's reading for any single work must always be open-ended, as readers continually hear echoes of new sources. This open-endedness suggests a fundamental problem with our critical methods: the test of verbal echo turns out to be fraught with uncertainties.[18] First, poetic passages sound variously to various ears; one scholar's echo, signalling indebtedness, is another scholar's coincidence, signifying nothing. Second, even when readers agree that two lines in Shakespeare sound like two lines, say, in Horace, they must still wonder just what the resemblance means. Did Shakespeare remember the whole text and context or just a few lines? Did he, in the age of collection, commonplace, and anthology, ever read the whole text at all? Did some intermediary recall the original and pass it on to Shakespeare? Third, even in the best of circumstances, when readers agree that a clear pattern of echoes identifies a source text, they must still be open to other influences, literary and cultural. A Shakespearian text registers always a variety of sources—other books read, Shakespeare's own previous writing, the plays of his company and rivals, contemporary literature, recent news and events. Reliance on verbal echo can obscure these rich sources and oversimplify the picture.

Beyond the uncertainties of method, the test of verbal echo has one other important limitation: it can neither recognize nor measure non-verbal evidence. Readers must use a different intuition to evaluate plot and character, for example, the organization of a revenge play like *Titus Andronicus* or *Hamlet*, or the villain as hero in Richard III (*Richard III*) and in Falstaff (*1, 2 Henry IV*). Then as now, playwrights did not write plays simply by reading books and adapting language; instead, they imitated rhetoric, image, structure, rhythm, and idea. Sometimes they took the content, sometimes the form—sometimes the wine, in other words, sometimes the bottles. And they manipulated familiar traditions, the rich and capacious treasury of dramatic resources created by writers from antiquity, the Middle Ages, and the early Renaissance. Like his fellow playwrights, Shakespeare read traditions as well as texts, shaping and reshaping them with fluency and sophistication.

Perhaps a recent cinematic example may clarify the nature of traditions. Everyone remembers the great success of Lucas' original *Star Wars*, a fantastic and innovative adventure story featuring the forces of good against the evil Empire. Fewer recognize that conventions from westerns give the space film much of its impact. The dashing, lone gunslinger becomes Hans Solo; the alien sidekick—Tonto, if you will—gets fur and a new name, Chewbacca. The great western landscape stretches to the universe; the simple homesteaders who get slaughtered live on a desolate planet; the boy who grows to manhood and revenge is reborn as Luke Skywalker. The traditional bar scene becomes spectacularly (and comically) intergalactic; fights with knives, guns, and horses turn into battles with lightswords, laser pistols, and spaceships; the comical townspeople find new life as robots. The villainous gunman, gang, or greedy landowner becomes Darth Vader (the villain always wears black) and the omnivorous Empire. Characters, scenes, and situations from westerns, creatively transformed, shape the entire film and evoke our responses. There may be no direct quotations of individual westerns in the space film, no verbal echoes of this or that dialogue, no direct imitations of any particular scene. And neither the writer nor the viewers need ever name the original films that shaped the genre—*High Noon, Shane, The Man Who Shot Liberty Valance, Gunfight at the OK Corral,* and many others—to appreciate their force in *Star Wars.* These films created traditions that have become part of a powerful cinematic vocabulary employed in countless adaptations. Later writers use this vocabulary, and later audiences respond to it, even if they are completely unfamiliar with the originating texts.

Recent scholars of Shakespeare's reading have called increasing attention to his creative use of traditions. Accordingly, this introduction to Shakespeare's reading will explore his use of both texts, the books-on-the-desk, and traditions, those inherited strategies and expectations about character and action. The discussion proceeds generically, beginning with Shakespeare's non-dramatic works, then moving through the Histories, Comedies, Tragedies, and Romances. Organizing the discussion this way, we can sample significant source texts and begin to understand Shakespeare's habits of appropriation. The aim is not a comprehensive account of any single text, tradition, or Shakespearian work, but an overview.

Shakespeare's texts range from the classical (Ovid, Plautus, Plutarch), to the medieval (Chaucer), and the contemporary (Holinshed, Fiorentino, *King Leir,* and Greene). They include poetry (Ovid, Chaucer), prose (Holinshed, Fiorentino, Greene) and drama (Plautus, *King Leir*). Shakespeare, as we shall see, reads widely and eclectically, always combining these texts with others. The principal source texts and Shakespearian works appear in Table 1 (see next page).

Table 1.   Principal source texts for Shakespeare's works.

Text	Shakespeare
	Poems:
Ovid, *Metamorphoses*	*Venus and Adonis*, Sonnets
Ovid, *Fasti*	*The Rape of Lucrece*
	Histories:
Holinshed, *Chronicles*	*Richard II, Henry V*
	Comedies:
Plautus, *Menaechmi*	*The Comedy of Errors*
Fiorentino, *Il Pecorone*	*The Merchant of Venice*
	Tragedies:
Plutarch, *Lives*	*Julius Caesar*
Anon., *King Leir*	*King Lear*
	Romances:
Greene, *Pandosto*	*The Winter's Tale*
Chaucer, *The Canterbury Tales*	*The Two Noble Kinsmen*

Table 2.   Principal traditions behind Shakespeare's works.

Tradition	Shakespeare
	Poems:
Italian Love Poetry (Petrarch)	Sonnets, *Romeo and Juliet*
	Histories:
The Vice Figure	*Richard III, 1 Henry IV*
	Comedies:
A Classical Conflict: Fathers vs. Lovers	*A Midsummer Night's Dream, All's Well That Ends Well, Othello*
	Tragedies:
Senecan Revenge	*Titus Andronicus, Hamlet*
	Romances:
The Pastoral Genre	*As You Like It, The Tempest*

The Principal traditions and Shakespearian works appear in Table 2. These traditions represent various types and modes of influence. Italian love poetry originates in the Renaissance and primarily shapes rhetoric. The Vice figure is a character who swaggers through medieval morality plays and onto Shakespeare's stages. The conflict between fathers and young lovers motivates much classical comedy and forms a flexible and popular configuration for later playwrights. The ancient dramatist Seneca provides a model for revenge action. Finally, the pastoral genre, which sings of shepherds and the simple, natural life, originates in classical poetry and develops through the centuries to encompass rhetoric, character, configuration, and action. To create his art Shakespeare read these traditions as well as specific texts.[19]

2

Poems

Early in his career Shakespeare wrote poems as well as plays. The sensual and melodic *Venus and Adonis* (1593), for example, tells of Venus' ill-fated love for Adonis, gored to death by a boar. *The Rape of Lucrece* (1594) more soberly recounts Lucrece's violation by Tarquin, her suicide, and the consequences for Rome. Shakespeare's sonnets, probably composed in the 1590s, sing of desire, love, frustration, the decaying effects of time, and the power of art.[1] All these works owe variously to an ancient Roman poet, Ovid—witty rhetorician, love poet, master of metamorphoses, the man 'for the elegancy, facility, and golden cadence of poesy', as Holofernes put it in *Love's Labour's Lost* (4. 2. 122–3). *Venus and Adonis* borrows directly from Ovid's *Metamorphoses*, an important treasury of myth and material. *The Rape of Lucrece* draws upon another poem of Ovid, the *Fasti*, a poetic celebration of the myths and feast-days in the Roman calendar. Shakespeare's sonnets owe to Ovid too, particularly the *Metamorphoses*, but derive more substantially from a later tradition—Italian love poetry. The sonnets everywhere echo the lyricism of Dante and Petrarch, mediated through countless European and English imitators and adapters. This lyricism shapes the plays also, especially the comedies and, climactically, a tragedy, *Romeo and Juliet*.

Text: Ovid's *Metamorphoses*

Ovid's *Metamorphoses*, an anthology of Greek and Roman legend, leads the reader from the creation myths up to the death and transformation of Julius Caesar into a star, and the birth of Augustus, the divine emperor. It tells of transformations strange and fantastical: human beings find themselves in extreme peril or passion and magically get changed into animals, insects, trees, rocks, flowers, springs, and constellations. This poem, both in the original Latin and in Arthur Golding's 1567 translation [Fig. 3] supplies Shakespeare throughout his career. The raped Lavinia uses the *Metamorphoses* as a stage prop in the early horror show, *Titus Andronicus*, which also depicts several Ovidian myths in the action—the world's four ages, and the story of Tereus, Philomel, and Procne. The rude mechanicals try desperately to act out an Ovidian story, Pyramus and Thisbe, for the

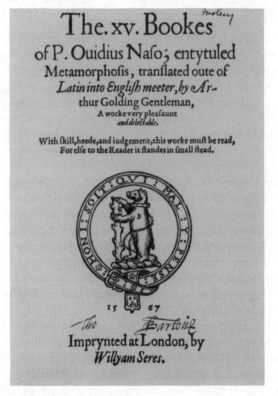

3. The title-page of Ovid's *Metamorphoses* in Arthur Golding's translation (1567). Note the didactic emphasis in the couplet, which exhorts readers to use 'skill, heede, and judgement'.

lovers of *A Midsummer Night's Dream*; Falstaff becomes an over-age Actaeon, transformed into a stag, in the conclusion of *The Merry Wives of Windsor*. In more subtle ways Ovid informs the monstrous changes in Shakespeare's great tragedies: Hecuba's grief, Niobe's lament for her dead child, and Ixion's folly and punishment variously shape Lear's anguished journey. The myth of Hercules colours Shakespeare's portrait of Antony in *Antony and Cleopatra*. In the late romances, Ovidian myths and moments continue to appear in various forms on stage: the legend of Proserpina, who returns to the earth in the spring, underlies *The Winter's Tale*; and specific texts, as we shall see, inspire climactic moments in *The Winter's Tale* and *The Tempest*.

Venus and Adonis. Early in Shakespeare's career writers like Thomas Lodge (*Scilla's Metamorphosis*, 1589) and Christopher Marlowe (*Hero and Leander*, wr. 1593, pub. 1598) read the *Metamorphoses* as an anthology of love and desire. They retold Ovidian stories as English love poems, thus fashioning a new style of mythological poetry—musical, rhetorical, and sexy. Shakespeare's *Venus and Adonis* belongs to this style, employing the same rhyme scheme as Lodge (verse stanzas rhyming ababcc) and recalling Marlowe in some particulars.[2] Shakespeare's erotic *Venus and Adonis* attracted contemporary admiration: in a Cambridge play, *The Return from Parnassus, Part One* (1598), Gullio vows to sleep with Shakespeare's *Venus and Adonis* under his pillow; Gabriel Harvey notes that 'the younger sort' take 'much delight' in the poem; a fellow poet, Richard Barnfield, thinks the 'honey-flowing vein' of Shakespeare's *Venus and Adonis* and *Lucrece* a guarantee of immortal fame.[3] The lush rhetoric delighted early readers but distressed some later ones: Edmond Malone, the first editor to provide a commentary for these poems (1780), complained of their 'wearisome circumlocution' (Vickers, vi. 287–8).

In *Venus and Adonis* Shakespeare combines two Ovidian tales of desire and transformation—the story of the principals (*Met*. 10. 503–739) and that of Salmacis and Hermaphroditus (*Met*. 4. 285–388).[4] The first contributes the general plot of the poem—Venus' love of Adonis, her warning about the boar, his death, her grief, his transformation into an anemone. The second, featuring the erotic, dominating female Salmacis and the beautiful, reluctant Hermaphroditus, supplies the characters and the dynamics of their relationship. Shakespeare collapses two distinct Ovidian narrators, Alcithoë in Bk. 4 and Orpheus in Bk. 10, into the uncharacterized teller of the tale, and adds lengthy argumentation—Venus' persuasions (8 ff., 95 ff. 751 ff.), Adonis' demurrals (409 ff., 769 ff.), the apostrophe to death (931 ff.), the prophecy about love (1135 ff.). He converts Ovid's light and rapid dactylic hexameter (a line of six metrical feet dominated by the dactylic foot consisting of a long followed by two short syllables) into a more leisurely six-line stanza of iambic pentameter (a line of five metrical feet dominated by the iambic foot consisting of a short followed by a long syllable). Each stanza begins with interlocking rhymes and concludes with a couplet (ababcc). The procession of self-contained stanzas, each with rhymed terminations, encourages dilation, digression, topical development, and rhetorical expansion rather than taut, continuous narration. Shakespeare expands Ovid's brief tales: the original 194 lines (not counting the Hippomenes–Atalanta insert, 10. 503–680) become an erotic, richly embroidered, aurally luxurious, and rhetorically intricate poem of 1,194 lines.

Both Ovid and Shakespeare preach throughout their poems, employing *sententiae*, wise sayings or general observations on life. Orpheus comments sagely, 'Winged Time glides by imperceptibly and deceives us, and nothing is swifter than the years' (*Met.* 10. 519–20). Likewise, Shakespeare's narrator reflects on beauty and love: 'Were beauty under twenty locks kept fast, | Yet love breaks through, and picks them all at last' (575–6). Both use rhetorical devices like *anaphora*, the repetition of introductory phrases; *antithesis*, answering and opposing words and phrases; *polyptoton*, the repetition of the same word in different forms. Moreover, Shakespeare imitates Ovid in his sudden shifts of style, particularly in the unpredictable change from high seriousness to bathetic humour. The famous Ovidian simile of Pyramus spouting blood like a leaky pipe (*Met.* 4. 121–4) (in the tale so important for *A Midsummer Night's Dream*) deflates tragic sentiment sharply and comically, as do some lines here. Confronted with the amorous goddess of love and beauty, Adonis petulantly prefers the company of animals: 'leave me here alone; | For all my mind, my thought, my busy care | Is how to get my palfrey from the mare' (382–4); ' "I know not love", quoth he, "nor will not know it, | Unless it be a boar, and then I chase it" ' (409–10).

Shakespeare imitates Ovid's imagery as well as his plot, characters, and rhetoric. The later poet does not translate literally, simply gathering and transplanting Ovidian blossoms into his text. Instead, as Renaissance theorists advised, he imitates creatively, apprehending the motive and style of Ovidian images and turning them into new creations. Ovid, for example, describes Hermaphroditus swimming:

> *desilit in latices alternaque bracchia ducens*
> *in liquidis translucet aquis, ut eburnea si quis*
> *signa tegat claro vel candida lilia vitro.*
>
> (4. 353–5)

Into the water lithe and baine [limber] with arms displayed [he] glides,
And rowing with his hands and legs swims in the water clear;
Through which his body fair and white doth glist'ringly appear,
As if a man an ivory image or a lily white
Should overlay or close with glass that were most pure and bright.

> (Golding, ed. Bullough, i. 172)

Describing Venus taking Adonis by the hand, Shakespeare recalls the white ivory, lilies, the action of enclosure, and the bold juxtaposition of the natural and artificial in simile:

> Full gently now she takes him by the hand,
> A lily prisoned in a jail of snow,
> Or ivory in an alabaster band.
>
> (361–3)

But here changing the visual display to white on white, he charges the imagery with the metaphor of imprisonment to suggest an erotic domination.

Shakespeare adapts Ovid's red-and-white imagery also. Salmacis finishes pleading with Hermaphroditus, who blushes:

> *nais ab his tacuit. Pueri rubor ora notavit;*
> *nescit, enim, quid amor; sed et erubuisse decebat:*
> *hic color aprica pendentibus arbore pomis*
> *aut ebori tincto est aut sub candore rubenti,*
> *cum frustra resonant aera auxiliaria, lunae.*
>
> (4. 329–33)

This said, the nymph did hold her peace, and therewithal the boy
Waxed red. He wist not what love was. And sure it was a joy
To see it how exceeding well his blushing him became.
For in his face the colour fresh appearèd like the same
That is in apples which do hang upon the sunny side,
Or ivory shadowed with a red, or such as is espied
Of white and scarlet colours mixed appearing in the moon,
When folk in vain with sounding brass would ease unto her done.
(Golding, ed. Bullough, i. 171)

Shakespeare focuses on the blush, expanding the red–white contrast throughout the poem. Adonis is 'rose-cheeked' (3), 'more white and red than doves or roses are' (10); Venus promises to make his lips 'red, and pale' with kissing (21), she being 'red and hot', he, 'red for shame, but frosty in desire' (35–6), ' 'Twixt crimson shame and anger ashy-pale' (76). Coming to Adonis, Venus' complexion signals the conflict within between fear and desire, 'How white and red each other did destroy!' (346). When Venus faints, Adonis 'Claps her pale cheek till clapping makes it red' (468). The boar, ironically, has a 'frothy mouth, bepainted all with red, | Like milk and blood being mingled both together' (901–2). Adonis' flower, the anemone, will be reddish-purple and white. These lines suggest the poetic competitiveness evident everywhere in Shakespeare, the urge to imitate, vary, and, finally, outdo the source.

Such bold competitiveness marks the larger contours of Shakespeare's borrowings as well as the specific details. Ovid writes two tales of female sexual desire, though his Venus is relatively imperial and restrained. She and Adonis recline together; she tells a story and gives kisses between the words (10. 559). This is their only physical demonstration of love. Shakespeare makes Venus the aggressor and the kiss an important and contested expression, requested (84), refused (90 ff.), recalled mythologically in the Narcissus story (161–2), entreated (209 ff.), finally granted after Venus' faint (479), passionately enjoyed (538 ff.), revealingly recollected after Adonis' death (1118). Powerful, dangerous, divine, Ovid's Venus, paired with an acquiescent Adonis, acts more like a *grande dame* and storyteller than like Shakespeare's desirous, devouring female.

Shakespeare's Venus, kindled into flame by male reluctance, owes more to Ovid's Salmacis. Gazing on her beloved's nude body, *Salmacis exarsit; flagrant quoque lumina* (4. 347), 'Salmacis burned; and her eyes spark fire'. Mad (*amens*, 4. 351), she embraces Hermaphroditus but he denies her the joy she craves (4. 368–9). So too Shakespeare's ardent Venus achieves coital embrace without full consummation. So near and yet so far. Salmacis clings to her lover so tightly that the gods finally join them into one being, *corpora iunguntur, faciesque inducitur illis | una* (4. 374–5), 'their bodies are joined, and the face for both is changed into one'. So Shakespeare's Venus hugs and kisses Adonis:

> Her arms do lend his neck a sweet embrace.
> Incorporate then they seem; face grows to face.
> (539–40)

She has much more to say than Ovid's desperate nymph. Shakespeare's Venus protests, pleads, grows angry, and extends the famous invitation:

> 'Fondling', she saith, 'since I have hemmed thee here
> Within the circuit of this ivory pale,
> I'll be a park, and thou shalt be my deer.
> Feed where thou wilt, on mountain or in dale;
> Graze on my lips, and if those hills be dry,
> Stray lower, where the pleasant fountains lie'.
> (229–34)

In the next stanza she promises 'sweet bottom-grass', 'high delightful plain', 'round rising hillocks', and 'brakes obscure and rough' (236–7). (For the full effect, imagine these lines spoken in the sexy female voice of your choice—that of Lauren Bacall, Kathleen Turner, or Sharon Stone, for example.) The lavish use of bawdy metaphors reveals a sexual frankness as well as a playfully poetic sensibility; the lines ring with a self-conscious theatricality that celebrates female desire and, in so doing, raises it beyond lust and obscenity.

Both Ovid (here and throughout Bk. 10) and Shakespeare show the destructive power of eros also. Ovid's Venus tells the story of Hippomenes and Atalanta (10. 560 ff.), in which desire leads Atalanta's unsuccessful suitors to death. There also *intempestiva cupido* (10. 689), 'incontinent desire', aroused by Venus, causes ultimately the punishment of Hippomenes and Atalanta. Ovid continually points to the irrational, predatory, and lethal aspects of eros. Salmacis' insatiable desire leads to a bizarre, permanent, physical union with Hermaphroditus; and, distraught, he charges the gods to make the fountain of Salmacis ever after enervating and enfeebling to men. *Eros* thus weakens and emasculates.

Ovid's dark portrayal of female desire—rapacious, deadly, male-devouring—inspires Shakespeare, particularly in his rendering of Adonis' death. Ovid describes the goring directly:

> *trux aper insequitur totosque sub inguine dentes*
> *abdidit et fulva moribundum stravit harena.*
>
> (10. 715–16)

> And hiding in his cods [testicles] his tusks as far as he could thrust,
> He laid him all along for dead upon the yellow dust.
>
> (Golding, ed. Bullough, i. 168)

Shakespeare relates the goring in the voice of Venus, who imagines the incident differently: she believes that the boar was amorous, the death, an accident:

> And, nuzzling in his flank, the loving swine
> Sheathed unaware the tusk in his soft groin.
>
> Had I been toothed like him, I must confess
> With kissing him I should have killed him first.
>
> (1115–18)

Here bestial eros, the boar's kiss, kills unwittingly; and Shakespeare's Venus admits that she, in her ardour, might well have killed her lover also. *Eros* leads irresistibly to *thanatos*, 'death', to the destruction of the male. Venus concludes her dazed reverie by staining her face with his congealed blood (1122), the rituals of love and death now indistinguishable.

Ovid's Venus ordains Adonis' final transformation into a flower, an anemone, as an enduring monument of her grief (10. 725–6). The story ends with a poignant observation: the anemone is *brevis*, 'short-lived', its blossom fragile and doomed to fall too easily (10.737–9). Ovid's strange, sad tale becomes an etiology story (one that explains origins), in this case the reason why all human love is painful and unsure.

Shakespeare has the anemone spring up unbidden from Adonis' blood. His Venus vows to carry the flower in her bosom, a private, rather than public, memorial of her love. Shakespeare's Venus prophesies, 'Sorrow on love hereafter shall attend' (1136), along with jealousy, fraud, madness, death, and war. This ending illustrates contemporary reading practices, particularly the habit of didactic interpretation. One Renaissance editor of Ovid, George Sabinus, for example, argued that the Salmacis–Hermaphroditus story taught the dangers of idleness, the Venus–Adonis story, the fragility of beauty. George Sandys drew a moral from the sad fate of Salmacis and Hermaphroditus closer to that of Venus: lovers always 'strictly embrace' 'to incorporate with the beloved; which, sith they cannot, [they] can never be satisfied'.[5] For him as for Shakespeare's Venus, the story teaches that there will always be pain, frustration, and dissatisfaction in human love.

Luxuriant, witty, overwrought, *Venus and Adonis* represents Shakespeare's first extended encounter with Ovid and reveals him as reader and writer. Like many in the Renaissance, Shakespeare reads Ovid as treasure-house of mythology and classical lore. He admires particularly Ovid's narrative complexity, the skill with visual detail and colour, the rhetorical wit and mastery, the portrayal of pathos and darker passions evident even in the bright and funny spots, the sympathy for human emotion and suffering combined with a capacity for detached (almost cruel) observation. Shakespeare shows early and late a deep and internalized appreciation of Ovidian style—the music, the vivid sensuality, the darting, rapid imaginative reach that begins with the colour of a blush and moves easily to fruit in sunlit orchards, painted ivory, and then, surprisingly and poignantly, to the moon in eclipse, as people below vainly beat bronze cymbals for its restoration. And, everywhere, the *Metamorphoses* furnishes Shakespeare's great theme of transformation.

Sonnets. In Anthony Burgess's entertaining novel, *Nothing Like the Sun: A Story of Shakespeare's Love-Life*, Anne Hathaway confronts her husband William Shakespeare:

> She said: 'There are little poems, and some are to men and some are of a black woman.' She snivelled. 'Thou didst never write such to me—'
> 'Sonnets? Is it sonnets? What is this about Field being

given my sonnets?'
'I know nothing of it.' WS was already out of bed, moonlit
in his shirt. 'Get back to bed', she ordered. 'You make it
clear that all they have said is true.'[6]

Like Anne, generations of critics have confronted Shakespeare about
his sonnets, charging that 'all they have said is true'. With varying
degrees of vexation and confidence, scholars have identified historical
persons in the figures of the sequence—the young aristocratic male
friend (1–126), the rival poet (78–80, 82–6), the dark lady (127–52).
Their hypotheses, sometimes belaboured, sometimes entertaining,
succeed only in being more or less plausible. For like *Venus and Adonis*,
Shakespeare's 'sugared sonnets', to quote Francis Meres (1598), derive
demonstrably from his reading, whatever other biographical inspira-
tions may have once existed.[7]

Shakespeare's sonnets recall Ovid's *Metamorphoses*, both in Latin
and in Golding's translation. Sonnet 114, for example, speaks of 'things
indigest', a variation on Ovid's famous opening, *chaos: rudis indigestaque
moles* (1. 7), 'chaos, a rude and shapeless mass'. Ovid's Bk. 15, particularly Pythagoras' discussion of vegetarianism, metempsychosis (rein-
carnation), and universal alteration and change contributes to the
sonnets more pervasively. Ovid compares the relentless passing of
time to the flow of rivers and the movement of ocean waves:

> *Ipsa quoque adsiduo labuntur tempora motu,*
> *Non secus ad flumen; neque enim consistere flumen*
> *Nec levis hora potest: sed ut unda inpellitur unda*
> *Urgeturque prior veniente urget priorem,*
> *Tempora sic fugiunt pariter pariterque sequuntur*
> *Et nova sunt semper.*
>
> (15. 179–84)

> The time itself continually is fleeting like a brook.
> For neither brook nor lightsome time can tarry still. But look,
> As every wave drives other forth and that that comes behind,
> Both thrusteth and is thrust itself: even so the times by kind,
> Do fly and follow both at once and evermore renew.
>
> (Golding, 15. ed. Rouse, 199–203)

Sonnet 60 illustrates Shakespeare's creative reading and remembering:

> Like as the waves make towards the pebbled shore,
> So do our minutes hasten to their end,
> Each changing place with that which goes before;
> In sequent toil all forwards do contend.
>
> (1–4)

The cumulative evidence in the sonnets suggests that Shakespeare regularly uses Golding's translation; in two particulars here, however, he draws closer to the Latin: Shakespeare's 'minutes' (2) recalls the specification of *tempora*, 'time' to the metonym *hora*, 'hours' (181); and 'sequent' (4) echoes *sequuntur* (183). Shakespeare imbues the Ovidian passage with deep pessimism and melancholy, emphasizing the relentlessness of Time's progress in order, finally, to proclaim his verse's power: 'And yet to times in hope my verse shall stand, | Praising thy worth despite his cruel hand' (13–14).

Sonnet 63, another on the theme of Time as the devourer of all things and on the lasting power of verse, also finds inspiration in Ovid. The Latin poet describes the progression of human life:

> *Inde valens veloxque fuit spatiumque iuventae*
> *Transit et emeritis medii quoque temporis annis*
> *Labitur occiduae per iter declive senectae.*
> *Subruit haec aevi demoliturque prioris*
> *Robora.*
>
> (15. 225–9)

> From that time growing strong and swift, he passeth forth the space
> Of youth, and also wearing out his middle age apace,
> Through drooping age's steepy path, he runneth out his race.
> This age doth undermine the strength of former years, and throws
> It down.
>
> (Golding, ed. Rouse, 15. 247–51)

Shakespeare personalizes the general metamorphoses:

> Against my love shall be as I am now,
> With time's injurious hand crushed and o'erworn;
> When hours have drained his blood and filled his brow
> With lines and wrinkles; when his youthful morn
> Hath travelled on to age's steepy night,

And all those beauties whereof now he's king
Are vanishing, or vanished out of sight.

(1–7)

The poet identifies himself and then his love as victims of a personified, injurious, blood-draining Time. Shakespeare reworks Golding's 'steepy path', which took liberties with Ovid's *iter declive*,
'downhill path', into 'steepy night', to suggest the increasing struggle
of advancing years and the contrast with 'youthful morn'. He reads
beyond Golding's inadequate 'drooping' for *occiduae*, 'setting', to catch
Ovid's central comparison of life to the sun's daily journey. Boldly, he
transforms *robora* (Golding's accurate 'strength') into 'beauties', converting the general grief about age into a personal lament for a loved
one. These beauties, the couplet promises, will endure in the 'black
lines' of the poet's verse. In Sonnets 60 and 63, then, Shakespeare
imitates Ovid only to repudiate him; he uses the great images of age,
alteration, and the destructive power of time to assert the immortalizing power of his poetry.

Text: Ovid's *Fasti*

The Rape of Lucrece. Probably the 'graver labour' promised in the
dedication to *Venus and Adonis*, *The Rape of Lucrece* appeared in 1594.
In it the tyrant Tarquin rapes the virtuous Lucrece, who then commits
suicide to preserve the family honour. Lucius Junius Brutus and other
Romans expel the wicked Tarquin family and establish the republic. In
accordance with conventional reading practices that sought moral and
political lessons in history, Shakespeare reads and writes the story of
Lucrece's rape and the aftermath didactically. The story illustrates the
dangers of lust and the virtue of chastity.

Shakespeare returns to Ovid for his material, this time to the *Fasti*
(2. 721–852)[8]. Again he greatly expands Ovid, 132 lines growing to 1,855.
The Latin elegiac meter, consisting of alternating hexameter (six feet)
and pentameter (five feet) lines, creates a varied narrative, one that
easily shifts pace, changes time or location, accommodates catalogues,
snatches of dialogue, explanatory parentheses, and stage directions.
Traditionally used for tragic themes, Shakespeare's rhyme royal
consists of seven-line stanzas rhyming ababbcc. This verse form

slows the pace for exposition and dilation, the last two couplets promoting reflection, sententiousness, and rhetorical questioning. The later poet cuts away most of the action; he expands rhetorically, providing debate, disputation, and declamation. The narrator and characters in this poem agonize, apostrophize, and digress; the language glitters with pun, proverb, conceit, antithesis, and allusion.

Shakespeare lavishly uses animal and military imagery to illustrate the dangers of lust. Various animals characterize Tarquin's desire as bestial and the rape as a kill: Tarquin acts like a predator, sometimes familiar, sometimes exotic: the 'night-owl' (360), the 'lurking serpent' (362), the 'grim lion' (421), the 'falcon tow'ring in the skies' (506), the cockatrice with 'dead-killing eye' (540), the griffin with 'sharp claws' (543). Lucrece is the helpless prey, the unsuspecting bird 'never limed' (88), a sleeping 'dove' (360), a 'white hind' (543), a 'weak mouse' (555), an 'unseasonable doe' (581). Images of war likewise identify Tarquin's action as a descent into sin. Unruly passions overthrow his reason; he besieges and sacks Lucrece's fair city. 'Affection' acts as a 'captain' (271) and leads the invader through the city walls, i.e. through the various doors and curtains to, finally, the 'ivory wall' (464) of Lucrece's body. Tarquin moves 'to make the breach and enter this sweet city' (469). These images portray Tarquin as a man whose lust has turned him into a beast dangerous to himself and to the city of Rome as well as to all civic and social order.

Shakespeare alters Ovid further to emphasize Lucrece's virtue, particularly her chastity. In Ovid Lucrece's beauty—her figure, hair, complexion, form, and face—(*Fasti* 2. 771-4) inflames Tarquin; in Shakespeare it is her chastity. He introduces the heroine in the first stanza as 'Lucrece the chaste' (7), and 'that name of chaste', he explains, sets 'This bateless edge' on Tarquin's 'keen appetite' (8-9). From the outset Shakespeare focuses on moral not physical excellence. Brutus later swears by 'chaste Lucrece' soul' (1839), thus beginning the long line of interpretation that viewed the suicide as a proof of chastity. Beautiful Roman wife becomes chaste, pre-Christian martyr. Shakespeare adapts the ancient Roman story for the instruction and improvement of his readers.

Like all such adaptation, however, Shakespeare's reading of classical history in this new Christian context presents unresolved tensions and problems. Lucrece's suicide makes sense as heroic sacrifice and expiation only in the original classical context of a shame–fame culture. In this culture the rape brings dishonour upon her husband and family. The rape-victim suffers a pollution from without that infects her being, regardless of personal choice. Lucrece rids herself of this pollution by suicide. Slaying herself, she asserts her fidelity and courage; she cleanses herself of sexual dishonour by claiming a different kind of honour, that of the Roman warrior. By her suicide Lucrece earns the only good afterlife available to the Roman, that offered by the memory of the living, in other words, fame.

Later generations admired Lucrece, but conceived the moral issues differently. St Augustine queried succinctly: *si adulterata, cur laudata; si pudica, cur occisa,* 'if she was made an adulteress, why has she been praised? If she was chaste, why was she slain?'[9] Employing a post-classical ethics of guilt and sin, Augustine asks whether Lucrece was an adulteress or rape-victim. If an adulteress, then she can deserve no praise; if a rape-victim, then the suicide, morally unjustifiable for a Christian, must be sinful rather than heroic. Often reviled today by people who have never read him, St Augustine here shows himself a proto-feminist: he treats Lucrece as an autonomous moral agent whose capacity for sin, like that of any man, resides wholly in her intellect, conscience, and will.

Well-articulated classical and Christian contexts oppose each other throughout Shakespeare's *The Rape of Lucrece*. Like Ovid's Lucrece, Shakespeare's heroine believes that the rape confers both a physical and moral stain. She laments her 'soul's pollution' (1157); she posits the interdependence of body and soul:

> Ay me, the bark peeled from the lofty pine
> His leaves will wither and his sap decay;
> So must my soul, her bark being peeled away.
> (1167–9)

Lucrece thinks herself infected by the pollution, that can visit the guilty and innocent alike, that requires the purgation of sacrifice and death. She blames herself for 'honour's wrack' (841), and worries about the defilement of her husband's stock (1063), the corruption of his bloodline and, by extension in a patriarchy, the order of the household and city itself. Through death she cleanses herself of shame and wins fame, a kind of immortality:

> For in my death I murder shameful scorn;
> My shame so dead, mine honour is new born.
> (1189–90)

In these passages Shakespeare clearly sets out the classical values by which Lucrece lives and dies.

But the poem outlines as well the competing Christian values which undermine the logic of Lucrece's suicide. The poem evokes the later values first in the imagery of Lucrece as 'earthly saint' and Tarquin as 'devil' (85), then in the depiction of Tarquin's inner struggle as a contest between passion and reason (183 ff.), a 'disputation' | 'Tween frozen conscience and hot-burning will' (246–7). In similar terms, Lucrece begs Tarquin by 'him', i.e. God, to command his 'rebel will' (624–5). Like some pious parson, the narrator preaches against Tarquin's 'drunken desire', 'lust', 'self-will' (703 ff.). According to this conception of the action, Tarquin sins and in so doing pollutes his own soul, not Lucrece's. Thus, Tarquin's 'soul's fair temple is defaced' (719), not his victim's; his soul is now a 'spotted princess' (721), hers immaculate.

This conflict in Shakespeare's poem between classical and Christian values remains unresolved. The narrator showers Lucrece with praise throughout but Brutus' final statement sounds more like criticism: 'Thy wretched wife mistook the matter so | To slay herself, that should have slain her foe' (1826–7). *Cur occisa?* 'Why was she slain?' indeed. Despite the unresolved tensions, Shakespeare's encounter with Ovid in *The Rape of Lucrece* proves fruitful. He endows Tarquin and Lucrece with an eloquence, emotional complexity, and ethical self-consciousness that anticipates later dramatic characters. Tarquin provides a prototype for other tyrants, particularly Macbeth, who approaches Duncan's chamber with Tarquin's ravishing strides and his inner turmoil (2. 1.55). Ovid's Brutus, *stulti sapiens imitator* (2. 717), 'wise though pretending to be fool', looks ahead to Hamlet, who also casts off pretence to become a revenger. Lucrece's struggle with Rome, which demands heroic constancy and self-sacrifice for the rewards of honour and fame, will reappear throughout the Roman plays, the chaste Roman matron herself evoked by name several times in *Titus*

Andronicus. Most important, Shakespeare's struggle to read antiquity didactically, evident here in all of its ambivalence, will produce in his later work wonderfully resonant clashes and dissonances.

Tradition: Italian Love Poetry (Petrarch)

Sonnets. Though no one has proved that he ever read a single Italian poem, Shakespeare shows a pervasive indebtedness to Italian love poetry for both the form and content of his sonnets. Italian influence flowed throughout Elizabethan literary culture, beginning with Thomas Wyatt's and the Earl of Surrey's Petrarchan adaptations in Tottel's *Miscellany* (1557), and culminating in the sonneteering vogue of the 1590s. At the end of the century virtually every aspiring poet wrote a sonnet sequence. These range from the derivative finger-exercises of Thomas Watson to the stately organ music of Edmund Spenser. In his sonnets Shakespeare often echoes his contemporaries, especially Edmund Spenser, Philip Sidney, Michael Drayton, Samuel Daniel, and Henry Constable, though the last two may, in fact, be echoing him.

The sonnet, or 'little song', usually but not always fourteen lines long, has deep origins in Italy, dating back at least to the thirteenth-century poet Giacomo da Lentini. Italian sonnets often took the form of an eight-line part, an octave (abbaabba) and a six-line part, a sestet (cdecde). Working in a language less generous than Italian with terminal rhyme, English sonneteers modified the sonnet form to three four-line units, quatrains, and a couplet (two rhymed lines) (abab cdcd efef gg), though many poets still changed rhetorical or logical direction in line nine. The English modification gave greater flexibility to the form while making the sonnet more discursive and argumentative. The ending rhyme of the couplet suggests a closure—personal, meditative, summary, or contradictory—that the lines sometimes poignantly fail to supply.[10]

In a slim volume of poetry and prose, *La Vita Nuova*, 'The New Life', Dante created the *dolce stil novo*, 'sweet new style' of Italian love poetry at the end of the thirteenth century.[11] This volume featured a personal lyric voice intensely experiencing the spiritual love of a lady. No mere object of desire, the narrator's beloved, Beatrice, whose name means 'bestower of blessings', lives and dies as an angelic presence who reflects God's love and beauty. Thus Dante decisively breaks with those medieval traditions that would clearly separate earthly and heavenly love. Indebted to Neoplatonic philosophy, completing his vision in the incomparable *La Divina Commedia*, Dante celebrates a love that ennobles and uplifts, that leads the lover to virtue and ultimately to union with God.

No one after Dante celebrated so purely, sweetly, and sublimely a love that led beyond the circling stars. Dante's great successor Petrarch, to be sure, praised Laura as an angelic presence in his *Rime sparse*, the remarkable collection that influenced so many poets.[12] There Petrarch tells of first seeing Laura on Good Friday, 6 April 1327, and of her dying on the same day and hour in 1348. He celebrates the lady as God's new creation, a new sun (4), a mortal who, like Christ, reflects God's love (144), the Platonic ideal of beauty (159). After her death (268), Laura continues to inspire and console the lover (279, 285). In his last poem (366) love of Laura becomes love of the Virgin Mary, the poetry of amorous praise now reformulated into a magnificent hymn.

But throughout the *Rime sparse*, Petrarch, unlike Dante, struggles with earthly desire, doubt, and disappointment. He suffers from unrequited *eros*, inflamed by the beloved's eyes, golden hair, white skin, and melodic voice. He experiences contrary passions:

> *Amor mi sprona in un tempo et affrena*
> *assecura et spaventa, arde et agghiaccia,*
> *gradisce et sdegna, a sé mi chiama et scaccia,*
> *or mi tene in speranza et or in pena.*
>
> (178, 1–4)

> Love spurs and holds me back at the same time,
> frightens and reassures, freezes and burns,
> is kind and rude; he calls me, throws me out;
> with hope he holds me now and then with grief.

Not ennobling, this love sometimes feels like a youthful error (1), an incurable wound, a yoke, a source of pain and grief (209), a labyrinth (211). On occasion, love of Laura is a culpable obsession, a bad habit (*l'usanza ria*, 81, 2), a stumbling block, an occasion of sin, a peril to his soul:

Allor errai quando l'antica strada
di libertà mi fu precisa et tolta,
ché mal si segue ciò ch' agli occhi agrada;
allor corse al suo mal libera et sciolta,
ora a posta d'altrui conven che vada
l'anima che peccò sol una volta.

(96, 9–14)

I first went wrong when I found my old road
of freedom was cut off and blocked to me—
it's bad to follow what the eyes find pleasing—
then it ran free and unbound to its harm,
now it is forced to do another's pleasure,
that soul of mine that sinned but only once.

Petrarch bequeathed to Europe this complex poetic legacy of intensely personal ecstasy and anguish expressed in complicated and demanding poetic forms. The speaker of Shakespeare's Sonnet 137 likewise complains about his eyes misleading him, 'Thou blind fool love, what dost thou to mine eyes | That they behold and see not what they see?' (1–2). Other sonnets show a similar consciousness of sin and entrapment: 'Love is my sin', declares the speaker of Sonnet 142 (1); Sonnet 146 begins with this address, 'Poor soul, the centre of my sinful earth'. 'My love is as a fever, longing still', laments the narrator of Sonnet 147, who describes himself as 'past care' and 'frantic mad'(1, 9–10).

Petrarch does not function as a source in the usual sense, as the book on the desk that Shakespeare read and revised. Instead, he acts as the originator of the great tradition that reached Shakespeare through many intermediaries. Consequently, his presence resides not in verbal echo caused by direct imitation but in inherited *conventions*, i.e. conspicuous features of subject-matter, form or technique that writers pass around to each other. Petrarch originated the rhetorical conventions of love poetry for the Italian, French, and English poets who came after. The example above, wherein the narrator laments the folly of his eyes and the fall of his soul into sin, provides just one example of a Petrarchan convention. Often, love enters the lover's heart through arrows from the lady's eyes. He typically suffers contrary passions but declares his humility and servitude. He praises the lady's celestial beauty, cataloguing excellences, but laments her absence and cruelty. The lover struggles with the mortality of the beloved, sometimes enduring the agony of her death. He proclaims the inadequacy or immortalizing power of his verse.

Petrarch also creates a resonant vocabulary of poetic imagery. The yearning lover, for example, often imagines himself as a ship at sea. Witness Petrarch's much-imitated 189, *Passa la nave mia colma d'oblio | per aspro mare a mezza notte il verno* (1–2), which received new life in Sir Thomas Wyatt's translation: 'My galley charged with forgetfulness | Thorough sharp seas in winter nights doth pass'.[13] Lost, buffeted by storms, Petrarch's traveller cannot see stars by which to navigate and ends in desperation:

> *Celansi i duo mei dolci usati segni,*
> *Morta fra l'onde è la ragion et l'arte*
> *Tal ch' incomincio a desperar del porto.*
> (12–14)

> The stars be hid that led me to this pain,
> Drowned is the reason that should me comfort,
> And I remain despairing of the port.
> (Wyatt)

In Sonnet 116 Shakespeare playfully reappropriates this image, turning it around to affirm a love that never alters or bends, that always shines for the lover:

> O no, it [love] is an ever fixèd mark
> That looks on tempests and is never shaken;
> It is the star to every wand'ring barque,
> Whose worth's unknown although his height be taken.
> (5–8)

True love endures, as constant as the North Star in the sky (the ever fixèd mark), well above the tempests below. Every lover in his ship (the wand'ring barque) can only wonder at its inestimable worth, ultimately mysterious, and trust in it for guidance. Unlike the Petrarchan lover, lost in storms at sea, these Shakespearian lovers sail safely, confidently, smoothly.

Petrarch did not just contribute images to later generations, but also images expanded into specific situations and responses. One example of this more complicated kind of convention occurs in Petrarch's 310,

wherein the beauties of spring intensify the loneliness and misery of
the unrequited lover. The poem begins, *Zefiro torna e 'l bel tempo
rimena | e i fiori et l'erbe, sua dolce famiglia* (1–2), 'Zephyr comes back
and brings with him fair weather and his sweet family of grass and
flowers'. In such weather, *ogni animal d'amar si riconsiglia* (8), 'every
living thing is bent on loving'. Not the speaker, alas, for whom *cantar
augelletti, et fiorir piagge* (12), 'the song of birds, the flowering of
meadows', are finally *un deserto et fere aspre et selvagge* (14), 'a desert
now, wild savage beasts'. The freshness, colour, and simplicity of the
images set up the climactic counterturn that powerfully conveys the
speaker's anguish and desolation.

In Sonnet 98 Shakespeare brilliantly adapts this seasonal convention:

> From you have I been absent in the spring
> When proud-pied April, dressed in all his trim,
> Hath put a spirit of youth in everything,
> That heavy Saturn laughed and leapt with him.
> Yet nor the lays of birds nor the sweet smell
> Of different flowers in odour and in hue
> Could make me any summer's story tell,
> Or from their proud lap pluck them where they grew;
> Nor did I wonder at the lily's white,
> Nor praise the deep vermilion in the rose.
> They were but sweet, but figures of delight
> Drawn after you, you pattern of all those;
>   Yet seemed it winter still, and, you away,
>   As with your shadow I with these did play.

The sonnet preserves the essential contrast between the bright and
beautiful spring weather—again suggested by bird song and flowers—
and the speaker's misery, this time imaged as winter. But lines 9–12
effectively vary the standard comparison of the beloved's complexion
to flowers; this lily's white and rose's vermilion only distantly and
palely imitate the beloved, who is a 'pattern of all those'. 'Pattern'
here, like 'figures' above and 'shadow', alludes to the Platonic doctrine
of ideal forms, which holds that the physical particulars we perceive
only distantly and palely imitate the true substance, or non-physical
ideal form. The language throughout is suggestively sexual, especially

the possible connotations of 'proud', 'spirit', 'leapt', 'proud lap', 'pluck', 'rose', and 'play'. The couplet begins with a simple declarative statement, 'Yet seemed it winter still', which concludes in the mournful, elliptical phrase 'and, you away'. This line recalls the beloved's absence in line 1; the omission of the participle (you *being* away) makes the construction stark and disconnected. The strong middle caesura in the last line (the pause between 'shadow' and 'I') emphasizes the speaker's disappointment at being left with 'shadow' not substance, and sets up the bitter end verb, 'play'.

Shakespeare not only adopts his Petrarchan legacy but sometimes rejects it. Sonnet 21 explicitly abjures standard images and conceits, particularly similes that have become worn and lifeless. The speaker of Sonnet 130 pointedly refuses to write the conventional catalogue of his lady's excellences; instead, he takes each literally and denies its applicability to her:

> My mistress' eyes are nothing like the sun;
> Coral is far more red than her lips' red.
> If snow be white, why then her breasts are dun;
> If hairs be wires, black wires grow on her head.
> I have seen roses damasked, red and white,
> But no such roses see I in her cheeks;
> And in some perfumes is there more delight
> Than in the breath that from my mistress reeks.
> I love to hear her speak, yet well I know
> That music hath a far more pleasing sound.
> I grant I never saw a goddess go:
> My mistress when she walks treads on the ground.
>   And yet, by heaven, I think my love as rare
>   As any she belied with false compare.

At first the poet appears to mock his lady. But actually he mocks the Petrarchan fictions in circulation, particularly the far-fetched comparisons of the lady's eyes to the sun, lips to coral, skin to snow, breath to perfume, voice to music, and so on. As Dogberry put it elsewhere, 'comparisons are odorous' (*Much Ado About Nothing*, 3. 5. 15), especially these standard Petrarchan ones. Despite the scorn of such rhetoric, the end couplet indulges in a little oath-taking ('by heaven'), compliment ('rare' means 'splendid', 'marvellous', and 'unusual'), and simile ('as . . . as'). The last line, which may be paraphrased, 'as any woman lied about with false comparisons', asserts that the poet's lady is finally as rare as any other poet's lady. Here Shakespeare fluently adapts his Petrarchan legacy: denial effects praise of another sort.

Romeo and Juliet. Shakespeare's reading of Italian love poetry and of Petrarchan tradition culminates in his plays, especially in *Romeo and Juliet.* This play, based on Arthur Brooke's dull poem, *Romeus and Juliet* (1562), recalls the teasing anti-Petrarchan manner of Sonnet 130, as the witty Mercutio mocks Romeo, tearful and love-sick for Rosaline: 'O flesh, flesh, how art thou fishified! Now is he for the numbers that Petrarch flowed in. Laura to his lady was a kitchen wench' (2. 2. 35–8). Mercutio here identifies Romeo's adolescent infatuation, with its attendant exaggeration, as Petrarchan misery; perhaps this lover too will write sonnets to a lady he thinks more beautiful than Petrarch's Laura. In the beginning of the play Romeo makes a splendid target for Mercutio's abuse. We first see him moaning about his great love, one Rosaline whom we never meet; he self-consciously adapts Petrarch's contrary passions into a series of glib paradoxes:

> Why then, O brawling love, O loving hate,
> O anything of nothing first create;
> O heavy lightness, serious vanity,
> Misshapen chaos of well-seeming forms,
> Feather of lead, bright smoke, cold fire, sick health,
> Still-waking sleep, that is not what it is!
>
> (1. 1. 173–8)

The Petrarchan passions degenerate here into an artificial list, a series of hollow mannerisms. Shakespeare portrays adolescent love in all its intensity, self-absorption, and silliness; Benvolio laughs and so do we.

Some think that Romeo outgrows such Petrarchan ecstasies and anguishes when he meets Juliet. Not so. Instead, Shakespeare transforms Petrarchan conventions into beautiful expressions of intimacy and love. Consider the lovers' first words to each other, which form a perfect English sonnet:

> ROMEO (*to Juliet, touching her hand*)
> If I profane with my unworthiest hand

This holy shrine, the gentler sin is this:
My lips, two blushing pilgrims, ready stand
To smooth that rough touch with a tender kiss.
JULIET   Good pilgrim, you do wrong your hand too much,
Which mannerly devotion shows in this.
For saints have hands that pilgrims' hands do touch,
And palm to palm is holy palmers' kiss.
ROMEO   Have not saints lips, and holy palmers, too?
JULIET   Ay, pilgrim, lips that they must use in prayer.
ROMEO   O then, dear saint, let lips do what hands do:
They pray; grant thou, lest faith turn to despair.
JULIET   Saints do not move, though grant for prayers' sake.
ROMEO   Then move not while my prayer's effect I take.

He kisses her
(1. 5. 92–105)

The private voice of the Petrarchan lover becomes a conversation between two speakers, whose participation in the verse form, replete with answering rhymes, expresses their intimacy, sensuality, and exclusivity. To the objection, 'No one ever talks like that', there is a simple answer: 'We would if we could.' Sceptics who think such language artificial may try a simple experiment: recall your greatest love scene—the passionate avowals, desperate promises, tender blandishments. Now imagine playing that scene in a theatre. Such love-talk may sound very well to its intended audience of one, but it would be hesitant, banal, and ridiculous on stage. Theatre demands a language that is private and public, particular and universal, a language, in other words, created by tradition and shaped by convention. The immediate and unpractised sonnet-speaking of Romeo and Juliet suggests that these two were made for each other. The religious imagery (pilgrims, saints, devotion, and prayers) gives solemnity and seriousness to the meeting. The Petrarchan lover—yearning, inspired, wondering—turns Montague; the Petrarchan lady—holy, distant, beautiful, gracious—turns Capulet. Rhetorical desire, voiced in numberless sonnets, finally finds theatrical fulfilment on stage as the lovers stop talking and kiss.

The play ends, however, not in theatrical fulfilment but in tragedy: Romeo confronts the death of Juliet. We recall Petrarch confronting the death of Laura in 268:

Che debb' io far? che mi consigli, Amore?
Tempo è ben di morire
ed ò tardato più ch' i' non vorrei.
Madonna è morta et à seco il mio core.

(1–4)

What will I do? Can you advise me, Love?
Now is the time to die,
And I have put it off more than I should.
My lady's dead and with her is my heart.

Love itself grieves too, says the speaker, *perch' ad uno scoglio | avem rotto la nave, | et in un punto n'è scurato il sole* (15–17), 'because on the same rock we both have wrecked our ship and seen the sun turn dark at the same time'. In the following poems the speaker struggles with Death personified, who has broken the knot of life and stamped out the scattered fire (*Morte . . . rotto 'l nodo, e 'l foco à spento et sparso*, 271, 14–15).

Romeo too struggles with Death personified, 'the lean abhorrèd monster' that keeps Juliet 'in dark to be his paramour' (5. 3. 104–5). For fear of that, he resolves to stay with her always. At the end of the play he actualizes Petrarch's death-wish by committing suicide. Like Petrarch above and in the poem we noted earlier, 189, *Passa la nave mia colma d'oblio*, 'My galley charged with forgetfulness', Romeo imagines himself as a ship at sea; he addresses the poison:

Come, bitter conduct, come unsavoury guide,
Thou desperate pilot, now at once run on
The dashing rocks thy sea-sick weary barque!

(5. 3. 116–18)

Petrarchan conventions create a powerful language of desolation, as Romeo radically translates the conventional metaphor. Instead of the lover desiring a safe port from seas of unrequited love and suffering, Romeo wants shipwreck. His flesh is world-wearied; the constellations above that should guide navigation are merely a yoke of inauspicious stars. The world without Juliet can afford no joy or hope, no safe port.

In similarly radical fashion, Romeo adapts other conventional Petrarchan imagery. At Laura's death, Petrarch's sun turned dark, *è scurato il sole* (268); Death extinguished the fires of life, *'l foco a spento et sparso* (271). After killing Paris, Romeo finds Juliet in her tomb:

> A grave—O no, a lantern, slaughtered youth,
> For here lies Juliet, and her beauty makes
> This vault a feasting presence full of light.
>
> (5. 3. 84–6)

Here we witness the unspeakably painful intimacy of bride and groom reunited in a moment of love and death. The tomb must be some sort of dark, enclosed burial chamber; in contrast, a 'lantern' in Elizabethan parlance denoted a light, and also a 'lanthorn', a tower room, glassed on all sides, a place, in other words, high and bright, opposite to a tomb. 'Vault' means 'tomb' but also metaphorically the sky, all that is under the sun; a 'feasting presence' is a festival chamber, recalling, of course, the colourful Capulet ball where the lovers first met. Juliet's beauty then transforms the dark tomb and the whole dark world into a grand festival of light.

This praise is more than mere hyperbolic compliment, more than the mere recognition of fair features; it is a hard-won assertion that contradicts the bawdier perspectives on human love represented by the Nurse's earthy humour and Mercutio's satirical wit. Moreover, it contradicts conventional moralistic perspectives—derived from Augustine and Boethius—that would view such love as a downward spiral of sensual confusion, perilous to soul as well as to body. Romeo perceives heavenly as well as earthly beauty in the beloved. The distinction between the two, as well as the possible connections, occupied Dante and Petrarch as well as the great Italian Neoplatonists—Ficino, Mirandola, Bembo, and Ebreo. These figures and traditions furnish the intellectual context for the language and action of Shakespeare's play. In this context love is simply the attraction of the soul to what it perceives as true and beautiful in the beloved; love then provides the means by which one can ascend from sensual worldly attachments to union with God, source of all truth and beauty. This matrix of ideas underlies Romeo's praise here, giving it point, and resonance and power; it enables his assertion that her beauty outlives life itself and transforms the world.

In the last act other Petrarchan images assemble themselves into new shapes and meanings. In different senses we witness on stage the 'Misshapen chaos of well-seeming forms', the 'Still-waking sleep, that is not what it is' (1. 1. 176, 178). The last moments recreate Petrarchan paradox into high tragedy. 'Thy drugs are quick! Thus with a kiss I die' (5. 3. 120), Romeo says. 'Quick' means here 'speedy' and also 'living' or 'life-giving', thus suggesting some new life in union with Juliet. She shows herself mistress of the same paradox with her invocation, 'O happy dagger, | This is thy sheath! There rust, and let me die' (5. 3. 168–9). Romeo and Juliet both pronounce the same last word, 'die', a linguistic sign of their unity, entirely apt for the two speakers whose first exchange constituted that beautiful sonnet. Moreover, the sounding of their last word 'die' makes for a highly charged dramatic rhyming because the word meant in Elizabethan English to expire and also to experience sexual climax. (The entire play is really in some sense an expansion of this pun.) The two lovers are none and they are also one again, joined in a moment of love and suffering and sacrifice—self-immolation and self-fulfilment, death and life. Hector Berlioz represented the paradoxes in his choral symphony (1839) by daringly juxtaposing music of frenzied joy, rephrasings of the love theme, with sombre and darker strains, concluding finally in the plaintive sound of a solitary oboe.

The rhetorical tradition of Italian love poetry pervasively informs Shakespeare's work, beginning with the sonnets. This tradition runs wide and deep in the non-dramatic work, especially the comedies. *The Two Gentlemen of Verona* and *Love's Labour's Lost*, for example, take an irreverent view of Petrarchan conventions and subject them to sceptical scrutiny and healthy laughter. The lovers in these plays learn that love on this planet requires them to shed stereotypical poses and expressions and to confront hard truths about themselves and the world. The two gentlemen and their ladies grapple with jealousy, anger and betrayal; the lovers in *Love's Labour's Lost* discover, among other things, the inadequacy of rhetorical conventions, including Petrarchan ones, 'Taffeta phrases, silken terms precise, | Three-piled hyperboles, spruce affectation, | Figures pedantical' (5. 2. 407–9). Shakespeare's encounter with Italian love poetry reaches a profound culmination in *Romeo and Juliet*; there, sadly and gloriously, two lovers translate Petrarchan rhetoric into tragic reality.

3

Histories

In order to write his plays about English history Shakespeare turned to contemporary history books, called chronicles, particularly those by Edward Hall and Raphael Holinshed.[1] Recounting the past sequentially, these books discussed politics, weather, local events, disasters, and marvellous occurrences like the birth of a baby with two heads. The chronicle accounts of kings, queens, rebellions, battles, wars, councils, and the like entertained as well as informed; they provided a long-running series on the lives of the rich and famous, who happened also to be the royal, the powerful, the good, and the evil. The millions of people today who eagerly read historical novels, watch BBC specials or films like Oliver Stone's *JFK*, or devour materials on Princess Diana's life and death, would have turned to chronicles in Shakespeare's day. They substituted for our histories, docu-dramas, journals, films, and in some cases, even our soap-operas. Chronicles offered the excitements of historical research as well as those of popular non-fiction and fiction.

Confronting so rich a record of human achievement and folly, chroniclers often read in English history political and moral truths. Everywhere they saw, or at least said they saw, the evils of dissension and rebellion, for example, or the inevitable workings of divine justice. Shakespeare inherited these thematic focuses as he shaped chronicle materials, often loose, formless, into sharp conflicts between compelling individuals; sometimes he darkened these conflicts into tragedy, as in *Richard II*; sometimes he brightened them into comedy, as in *Henry V*.[2] To some extent, Shakespeare created the form of the history play as he went along. But he also drew continually upon other parts of his dramatic heritage, specifically on the medieval morality plays, which featured a witty, swaggering, theatrical villain—the Vice.

Text: Holinshed's *Chronicles*

Richard II. To write history plays, Shakespeare turned frequently to Raphael Holinshed's *The Chronicles of England, Scotland, and Ireland* (1577; 2nd edn., 1587). For Elizabethans Holinshed's account of King Richard II's deposition and murder made for exciting, even scandalous, reading. It raised all the hottest political issues of the day—the nature of the tyrant and good king, the ethics of rebellion, the dilemma of regicide. The official Tudor view on these matters, articulated by the government and Anglican Church, held that kings ruled by divine right and that rebellion for any reason was wrong. The 'doctrine of passive obedience' enjoined each citizen simply to do his or her daily work and to endure the occasional bad king as a test or punishment from God. Many disagreed. The tremendous upheaval of the Reformation and Counter-Reformation ignited contrary arguments by Protestants and Catholics alike. Philosophers and political theorists like John Ponet, Christopher Goodman, the author of *Vindiciae Contra Tyrannos*, and the learned Jesuits—Robert Persons, Francisco Suarez, and Juan de Mariana—debated fiercely the duties of kings and subjects and the foundations of civil order. Some posited a social contract between rulers and the ruled which was in extreme cases revocable by the people; in this view sovereign and subject were each reciprocally responsible to each other.

   In the turbulent closing years of the sixteenth century these issues took on particular urgency. Because Pope Pius V had excommunicated Elizabeth and called for her deposition (*Regnans in Excelsis*, 1570), many regarded all Catholics as potential rebels and traitors. Trouble threatened from Puritans on the left as well as from Catholics on the right. Elizabeth's Act Against Seditious Sectaries (1593), aimed against radical Puritans, and later legislation against Catholics resulted in governmental harassment and capital punishments. By the end of the sixteenth century audiences of *Richard II* also witnessed public executions, wherein an official often slit open the chest and stomach of a convicted traitor, pulled out the warm entrails, chopped up the body, hung the pieces on hooks, and finally staked the head on a pole as a warning. Such barbaric measures responded to threats of rebellion both imaginary and real. In 1601, for example, the brilliant and ambitious Earl of Essex marched against Elizabeth. Some of his supporters cited the story of Richard II as a justification for their actions, even going so far as to pay Shakespeare's company to perform a play, almost certainly Shakespeare's own, about the reign. Legend has it that Queen Elizabeth commented on the performance: 'I am Richard II. Know ye not that?' Shakespeare's deposition scene, 4. 1, excruciating for royalists, did not appear in the first three Quarto editions of the play (1597, two in 1598), those printed during Elizabeth's lifetime. Later, nervous government officials closed Nahum Tate's adaptation of *Richard II* (1680) before opening night.

Holinshed provides ample material for a play that dramatizes all the explosive political questions of Shakespeare's day. How could one distinguish between a tyrant and a just king? Could deposition and/ or regicide ever be justified? Under what circumstance and by whom? Grappling with these questions, Shakespeare's *Richard II* turns Holinshed's account into a conflict between two living men—Richard and Bolingbroke. To transform history into drama, Shakespeare, here as elsewhere, focuses on the individuals as antagonists in the story. In *1 Henry IV* he employs the same strategy, creating for Prince Henry a rival in the fiery, young Hotspur, though Hotspur was actually older than Henry's father; Shakespeare then invents a climactic battle between the two young warriors at Shrewsbury.

Shakespeare plays up the conflict between King Richard and rebel Bolingbroke, portrayed as two mighty opposites. In the first two acts Richard acts the tyrant. He clashes with Bolingbroke's dying father, the loyal Gaunt, in a scene invented by Shakespeare. Gaunt sharply criticizes the King for all his crimes: the cultivation of flatterers, the irresponsible extravagances, the leasing-out of land for money, the killing of a relative, Gloucester. Richard's callous anger and his immediate seizure of Gaunt's possessions at his death prove some of the charges all too true. Here Richard steals Bolingbroke's patrimony, directly violating the very principle of inheritance by which he rules. This arrogant offence against tradition and order draws protest from the loyal York and gives dangerous provocation to rebellion. Shakespeare, however, depicts Richard as both rightful anointed king as well as capricious tyrant. Richard later defends himself by asserting the divine right of kings to rule:

> Not all the water in the rough rude sea
> Can wash the balm from an anointed king.
> The breath of worldly men cannot depose
> The deputy elected by the Lord.
>
> (3. 2. 50–3)

The ringing rhetoric articulates orthodox Tudor doctrine.

Richard's rival, Bolingbroke, establishes himself as someone to be reckoned with in the opening confrontation with Thomas Mowbray. He accuses Mowbray of treason and agrees to a trial by combat. Richard arbitrarily and surprisingly halts the trial and banishes both Mowbray and Bolingbroke. In Holinshed's *Chronicles* nobles, prelates, and magistrates invite Bolingbroke to return from banishment, 'promising him their aid, power, and assistance, if he, expelling King Richard as a man not meet for the office he bare, would take upon him the sceptre, rule and obedience of his native land and religion' (Bullough, iii. 397). This Bolingbroke returns at the urging of the nobility to restore order to England. The *Chronicles* thus define the conflict as a struggle between the Crown and the upper class. Shakespeare, however, again focuses on the individuals. Exiled and disinherited, Bolingbroke returns to reclaim his land and titles. Uninvited and therefore more suspicious, Shakespeare's Bolingbroke defies the King in an act of personal will and daring. Privately, Northumberland, Ross, and Willoughby hope that Bolingbroke's return can help them 'shake off our slavish yoke, | Imp out our drooping country's broken wing, | Redeem from broking pawn the blemished crown' (2. 1. 293–5). In public, however, Northumberland tells the King a different story: Bolingbroke returns merely to claim what is his: 'His coming hither hath no further scope | Than for his lineal royalties, and to beg | Enfranchisement' (3. 3. 111–12).

Bolingbroke's return necessarily has wider implications and consequences, the 'further scope' that Northumberland denies. The realities of power, Shakespeare shows us, cannot be neatly contained, categorized, or circumscribed. An individual who comes in arms against a king necessarily undermines his sovereignty and the law and order of the realm. The king who submits to a subject for any reason can no longer call himself a king; the subject who commands the supreme ruler, becomes, *ipso facto*, the supreme ruler. Richard immediately understands the significance of acceding to Bolingbroke's demand for his possessions and freedom:

> What must the King do now? Must he submit?
> The King shall do it. Must he be deposed?
> The King shall be contented. Must he lose
> The name of King? A God's name, let it go.
>   (3. 3. 142–5)

Shakespeare conveys the significance of Richard's capitulation by imagery and symbolic stage action. He stages a dialogue between Richard 'on the walls', i.e. on the upper gallery above the Elizabethan stage, and Bolingbroke and the others below, i.e. on the stage itself. Called down from the battlements, Richard registers in anguish the symbolic significance of the descent.

> Down, down I come like glist'ring Phaethon,
> Wanting the manage of unruly jades.
> In the base court: base court where kings grow base
> To come at traitors' calls, and do them grace.
> In the base court, come down: down court, down King.
>   (3. 3. 177–181)

Richard's physical descent neatly reflects his fall from power: he exits from the gallery above and re-enters the stage itself, thus physically and visually brought low to the commoners' level. Richard describes himself in mythological terms, as Phaethon, who could not control the chariot of the sun and scorched the entire earth. The allusion suggests the universal chaos caused by the descent. Holinshed, by contrast, has the king come forth 'from the inner part of the castle' to Bolingbroke in the 'utter ward' or outer circuit of the walls (Bullough, iii. 404). Shakespeare invents a speech and stage action that strikingly dramatizes the shift in power.

Adapting Holinshed, Shakespeare frequently employs such symbolic stage action. In the very next scene, unprecedented in Holinshed, the Queen and her ladies enter a garden, seeking diversion. They eavesdrop on the arriving caretakers, who lament Richard's gross negligence by comparing England to an unkept garden,

> ... full of weeds, her fairest flowers choked up,
> Her fruit trees all unpruned, her hedges ruined,
> Her knots disordered, and her wholesome herbs
> Swarming with caterpillars?
>
> (3. 4. 45–8)

The setting for the specific scene in the play becomes a metaphor for the kingdom, wherein Richard's negligence has allowed noxious practices to flourish and to suppress natural virtue and productivity. After the men predict the King's imminent deposition, the Queen steps forward to rebuke them:

> Thou, old Adam's likeness, set to dress this garden,
> How dares thy harsh rude tongue sound this unpleasing news?
> What Eve, what serpent hath suggested thee
> To make a second fall of cursèd man?
>
> (74–7)

The garden setting now widens from a metaphor for England to one for Eden, the original paradise on earth. The Queen's protest recalls the primal sin, re-enacted all too plainly by the present generation. This time Richard plays the role of erring humanity; and England, 'this other Eden, demi-paradise' (2. 1. 42), as Gaunt put it earlier, falls again from grace. Again, Shakespeare uses language and stage action to widen perspective and deepen significance.

In the deposition scene itself, 4. 1, Shakespeare again departs from Holinshed to create resonant stage symbols. He adds to Holinshed's account (perhaps from Froissart, Hall, or Daniel) the highly charged handing-over of crown and sceptre: 'I give this heavy weight from off my head, | And this unwieldy sceptre from my hand' (194–5). The ceremonial king of the first two acts, secure in his power and panoply, appears now a crushed and naked human being. No wonder Richard calls for a looking-glass to see himself and then dashes the mirror to the ground, unable to endure the pain of such self-knowledge. This gesture, also invented by Shakespeare, has additional overtones. Since mirrors served as conventional iconographical attributes of *vanitas*, or 'pride', the breaking suggests a rejection of the pride that led to so many 'weaved-up follies' (219). The gesture also warns against the simple, moralistic reading of Richard's story as a mirror for magistrates, as a cautionary history lesson for future rulers. This suffering human being refuses to be translated into political bromides or moral clichés.

Shakespeare further complicates Holinshed's reading of Richard's history by expanding the women's roles.[3] Insisting on the importance of family bonds, these women register the cost of both tyranny and rebellion. Grieving over the death of her husband and calling for retribution, the Duchess of Gloucester acutely and personally reveals the effects of Richard's tyranny. Early on she confronts Gaunt and demands justice for the King's murder of her husband. Deborah Warner's 1995 production realized the potential of this scene, often cut, by featuring an elderly Duchess on crutches slowly making her way across stage to berate and beg an immobile and powerful Gaunt. Her dignified, ceremonious entrance and physical weakness enhanced by contrast the intensity and power of her speech, 'One vial full of Edward's sacred blood ... is cracked' (1. 2. 17, 19). The Duchess tries to goad Gaunt to action:

> Call it not patience, Gaunt, it is despair.
> In suff'ring thus thy brother to be slaughtered
> Thou show'st the naked pathway to thy life,
> Teaching stern murder how to butcher thee.
>
> (29–32)

Gaunt resists, but the Duchess' vindictive anger rings in the memory, a powerful witness against Richard.

Queen Isabel, largely invented by Shakespeare from the historical 11-year-old, first appears in 2. 2, sensing some 'unborn sorrow, ripe in fortune's womb' (10). Bolingbroke's arrival in England confirms these fears and, once again, Shakespeare invents a scene starring a woman to explore history in terms personal and familiar. Like the Duchess of Gloucester, the Queen can only express her shock and dismay. Her reaction becomes refined later into a poignant sorrow as Shakespeare stages the enforced parting of King and Queen, or more precisely, that of husband and wife. Richard says,

> Doubly divorced! Bad men, you violate
> A twofold marriage: 'twixt my crown and me,
> And then betwixt me and my married wife.
>
> (5. 1. 71–3)

The Queen asks to be allowed to accompany her husband; North-umberland replies, 'That were some love, but little policy' (84). Prac-tical politics demands separation, lest the exiled couple arouse sympathy and support or produce an heir to challenge Bolingbroke. The force of history shatters the marriage and, again, a woman's grief expresses the kingdom's misery.

Shakespeare invents the Duchess of York to assert in a different way the importance of domestic concerns over civil imperatives, of private needs over public necessities. The father, York, discovers his son's involvement in a conspiracy against the new King Henry and promptly reveals all. In 5. 3 the Duchess interrupts York's interview with the King and begs for mercy. Kneeling, she dominates the scene with urgent supplication and finally forces the King to grant her son pardon. Mother knows best, it seems, as the scene totters (disruptively and typically for Shakespeare) on the edge of comedy. The Duchess' sheer force of will gains pardon for a convicted traitor against the Crown, suspends the mechanisms of law and punishment, and alters the course of history.

As the scenes of descent and deposition suggest, Shakespeare's portrayal of King Richard the tyrant gradually yields to his portrayal of Richard the suffering man and poet. Holinshed suggests this change and dual portrait, first enumerating Richard's crimes and then imagin-ing sympathetically his sorrows:

For was it no hurt, think you, to his person, to be spoiled of his royalty, to be deposed from his crown, to be translated from principality to prison, and to fall from honour into horror? All which befell him to his extreme heart grief. (Bullough, iii. 403)

But Holinshed never gives the suffering Richard his own voice. At one point, he relies on a Latin quotation which Richard 'might very well have said': '*Heu quantae sortes miseris mortalibus instant!*',[4] ('Alas, what fates oppress wretched mortals!'). At the deposition, Holinshed's Richard 'with glad countenance' reads his own resignation:

I resign all my kingly dignity, majesty, and crown, with all the lordships, power, and privileges to the foresaid kingly dignity and crown belonging, and all other lordships and possessions to me in any manner of wise pertaining, of what name, title, quality, or condition soever they be, except the lands and posses-sions for me and mine obits purchased and bought. And I renounce all right and all manner of title of possession, which I ever had or have in the same lordships and possessions or any of them, with any manner of rights belonging or appertaining unto any part of them.   (Bullough, iii. 406–7)

So Richard drones on in dry legalese.

Shakespeare's Richard, in contrast, confronts Bolingbroke face to face, king now of only his 'griefs' (4. 1. 183):

> With mine own tears I wash away my balm,
> With mine own hands I give away my crown,
> With mine own tongue deny my sacred state,
> With mine own breath release all duteous oaths.
> All pomp and majesty I do forswear.
> My manors, rents, revenues I forgo.
>
> (4. 1. 197–202)

This Richard's voice eloquently expresses sorrow and dignity. The fourfold repetition, 'with mine own', gives a ritualistic gravity to the renunciation while suggesting the personal loss and devastation. Instead of reading with 'glad countenance', Shakespeare's Richard refuses to read the official documents of accusation: 'Mine eyes are full of tears; I cannot see' (234).

Shakespeare's portrayal of Richard as suffering man and poet comes to a climax at the end of the play. Imprisoned in Pomfret castle, Richard compares 'this prison where I live unto the world' (5. 5. 2), and reflects on his own mortality:

> But whate'er I be,
> Nor I, nor any man that but man is,
> With nothing shall be pleased till he be eased
> With being nothing.
>
> (38–41)

Richard realizes that he is 'but man', destined to struggle and, finally, to find relief only in easeful death. He hears music and rues his own follies:

> And here have I the daintiness of ear
> To check time broke in a disordered string;
> But for the concord of my state and time

Had not an ear to hear my true time broke.
I wasted time, and now doth time waste me.
(45–9)

Richard reproaches himself for squandered opportunity and misrule. The poignant line, 'I wasted time, and now doth time waste me', summarizes Richard's life with cold precision and hints at the operation of divine justice. The eloquent sorrow and acknowledgement of guilt distinguish Shakespeare's Richard from Holinshed's, who shows no such poetic or moral capacity. Shakespeare rouses the former king from melancholy to indignation at the news of Bolingbroke riding his horse, the roan Barbary. The murderers enter and Richard dies in valiant struggle.

Holinshed and Shakespeare assess differently the meaning of Richard's life and death. The historian finds fault with Richard, but judges him 'a prince the most unthankfully used by his subjects'. Holinshed condemns the rebellion: though the commons, nobles, and clergy all prospered during his reign, their ingratitude stirred up such malice 'till at length it could not be assuaged without peril of destruction to them both' (Wallace and Hansen, 49). Concluding, Holinshed finds universal truths in the story: 'such misfortune (or the like) oftentimes falleth unto those princes, which when they are aloft, cast not doubt for perils that may follow. He was prodigal, ambitious, and much given to the pleasure of the body' (Bullough, iii. 408). 'The wrath of God was whetted and took so sharp an edge that the same did shred him off from the sceptre of his kingdom' (Wallace and Hansen, 49).

Less didactically, Shakespeare reads Richard's story as tragedy, as the suffering and fall of a great man. To our eyes this tragedy illustrates not providential law but human fortune. Recent productions have focused on the arbitrariness of kingship, not on its divinely appointed inevitability, and on the players who assume the royal role—Richard and Bolingbroke—or who have it thrust upon them by fate and history. John Barton's 1973 Royal Shakespeare Company production, for example, emphasized these ideas by having Richard Pasco and Ian Richardson alternate the roles of Richard and Bolingbroke. The play began with Shakespeare presenting the crown and robe to the actor who was to play Richard for the performance; the crown and robe, of course, went to Bolingbroke during the course of the show. The next night the actors switched roles.[5] This production thus demonstrated the theatricality of kingship and the powerlessness of those who live and die trying to play the king. Such a spectacle teaches moral and political lessons, but it also arouses wonder, terror, and pity.

Henry V. Holinshed reads Henry's story as a heroic epic. In his view, echoed by Shakespeare's Chorus and Henry himself, the warrior-king Henry triumphs over the French and fulfils England's imperial destiny. Henry wins in war and, finally, in love as he woos the princess, Katherine of France. Shakespeare, however, reads and writes a more ambivalent story, one that reveals the darker aspects of self-interest and self-delusion in the heroic action.

Holinshed praises Henry as 'a pattern in princehood, a lodestar in honour, and mirror of magnificence' (Bullough, iv. 408). He summarizes the King's character in terms equally hyperbolic:

> This Henry was a king, of life without spot, a prince whom all men loved and of none disdained, a captain against whom fortune never frowned, nor mischance once spurned, whose people him so severe a justicer both loved and obeyed (and so human withal) that he left no offence unpunished, nor friendship unrewarded, a terror to rebels and suppressor of sedition, his virtues notable, his qualities most praiseworthy.   (Bullough, iv. 406)

Such praise reflects a conventional Tudor understanding of history. According to this understanding, the sin of Richard II's deposition, which produced the chaos of civil war during the reign of Henry IV, finally receives expiation in the reign of Henry V, who restores England to triumphant monarchy.

From the outset, Shakespeare dramatizes this Tudor reading in the figure of the Chorus, who explains the action, and directs the audience's response. The Chorus refers to Henry as 'the mirror of all Christian kings' (2. o. 6) and, later, again in terms theological, as 'this grace of kings' (28). Whoever beholds this 'royal captain' (4. o. 29) inspiring his troops, the Chorus explains, will cry, 'Praise and glory on his head!' (31). Henry walks among his outnumbered soldiers at Agincourt, 'with cheerful semblance and sweet majesty' (40). 'Every wretch . . . plucks comfort from his looks' (41–2). Henry has a majestic presence, bestowing on all 'a largess universal, like the sun' (43). After the great victory, Henry proves himself a moral, as well as military, exemplar: 'Being free from vainness and self-glorious pride', he gives 'full trophy, signal, and ostent | Quite from himself, to God' (5. 0. 20–2). After the play the Chorus supplies an epilogue to point the moral and adorn the tale. 'Small time, but in that small most greatly lived | This star of England' (5–6). Though he reigned only nine years, Henry passes the bounds of ordinary history and mortality and moves into the realms of myth and legend.

The Chorus thus actively promotes Holinshed's reading of Henry's story as heroic epic. And the text certainly supports such a reading. Shakespeare endows Henry with an eloquent and mesmerizing voice. From the beginning Henry V expresses in rhetoric his sovereignty and divine right to rule. Mocked by the French gift of tennis balls, he resolves to 'Be like a king', and show his 'sail of greatness' (1. 2. 274). Henry promises to 'dazzle all the eyes of France' (279):

> And tell the pleasant Prince this mock of his
> Hath turned his balls to gunstones, and his soul
> Shall stand sore chargèd for the wasteful vengeance
> That shall fly from them—for many a thousand widows
> Shall this his mock mock out of their dear husbands,
> Mock mothers from their sons, mock castles down;
> Ay, some are yet ungotten and unborn
> That shall have cause to curse the Dauphin's scorn.
> But this lies all within the will of God.
>
> (281–9)

Offended majesty confronts insult and rises to menacing prophecy. Beginning in icy calm and self-possession, his rhetoric bespeaks command. The repetition of 'mock' contemptuously throws the insult back in the Dauphin's face while portraying the consequences in French blood and grief. These consequences seem all the more affecting because they are tinged with the speaker's melancholy compassion for the future French victims, the 'dear' husbands and lamented sons. The concrete images—gunstones, toppled castles—paint a vivid picture of a war that stretches on indefinitely; the couplet's rhyme— 'unborn' and 'scorn'—lays the responsibility for such destruction squarely on the Dauphin. Henry's abrupt resignation to divine will ('But this lies all within the will of God') shows him a Christian king, raising his 'rightful hand' in a 'well-hallowed cause' (293).

To a greater degree than Holinshed's king, this Henry performs his kingship in language. Similar royal performances include the discovery of treason and formal accusation of Cambridge, Scrope, and Grey (2. 2. 76 ff.) and the speech before Harfleur ('Once more unto the breach' 3. 1. 1 ff.), wherein Henry exhorts the troops, 'imitate the action of the tiger. | Stiffen the sinews, conjure up the blood, | Disguise fair nature with hard-favoured rage'; 'Cry "God for Harry! England and Saint George!"' (6–8, 34). The St Crispin's day speech, of course, chanted dutifully by generations of schoolchildren, provides the most famous example of royal rhetoric in action. (Olivier's rendition in the overtly patriotic film version, 1944, still has the power to enthrall.) Exhausted, outnumbered, facing almost certain defeat, Henry rallies his troops. Holinshed provides the germ of the speech:

I would not wish a man more here than I have; we are indeed in comparison to the enemies but a few, but if God of his clemency do favour us and our just cause, as I trust he will, we shall speed well enough. But let no man ascribe victory to our own strength and might but only to God's assistance, to whom I have no doubt we shall worthily have cause to give thanks therefore. And if so be that for our offences' sakes we shall be delivered into the hands of our enemies, the less number we be, the less damage shall the realm of England sustain.   (Bullough, iv. 394)

Should the English win, Henry preaches, they must ascribe their victory to God; though the human mind is 'prone to pride', all must guard against crediting their 'own puissance'.

Shakespeare converts the speech to a supple blank verse that conveys Henry's confidence, faith, courage, and humanity. Warwick wishes for more men; Henry replies sharply:

> What's he that wishes so?
> My cousin Warwick? No, my fair cousin.
> If we are marked to die, we are enough
> To do our country loss; and if to live,
> The fewer men, the greater share of honour.
>   (4. 3. 18–22)

In balanced phrases and run-on lines, Henry courageously resigns all to God's will. He stirs the men by introducing the theme of honour, by rejecting 'outward things' like gold and garments (27), and by articulating the ancient warrior ethic:

> God's peace, I would not lose so great an honour
> As one man more methinks would share from me.
>
> (31–2)

Instead of wishing for more men, Henry offers leave for those who have no stomach for the fight: 'We would not die in that man's company | That fears his fellowship to die with us' (38–9). Dismissing fears of death, Henry envisions victory and triumphant recollection of the battle.

> He that shall see this day and live t'old age
> Will yearly on the vigil feast his neighbours
> And say, 'Tomorrow is Saint Crispian'.
> Then will he strip his sleeve and show his scars
> And say, 'These wounds I had on Crispin's day'.
> Old men forget; yet all shall be forgot,
> But he'll remember, with advantages,
> What feats he did that day.
>
> (44–51)

For his desperate, frightened troops, Henry re-imagines the battle as a triumphant and defining moment. God ultimately orders the outcome, but men who fight courageously will be rewarded with fame ever after. Unlike Holinshed's Henry, this one emphasizes human effort, justifiable pride in the imagined victory, and the rewards of honour and glory. Henry concludes with a personal touch, uniting himself to his troops in the mystical communion of battle:

> We few, we happy few, we band of brothers.
> For he today that sheds his blood with me
> Shall be my brother.
>
> (60–2)

The battle becomes a sacrament that 'shall gentle' the condition of all soldiers, howsoever vile; those who miss it will forever regret their absence and 'hold their manhoods cheap' (63, 66) in the company of these veterans.

Henry does not always speak so inspirationally. Shakespeare adds to the chronicle account, perhaps from Tacitus' *Annals* (tr. 1598) or the 'disguised king' plays of the 1590s, Henry's night-time conversation with some ordinary soldiers in camp. This episode reveals the man behind the 'ceremonies', i.e. the royal robes and all the rhetoric of kingship. Wearing Sir Thomas Erpingham's cloak as a disguise, Henry protests the king's humanity to the ordinary soldiers, Williams and Bates:

> I think the King is but a man, as I am. The violet smells to him as it doth to me; the element shows to him as it does to me. All his senses have but human conditions. His ceremonies laid by, in his nakedness he appears but a man. (4. 1. 101–5)

Not recognizing his sovereign, Williams brusquely objects that the King will have a 'heavy reckoning to make' 'if the cause be not good' (133–4). All the slaughtered soldiers will rise to confront him on the last day, some crying for their wives, some for their unexpiated sins. Henry answers the imagined charges of the second group: 'Every subject's duty is the King's, but every subject's soul is his own' (175–6). But he never proves to the fighting men in the trenches that his cause is good; consequently, he cannot respond to the imagined charges of the first group, to the cries of grief and accusation from the dead who have left behind shattered families in a war that proves to be unjust. The awful weight of this responsibility, Henry confesses in soliloquy, lies heavily on the crowned head: 'What infinite heartsease | Must kings neglect that private men enjoy' (233–4). Neither the sceptre nor the robes 'of gold and pearl' can bring a king so sound a sleep as that enjoyed by the wretched slave with vacant mind (259 ff.). The scene ends with Henry's prayer that God forgive the sin of Richard's deposition, and steel the soldiers for battle.

Shakespeare thus endows Henry with a private voice as well as a public one. The conversations with the soldiers and with himself in soliloquy reveal the man beneath the royal robes, the mortal who struggles to uphold the weight of royal responsibility. The private prayer from a very human hero receives a positive answer in the battle of Agincourt. 'By divine persecution', Holinshed writes, 'the less number vanquished the greater' (Wallace and Hansen, 41). To magnify Henry's achievement Shakespeare suppresses Holinshed's notice of the French king's madness and the French nobles' division and increases the margin of victory, tallying the losses at 10,000 French to 29 English. His Henry attributes the lopsided victory to God and makes sure everyone else does too: 'be it death proclaimèd through our host | To boast of this, or take that praise from God | Which is his only' (4. 8. 114–16). In Henry's view God has forgiven the sin of Richard's deposition and enabled the victory. The triumphant march of British armies across French soil concretely expresses heavenly favour. Henry rules England by divine right, and France too. In 1859 Charles Kean emphasized the point by staging Henry's victorious return home: after he had ridden by a London gatehouse transformed into a triumphal arch, girls robed as angels greeted the conquering King, showering him with gold.[6] The final celebratory wooing of Princess Katherine ensures the victory for generations to come.

Or so it seems. While praising the 'star of England', the Chorus's Epilogue reminds us that Henry's successor, Henry VI, lost France and made England bleed (12). This sour note hardly untunes the joyous harmonies of the close; when heard with other discordances, however, it grows disturbingly to something of great constancy. As in *Richard II*, Shakespeare here questions the self-congratulatory formulations of Tudor historiography. He darkens Holinshed's portrait of Henry and refuses to reduce the war against France to a simple conflict between good and evil. In this play history remains to some extent unreadable—a sequence of confusing events undertaken by people of mixed motivations to uncertain ends.

Against the praise of the Chorus, Shakespeare presents an ambivalent hero from the outset. Holinshed notices that the clergy originally promoted the invasion of France so that Henry would 'not regard the importunate petitions of the commons' (Bullough, iv. 378) which mandated the transfer of Church lands to the Crown. To save their own wealth the clergy persuade the King to help himself to France. Shakespeare opens his play with the Archbishop of Canterbury and the Bishop of Ely similarly plotting some 'prevention' (1. 1. 22) against the bill that would take 'the better half' (8) of their possessions. Canterbury reveals that he already offered Henry, 'as touching France' 'a greater sum' (80) than the Church ever gave to his predecessors. The language of business acquires the dubious sanction of the lawcourt in the next scene, where Canterbury delivers a long, convoluted justification for the invasion. Ely beats the patriotic drum, exhorting Henry to remember his ancestors, 'and with your puissant arm renew their feats. | You are their heir' (1. 2. 116–17). To the objection that the invasion would leave vulnerable the Scottish border, Canterbury in polished rhetoric compares the well-ordered commonwealth to the beehive, wherein each individual does his job. He concludes triumphantly, if none too logically, that a mere fraction of the English army would 'make all Gallia shake' (216). Caught up in nationalist fervour, dazed by the prospect of international acquisitions, everyone seems to forget about logic and, of course, Church lands.

The scene with Canterbury and Ely suggests that Henry's holy war may in reality be unjustified aggression motivated by clerical and royal self-interest. The patriotism that sustains the endeavour (and that is evoked by it in performance) also disturbs, appearing sometimes as self-sacrificing love of country and sometimes as chauvinistic chest-thumping and bullying. Upon being asked if he were planning to attend a performance of *Henry V*, a witty colleague once quipped: 'I think I'll drop in for the humiliation of the French.' Reductive and unfair, the wit nevertheless draws blood as a brutal summary of the action. The victory at Agincourt in this play magnifies the blessed and courageous English army at the expense of their proud enemies. Any construction of English patriotism in performance of this play depends heavily upon the depiction of the French. Some productions (including Olivier's film) contrast the foppish, boastful French with the plain, tough English soldiers. Others challenge the flag-waving by dignifying the French, as Michael Langham did in 1956 in Stratford, Ontario, where he invited French-Canadian actors to play French roles, thus evoking Canadian politics. Still others (including Noble's 1984 Royal Shakespeare Company production and Branagh's 1989 film) undermine the patriotic reading by emphasizing the brutality of war and its terrible cost in human suffering.

The play itself seems designed to question its own patriotic assumptions and assertions. Holinshed's invading Englishmen become Shakespeare's multinational force, conspicuously featuring the Welsh Fluellen, the Irish MacMorris, and the Scottish Jamy, each speaking with a thick regional accent (e.g. 3. 2). The idealized dream of British unity and co-operation against a common enemy creaks and cracks throughout the play. The Welshman Fluellen thrashes Pistol for

mocking the Welsh custom of wearing a leek on St David's day (5. 1).
Alluding to current events, the Chorus anticipates Essex's return from
Ireland, 'Bringing rebellion broachèd on his sword' (5. 0. 32). How
must original audiences have viewed the Irish MacMorris? Barrie
Rutter, who played the role 'with IRA fervour' before the royal family
in one performance of Terry Hands's 1975 production, sensed modern
audience discomfort: 'I could feel them freezing in their seats. Oh-
God-not-in-front-of-our-monarch vibrations came welling up out of
the stalls.'[7] King Henry himself recalls traditional Anglo–Scottish
enmity and prepares for invasion:

> For you shall read that my great-grandfather
> Never unmasked his power unto France
> But that the Scot on his unfurnished kingdom
> Came pouring like the tide into a breach
> With ample and brim fullness of his force
> Galling the gleanèd land with hot assays,
> Girding with grievous siege castles and towns.
>   (1. 2. 146–52)

Olivier cut all reference to the Scottish threat from his nationalistic
production; such moments insistently unsettle those who believe in
the united kingdom and the unrealized dream of British nation-
hood.

   Another group of invented characters also casts long shadows on
Henry and the invasion. Here, as elsewhere, Shakespeare adds to his
sources a comic cast of characters and subplot. Pistol, Bardolph, and
Nym go to France to steal. As Pistol says, 'Let us to France, like
horseleeches, my boys, | To suck, to suck, the very blood to suck!' (2. 3.
51–2). Simple thieves, cowards, and profiteers, these characters puncture the rhetoric of divine right and British imperialism. Bardolph
even offers a parody of Henry's battle cry, 'Once more unto the breach'
(3. 1. 1 ff.), echoing him with 'On, on, on, on, on! To the breach, to the
breach!' (3. 2. 1–2); Bardolph's friends, Nym and Pistol, refuse to budge
until Fluellen beats them forward. Bardolph gets hanged for robbing a
church (3. 6. 102). The blustering Pistol frees his prisoner for ransom:
'As I suck blood, I will some mercy show' (4. 4. 61); beaten finally by
Fluellen and exposed as a coward, Pistol resolves to turn bawd and
cutpurse. The ignominious careers of these characters reflect ironically

on the pretensions of the English invaders: Henry and his army may be simply a grander, more pompous version of these selfish lowlifes.

On occasion, even Henry himself invites such sceptical demythologizing. Outside the town of Harfleur with his army, he threatens to be unable to stop his troops from raping 'the shrill-shrieking daughters', from dashing fathers' 'reverend heads' against walls, from spitting 'naked infants' upon pikes (3. 3. 118–21). The town surrenders without any bloodshed but the audience may shrill feel discomfited by such rhetoric, unprecedented in Holinshed. Later, upon hearing of French reinforcements, Henry orders the soldiers to kill their prisoners (4. 6. 35–7), a precautionary strike that appears as such in Holinshed (Bullough, iv. 397).[8] In the next scene, however, Gower reports approvingly that the King gave this order to get revenge for the sacking and burning of his tent (4. 7. 7–10); this news prompts Fluellen's comparison of Henry to Alexander the Pig, the mispronunciation (Pig for Big) being humorously deflating if not intentionally ironic. Soon after, Henry enters angrily, having heard presumably about the French slaughter of the boys guarding the luggage; he orders a herald to tell the French to join combat immediately:

> Besides, we'll cut the throats of those we have,
> And not a man of them that we shall take
> Shall taste our mercy. Go and tell them so.
> (4. 7. 61–3)

Henry here echoes Pistol: '*Couple a gorge*' (2. 1. 69), 'Cut the throat!' The King's language again strains credulity and disturbs; the changing rationale for the prisoners' slaughter—precaution, revenge, threat—suggests the capricious cruelty of the invader rather than the mercy of the self-proclaimed Christian king.

The last scenes of the play similarly furnish Henry's sceptics and adulators alike. In 5. 2, a scene created from Holinshed's mere mention of Henry's love for Katherine (Bullough, iv. 403–4), the King woos Katherine like a plain English soldier:

A good heart, Kate, is the sun and the moon—or rather the sun and not the moon, for it shines bright and never changes, but keeps his course truly. If thou would have such a one, take me; and take me, take a soldier; take a soldier, take a king. (162–7)

Such charming nonsense distracts neither the wooer nor the audience from Henry's imperial designs; winning Katherine, Henry secures his conquest for the future:

I love France so well that I will not part with a village of it, I will have it all mine; and Kate, when France is mine, and I am yours, then yours is France, and you are mine. (173–6)

Again, as in *Richard II*, Shakespeare expands female character: Holinshed's Katherine appears finally as an article in the peace treaty (Bullough, iv. 406). Shakespeare's Katherine appears in 3. 4, prophetically learning English, the language of the future conqueror. She appears again in 5. 2, where she speaks French and English, flirts, plays coy, grants a kiss. (An inventive Shenandoah Shakespeare Express director had Katherine's French maid speak the line, 'de tongeus of de mans is be full of deceits' (5. 2. 120), with a cleverly appropriate mispronunciation of the last word, 'de-*sheets*'.) The private love chat *à deux* concludes with a public ratification of the proposed marriage, negotiation of the final terms, and the official naming of Henry as *Haeres Franciae* (337), 'heir of France', thereby disinheriting Katherine's brother, the Dauphin.

Shakespeare finds in the *Chronicles* plots, characters, and ideas. Reading against Holinshed, he turns *Richard II* into tragedy, reshaping the facts of revolt and deposition into the moving story of a flawed, suffering man. Reading against Holinshed later, Shakespeare writes *Henry V* as problem comedy. The play features humorous characters, triumphant intrigue, restoration of loss, and even the culminating wedding; Henry's glorious triumph, however, also appears as grand theft and murder.

Tradition: the Vice Figure

The famous film-maker Alfred Hitchcock, it is said, believed in an eleventh commandment: 'Thou shalt not get caught.' Hitchcock shrewdly suggests here a fundamental principle of audience psychology: we tend to identify with those who act out forbidden impulses; like children, we all secretly wish to escape the adult laws of consequence, responsibility, and punishment. The master of the modern suspense film exploited these principles as did medieval drama, a rich and important part of Shakespeare's literary heritage.[9] In the late fourteenth and early fifteenth centuries the morality play told the story of a representative human figure (Humanum Genus, Everyman, Mankind, Youth), surrounded by personified abstractions of good (Courage, Conscience, Despair) and evil (Avarice, Pride, Lust).[10] The human figure usually falls into sin and recovers through God's grace and repentance. From the early and elaborate *The Castle of Perseverance* (*c.*1425), through the stark *Everyman* (*c.*1490) to William Wager's *Enough is as Good as a Feast* (*c.*1560), the Vice figure, who appears under many different names, stars in the show. Opposed to various virtues, Vice acts as a nimble trickster and master rhetorician who entertains the audience even as he outrages them. The Vice figure animates Shakespeare's plays, particularly the characters of Richard III and Falstaff.[11]

Richard III. Shakespeare's *Richard III* provides the lead actor with one of the great villain roles in world theatre. To get and keep the crown Richard has executed his brother George, Duke of Clarence, along with the Queen's faction, Rivers, Vaughan, and Grey, the Lord Hastings, his trusted ally Buckingham, his wife Anne, and his nephews, the two young princes. The appeal of the role, however, lies not so much in the villain's evil (others can match Richard in this regard) but in his style—in the audacious, witty, theatrical, defiantly self-congratulatory way he performs his wickedness. This style, especially evident in the first half of this play, Richard owes to the traditional Vice. Richard opens the play by cheekily announcing to the audience his evil intention and purpose:

> I am determinèd to prove a villain
> And hate the idle pleasures of these days.
> Plots have I laid, inductions dangerous.
> (1. 1. 30–2)

This sort of brash opening revelation typifies the Vice. Witness Detraction at the beginning of *The Castle of Perseverance*:

> All things I cry against the peace
> To knight and knave: this is my kind [nature]
> Ya![12]

The use of direct address, usually continued in soliloquy and aside, establishes a rapport with the audience, who become involuntary confidants. Richard, like the Vice figures before him, keeps up a conversation with the audience; he thus evokes sympathetic laughter as he provokes intellectual and moral disapproval.

At one point Richard himself recognizes explicitly his adoption of the Vice's verbal facility and linguistic style. Overheard muttering a threat to Prince Edward, 'So wise so young, they say, do never live long' (3. 1. 79), Richard recovers quickly:

> I say, 'Without characters fame lives long'.
> (*Aside*) Thus like the formal Vice, Iniquity,
> I moralize two meanings in one word.
>   (81–3)

The capacity to 'moralize two meanings in one word', to deceive by clever use of language, characterizes Richard and the 'formal' (i.e. conventional) Vice. Moreover, Bernard Spivack notes, this quick-witted ability in deceptive rhyme functions as a 'prominent signature' of the Vice.[13] Throughout the play Richard employs other rhetorical tricks and mannerisms from the Vice's repertoire. He frequently uses proverbs and false tears; he mouths pieties, lamenting the world's decline (1. 3. 70), invoking the name of Jesus (136), thanking God for his humility (2. 1. 73), expressing faith in eventual punishment of the wicked (140). He sermonizes on the failings of his victims, mocking, for example, his brother's gullibility, as he sends him to the Tower: 'Simple plain Clarence, I do love thee so | That I will shortly send thy soul to heaven' (1. 1. 118–19). He uses the resources of theatre, acting parts and staging scenes.

Richard shows off all his tricks in seducing Lady Anne over the body of her fiancé, whom he slew earlier. In a scene Shakespeare invented, Richard swears by Saint Paul (1. 2. 36), preaches charity (49, 68–9), practises disputation and outright flattery (114 ff.). He gives up his sword and histrionically lays his breast open for the blow. In the film *Looking for Richard*, Al Pacino circled with predatory intensity a young, innocent, dark-eyed, and vulnerable Winona Ryder. Anne finally yields, mastered by Richard's rhetorical and theatrical brilliance. Exultant in soliloquy, Richard scorns Anne's weakness and inconstancy:

> Was ever woman in this humour wooed?
> Was ever woman in this humour won?
> I'll have her, but I will not keep her long.
> What, I that killed her husband and his father,
> To take her in her heart's extremest hate,
> With curses in her mouth, tears in her eyes,
> The bleeding witness of my hatred by,
> Having God, her conscience, and these bars against me.
>
> .   .   .   .   .   .
>
> Upon my life she finds, although I cannot,
> Myself to be a marv'lous proper man.
> I'll be at charges for a looking-glass
> And entertain a score or two of tailors
> To study fashions to adorn my body.
>
> (1. 2. 215–22, 240–4)

The Vice can be alluring, dangerous, charming, downright sexy; but the preening self-congratulation, laced with contempt for Anne, expresses a frightening malevolence.

As this passage indicates, Richard directly opposes the workings of conscience in others as well as in himself. Plays like *Mundus et Infans.* (*c.*1508), *Impatient Poverty* (*c.*1547), and *Appius and Virginia* (*c.*1564) likewise feature a Vice who opposes a Conscience figure. Shakespeare weaves this opposition throughout the rhetoric and action of *Richard III.* Hired by Richard to kill Clarence, the unnamed murderers decide to dispense with conscience:

> SECOND MURDERER I'll not meddle with it. It makes a
> man a coward. A man cannot steal but it accuseth him.
> A man cannot swear but it checks him. A man cannot
> lie with his neighbour's wife but it detects him. 'Tis a
> blushing, shamefaced spirit, that mutinies in a man's
> bosom. It fills a man full of obstacles.
>
> (1. 4. 131–6)

After killing the two young princes, Dighton and Forrest flee 'with conscience and remorse' (4. 3. 20). Having committed sin, they begin to enact a familiar morality-play pattern of repentance. Playing the Vice before his death, Richard scorns conscience directly:

Conscience is but a word that cowards use,
Devised at first to keep the strong in awe.
Our strong arms be our conscience; swords, our law.
            (5. 6. 39–41)

This sinner defiantly refuses to repent. Consigning all moral scruple to cowardice, Richard here recognizes no higher moral authority than the will to power. The familiar opposition between Vice and Conscience here shows the King's moral depravity and inhumanity.

Despite his surging comic energy, the Vice often brings death to his victims. The misled Dalila of *Nice Wanton* (*c.*1550) dies crooked, lame, starving; her brother Ismael gets executed for burglary and murder. The irrepressible Nichol Newfangle scorns his victims Cutpurse and Pickpurse, who end up hanged for their crimes. Death often stalks the Vice himself. In *Mankind* (*c.*1470), New-guise enters the stage with a noose around his neck, having narrowly escaped hanging; in *Youth* (*c.*1520), a broken rope saves Riot at the gallows tree. Like his many predecessors, Richard leads victims to death. Queen Margaret calls him 'hell's black intelligencer, | Only reserved their factor to buy souls | And send them thither' (4. 4. 71–3). And Death, finally, comes for Richard himself and reveals momentarily the man behind the Vice. Sensing his end, Richard cries to the God he mocked before with such flippant arrogance: 'Have mercy, Jesu!' (5. 5. 132). The conscience so frequently violated and dismissed now stings the reprobate: 'O coward conscience, how dost thou afflict me?' (133). For this doomed man there will be no last-minute escape; he fears the approaching end: 'I shall despair. There is no creature loves me? | And if I die no soul will pity me' (154–5). This brief switch out of the Vice role, and then back into it for the last battle, poses a considerable challenge to actors: Olivier's film cut Richard's crisis of conscience as too compromising.

'Thou shalt not get caught.' Richard's sins finally do catch up with him: the procession of ghosts in 5. 5 provides a reckoning both arithmetical and moral. Eleven victims in all, Yorks and Lancasters alike, appear on stage to bless Richmond and curse Richard, their killer. Finally, Richmond, the anointed one, slays Richard, much to our relief and, it must be admitted, our sorrow. For part of us laments the loss of that voice and charm, whatever form Richard has taken—Laurence Olivier's jaunty, swaggering, eloquent grotesque (1955), Antony Sher's deformed but astonishingly athletic cripple, whose crutches doubled as weapons, mandibles, parts of a crucifix (1984), or Ian McKellen's malign, psychotic, neo-Nazi (1995) ('A jeep! A jeep! My kingdom for a jeep!'). And our sorrow actually pays tribute to the Vice figure, who supplied Richard with his charming style of verbal villainy. In *1 Henry IV*, the Vice will put on some weight and play a different role, that of Sir John Falstaff.

1 Henry IV. Shakespeare conjoins many figures in the fat person of Sir John Falstaff—the historical Sir John Oldcastle, the classical parasite and bragging soldier, the festive Lord of Misrule, and the Vice. Like Richard III, Falstaff explicitly identifies himself with the morality-play villain, threatening to beat Hal out of the kingdom with a 'dagger of lath [wood]' (2. 5. 137), a traditional weapon of Vice. Later, Hal calls Falstaff 'that reverend Vice, that grey Iniquity, that father Ruffian, that Vanity in Years' (2. 5. 458–9). Reprising the language and action of Vice throughout the play, Falstaff tempts Hal to indulgence and dissipation.

From the outset, Falstaff exhibits the Vice's familiar rhetorical style and tricks. He strikes virtuous poses: 'Before I knew thee, Hal, I knew nothing; and now am I, if a man should speak truly, little better than one of the wicked' (1. 2. 92–4). The Vice often enters the stage singing; Falstaff calls for music and laughter: 'Come, sing me a bawdy song, make me merry' (3. 3. 12–13). Like the Vice, Falstaff is a master of lies: he skilfully fabricates the non-existent fight against the men in buckram. He can also invent an excuse instantly to avoid getting caught. Exposed as coward in the Gadshill episode, Falstaff turns the tables on the accusing Prince, who robbed him in disguise: 'By the Lord, I knew ye as well as he that made ye. Why, hear you, my masters. Was it for me to kill the heir-apparent? Should I turn upon the true prince?' (2. 5. 270–2). Like his predecessors, Falstaff displays a knack for colourful insult (2. 5. 248–51) and for theatrical performance, wittily discharging his part in the 'play extempore' (2. 5. 282–3) just as he does in the larger play everywhere.

Falstaff plays the Vice in deeds as well as words. Spivack (87 ff.) compares Shakespeare's gormandizing knight to Gluttony in *Nature* (*c*.1495) as well as to Sensual Appetite in *The Four Elements* (*c*.1517), who tells a lie similar to Falstaff's story of the men in buckram. Regarding Falstaff in *1* and *2 Henry IV*, he writes: 'The robbery at

Gadshill, the tavern frolics, Doll Tearsheet meretrix, the endless jests about hanging, the antinomy of Falstaff and the Chief Justice, are all stock motifs of action, dialogue, and "character" in the moralities' (90). Moreover, as Falstaff leads Hal from the court world of responsibility into the tavern world of riot, he re-enacts the familiar role of tempter. In *Mankind* (*c.*1470) Mischief and his crew of engaging comic rascals—New-guise, Nowadays, and Naught—likewise lead the titular character from work to idleness, drunkenness, and foolery. In *Mundus et Infans* (*c.*1508) Folly leads Manhood Mighty to brothels and taverns; they even dine in Eastcheap. Hypocrisy in *Lusty Juventus* (*c.*1550) seduces the lead character with Wicked Fellowship and offers him a prostitute, Abominable Living, for a companion. Figures such as these furnish the prototypes for Falstaff, that 'abominable misleader of youth' (2. 5. 467–8), and his fellow roisterers at the tavern—Bardolph, Nym, Poins, and Doll Tearsheet.

Despite the gaiety here, death looms increasingly as Falstaff proceeds through Shakespeare's history plays. He leads his beggarly band of soldiers to slaughter: 'I have led my ragamuffins where they are peppered; there's not three of my hundred and fifty left alive, and they are for the town's end, to beg during life' (5. 3. 35–8). This cavalier dismissal of human life and suffering exposes the core of cruelty beneath the Vice's merry demeanour. For all the fun, Falstaff poses a real threat to the citizens and rulers of England. Finally death stalks Falstaff himself. In *2 Henry IV* the fat knight struggles with disease and old age. He cannot abide a reminder of his end, protests his youth to Justice Shallow but confesses poignantly to Doll Tearsheet: 'I am old, I am old' (2. 4. 273). Banished by the newly crowned Hal, condemned to prison by the Chief Justice, Falstaff dies finally, a broken man, babbling of green fields.[14] His last breath recalls ironically, perhaps, Psalm 23, with its promise of righteous living and trust in God's goodness and mercy.

The traditional Vice animates Shakespeare's Falstaff. But though Shakespeare replays the archetypal morality-play temptation of youth in *1 Henry IV*, he also subverts the familiar pattern.[15] Hal is no Everyman but a politic and sophisticated prince. He dallies in the tavern world to strike up popular admiration at his eventual reformation: 'I'll so offend to make offence a skill, | Redeeming time when men think least I will' (1. 2. 213–14). Henry manipulates the Vice instead of being manipulated by him (vice versa, indeed). Furthermore, unlike the unregenerate prince of at least one source, *The Famous Victories of Henry V*, Hal sojourns in the tavern world not to cancel but to complete his education. In the hereditary monarchies of Europe, the education of the Christian prince became a matter of constant discussion and supreme practical import. Although the people could not choose their ruler, they could at least train him for just and efficient administration. Guillaume Budé, Desiderius Erasmus, and Thomas Elyot all wrote treatises on the proper education of a Christian prince, outlining a rigorous course of study in languages, literature, history, philosophy, sciences, theology, and the social arts. Hal elects a different curriculum in the tavern, one whose advantages he summarizes pithily: 'I can drink with any tinker in his own language' (2. 5. 18–19). This understanding of common people and ability to communicate with them stands Hal in good stead during his reign as king, as Shakespeare illustrates in the Harfleur and St Crispin's Day speeches of *Henry V*.

Moreover, Falstaff does not merely function as the traditional Vice, tempting the Prince to sin. In the balanced architecture of the play, Falstaff and the tavern world call into question the character and values of the opposing court world. Robbing the travellers at Gadshill, Falstaff and his crew reflect ironically on their courtly betters. Falstaff steals crowns, but the King, we are insistently reminded, has stolen the crown. The rebels wish to steal it back and plunge England into civil war. The robbery suggests the greedy self-interest that underlies courtly pretension and rhetoric, even if Falstaff himself appears as an old, vain sinner, as in James Henry Hackett's long-running stage interpretation in the United States (1832–70).

Falstaff directly challenges courtly rhetoric and ideals, especially the concept of honour that motivates King and rebel alike. Hotspur expresses his devotion to this ideal of military daring and courage:

> By heaven, methinks it were an easy leap
> To pluck bright honour from the pale-faced moon,
> Or dive into the bottom of the deep,
> Where fathom-line could never touch the ground,
> And pluck up drownèd honour by the locks.
>
> (1. 3. 199–203)

Choleric, fearless, gallant, perhaps a bit mad, Hotspur lives up to the ideal of honour. Like many brave soldiers, however, he winds up dead. Falstaff wants nothing to do with such 'grinning honour' (5. 3. 59); his famous 'catechism' rejects such abstract ideals for the comfortable solidities of life and limb:

Can honour set-to a leg? No. Or an arm? No. Or take away the grief of a wound? No. Honour hath no skill in surgery, then? No. What is honour? A word. What is in that word 'honour'? What is that 'honour'? Air. A trim reckoning! Who hath it? He that died o' Wednesday. Doth he feel it? No. Doth he hear it? No. 'Tis insensible then? Yea, to the dead. But will it not live with the living? No. Why? Detraction will not suffer it. Therefore, I'll none of it. Honour is a mere scutcheon. And so ends my catechism. (5. 1. 131–40).

Honour can perform no helpful service to the living, nor can it rest with the dead because of detraction and slander. An empty sound, honour makes men 'food for powder' (4. 2. 65). It is mere ornament, a 'scutcheon', i.e. a heraldic emblem that was the lowest form of symbol, having no banner or other devices.

The Vice figure—deceitful, charismatic, theatrical—supplies Shakespeare here and throughout his career. In addition to these historical figures, the Vice enlivens some villains—Aaron in *Titus Andronicus*, Edmund in *King Lear*, and Iago in *Othello*. This last arch-deceiver plays hale drinking companion, honest friend, sage counsellor, pious homilist, and knowing informer; he works by skilful rhetoric and stage trick to goad Othello into a jealous frenzy. Out of the goodness of Desdemona, he boasts, he makes the net that enmeshes them all (2. 3. 352–3). In him and the others the Vice finds new life and new audiences to offend and to please.

4

Comedies

What did Shakespeare read in order to write his comedies? He read the classics, probably in Latin and in translation, especially Plautus (*c.* 250–184 BC) and Terence (*c.*190–159 BC).[1] These playwrights, heirs to Menander (fourth century BC) and other Greeks, gave to later generations a flexible repertory of comic characters—the old man (*senex*), wily servant (*servus callidus*), marriageable girl (*virgo*), young man (*adulescens*), braggart soldier (*miles gloriosus*), parasite (*parasitus*), and courtesan (*meretrix*). In their twenty-seven surviving Latin plays, still called New Comedy after two thousand years, these playwrights vary skilfully such dramatic devices as lock-outs, eavesdroppings, and disguises. Shakespeare also read later prose fiction, usually but not always translated from the Italian or French.[2] These tales display love thwarted, denied, troubled; they feature oaths, rings, adventures, impossible tasks and difficulties; they often end in wondrous reconciliations. From classical comedy, through numerous Continental, especially Italian variations, Shakespeare inherited an important dramatic tradition featuring an angry father blocking young lovers. Lysander in *A Midsummer Night's Dream*, who must confront Egeus, Hermia's father, comments aptly, 'The course of true love never did run smooth' (1. 1. 134). Here as elsewhere, the lovers must use their wits to defeat the old man. This conflict drives the plots of much Renaissance drama as well as those of books, films, and television situation comedies today.[3]

Text: Plautus' *Menaechmi*

The Comedy of Errors.

Two similar faces, neither of which taken by itself draws a smile, do so from their similarity when seen together. (Blaise Pascal, *Pensées*)[4]

Like Pascal, we find something oddly whimsical about such repetition, such duplication of the human and natural. Clones or identical twins unsettle and amuse because nature normally tends to infinite variation, to dissimilar snowflakes, elm trees, aardvarks. The doubling of one's face, so basic and private a marker of self, disables any pretension to dignity, individuality, and importance. Plautus' *Menaechmi* capitalizes on the comic possibilities of such doubling. The play presents separated identical twins, one of whom, Menaechmus the Traveller of Syracuse, appears in Epidamnus, the home of the other, Menaechmus the Citizen. The Citizen's family and friends confuse the two; eventually a doctor pronounces the Citizen mad. Finally, the twins meet each other and resolve the misunderstandings.

Even when he follows a source closely, Shakespeare reads eclectically, dipping into other texts and books, creating subordinate plot lines, adding characters and themes. Instead of the Plautine prologue, which explains the background, he here substitutes the adapted story of 'Apollonius of Tyre', probably as found in John Gower's *Confessio Amantis* (which will later supply *Pericles*). Arrested and condemned, Egeon, Syracusan merchant and father of the twins, relates his shipwreck, loss of wife and child, and fruitless wanderings. Shakespeare adds the Apollonius story to set up a familial, not merely fraternal, reunion. But the long tale of woe, so apparently different in style and tone from the raucous Plautine comedy, presents a distinct challenge to directors and actors. The BBC television version (1984) jazzed up the tale by staging it amidst the antics of Ephesian jugglers and magicians. Colin Romoff's 1953 production in South Africa with an all-black cast transposed the narration culturally: the arrest of a person for being in the wrong place at the wrong time had chilling contemporary application; audiences rejoiced at the final joyous overthrow of the law and liberation of the prisoner. Tim Supple's 1996 Royal Shakespeare Company production played the tale straight, finding in Egeon's pathos and yearning not merely a contrast to the Plautine action but its keynote.

Shakespeare changes the original setting from Epidamnus (which spurred some wordplay for Plautus on *damnum* or 'loss', 263–4) to Ephesus, replete with associations of witchcraft from another source, St Paul's epistles. The Traveller muses on the setting:

> They say this town is full of cozenage,
> As nimble jugglers that deceive the eye,
> Dark-working sorcerers that change the mind,
> Soul-killing witches that deform the body,
> Disguisèd cheaters, prating mountebanks,
> And many suchlike libertines of sin.
>
> (1. 2. 97–102)

This setting suggests the presence of dangers spiritual as well as material, the threat to self and soul, not merely to the wallet. St Paul may exert influence elsewhere, particularly in the transformation of Diana's temple to an abbey, the scene for the resolution. Paul's Epistle to the Ephesians probably also suggested Shakespeare's concern with marriage and the proper relations between husband and wife. Emphasis on these non-Plautine elements in performance can transform the rollicking Roman farce to romance. In this transformation the various losings and findings betoken larger mysteries of identity, marriage, reconciliation, and deliverance.

Naturally competitive, Shakespeare outdoes Plautus by doubling the joke, providing two sets of identical twins, the Antipholuses and their servants, the Dromios, instead of one. This change increases exponentially the number of mistakes and confusions. Delaying the entrance of the Traveller, Plautus focuses attention on the Citizen, on the premiss of a normal, if troubled, marriage; delaying the entrance of the Citizen, Shakespeare emphasizes the Traveller, thus increasing the sense of dislocation and disturbance from the start. Shakespeare also develops the character of the travelling twin. Plautus' Traveller, like many others in *Menaechmi*, hustles about the town, eager for gain. Mistaken for his brother, he accepts the courtesan's invitation: *mulier haec stulta atque inscita est quantum | perspexi modo | est hic praeda nobis* (439–41), 'This woman is a fool and also ignorant; I have just seen as much. There is booty for us here'. In the original text he uses the Latin

word *praeda*, 'booty', thus indicating rapacious interests. His Shakespearian counterpart, Antipholus of Syracuse, a melancholy, romantic
dreamer, instead searches for his lost mother and brother. He does not
hunt for spoil.

> He that commends me to mine own content
> Commends me to the thing I cannot get.
> I to the world am like a drop of water
> That in the ocean seeks another drop,
> Who, falling there to find his fellow forth,
> Unseen, inquisitive, confounds himself.
> So I, to find a mother and a brother,
> In quest of them, unhappy, lose myself.
> (1. 2. 33–40)

The searching, discontented Traveller fears losing himself in the
world's great ocean. When Adriana, the Citizen's wife, invites him
to dinner, he does not think her easy prey, but wonders about his
situation in amazement:

> Am I in earth, in heaven, or in hell?
> Sleeping or waking? Mad or well advised?
> Known unto these, and to myself disguised!
> I'll say as they say, and persever so,
> And in this mist at all adventures go.
> (2. 2. 215–19)

Suspended between waking and sleeping, madness and sanity, he
surrenders to the unfolding series of events.

Shakespeare softens the hard edges of the Plautine romp and
centres the play on love and marriage. Plautus' Traveller eats, drinks,
and makes merry with his brother's wife; Shakespeare's Traveller falls
in love with Adriana's sister, Luciana, invented, apparently, for this
purpose. He woos her in wonder: 'Are you a god? Would you create
me new? | Transform me, then, and to your power I'll yield' (3. 2. 39–
40). Previously, the single Luciana preached to Adriana about 'self-
harming jealousy' (2. 1. 101); now, mistaking the Traveller for the
Citizen, she finds Adriana's fears confirmed. Proven wrong, thoroughly confused and off balance, her own desires for love and marriage
can surface in the lyrical duet. Clifford Williams' 1962 Royal

Shakespeare Company production played up the romance in this scene, featuring a lovely and surprised Susan Maryott responding to the tender, smitten Alec McCowen. In *The Comedy of Errors* Plautus' spoil-hungry Traveller becomes a bewildered lover who will find a wife and reconstituted family; the unmarried Luciana will find a husband.

These findings occur through fortunate happenstance rather than witty intrigue. And Shakespeare qualifies the soaring violin music with a distinctly comic counterpoint. The Traveller's amorous poetry in 3. 2 precedes Dromio of Syracuse's comic prose, specifically his horrified account of Nell, the amorous kitchen wench affianced to his resident twin:

> Marry, sir, she's the kitchen wench, and all grease; and I
> know not what use to put her to but to make a lamp of her,
> and run from her by her own light. I warrant her rags and
> the tallow in them will burn a Poland winter. If she lives
> till doomsday, she'll burn a week longer than the whole
> world.   (3. 2. 96–101)

There follows a comedy routine wherein Antipholus feeds Dromio questions, and he responds with an inverted blazon, a catalogue of the lady's grotesqueries instead of her charms.

> ANTIPHOLUS S What complexion is she of?
> DROMIO S Swart like my shoe, but her face nothing like so
> clean kept. For why?—She sweats a man may go over-
> shoes in the grime of it.
>
> (102–5)

This is great fun in itself but the clowning also serves a serious purpose, qualifying the other love relationships in the play. Romantic rapture coexists with love amidst the potato peels. And this coexistence is typical: Shakespeare often adds comic characters to his source stories to reflect humorously and satirically on the main action.

Shakespeare also transforms Plautus' women. Plautus plays up the Courtesan and plays down the wife; Shakespeare again reverses the emphases. The seductive and aptly named Erotium becomes in his play the 'Courtesan', while the unnamed wife turns into Adriana. Plautus presents us with simple character types—the courtesan and nagging wife—in a businessman's fantasy: the Citizen sneaks out to escape his wife and enjoy the forbidden delights of exotic meals and sex with Erotium, to revel in *voluptas* (pleasure) instead of *negotium* (business). The cloak stolen from the wife for the Courtesan, we are told, smells of *furtum, scortum, prandium* (170), 'theft, whoring, lunch'. (Others have translated the Latin more colourfully, 'A raid! A jade! A meal!'; 'grabbing, grubbing, and rub-a-dub-dubbing'; 'pinching, lunching, wenching'; and the triumphant 'purloin, sirloin, her loin'.)[5] After discovering his brother, Menaechmus ends the play by offering to sell his wife to the highest bidder.

Shakespeare's Courtesan searches after her diamond ring, one more miscarried object, and recovers it at the conclusion. The playwright focuses more on the passionate wife, Adriana. Adriana confronts her supposedly errant husband (actually his twin) in high indignation, hosts the dinner, summons the doctor, pleads for her husband's release into her custody. In her character the playwright explores further the workings of love and marriage. She introduces the topic of gender inequity ('Why should their liberty than ours be more?' 2.1.10). Trying to reclaim her estranged husband, she articulates a vision of marital unity:

> How comes it now, my husband, O how comes it
> That thou art then estrangèd from thyself?—
> Thy 'self' I call it, being strange to me
> That, undividable, incorporate,
> Am better than thy dear self's better part.
>
> (2. 2. 122–6)

Adriana touches on the Plautine theme of identity from another angle, that of two selves becoming one in marriage. This mysterious transformation will appear elsewhere in the reunion of Egeon and his long lost-wife. In the course of the action Adriana and her husband show how hard it is to achieve and maintain marital harmony. They miscommunicate; they show insensitivity to each other—she in her jealousy, he in his questionable friendship with the Courtesan. At the end of the play, they are still working towards understanding and an uneasy peace.

Expanding the dinner sequence with reference to another play, Plautus' *Amphitruo*, Shakespeare alters the plot and creates the lockout scene (3. 1). In *Menaechmi* the husband finds his own door and that of Erotium locked against him (668 ff.); he thinks himself *exclusissimus* (698), 'utterly locked out'. In 3. 1 Antipholus the Citizen arrives with dinner guests to find his door shut against him. Shakespeare adds insult to injury: the Traveller's slave, Dromio, scorns the master from within:

> Mome, malt-horse, capon, coxcomb, idiot, patch!
> Either get thee from the door or sit down at the hatch.
>
> (3. 1. 32–3)

As in *Amphitruo*, a cheeky servant keeps watch while the wife innocently entertains an impostor she thinks is her husband. Converting the scene to rollicking long-line rhymes, Shakespeare emphasizes the servant's insolence and the husband's impotent fury. Trevor Nunn's musical production (1976) emphasized these aspects hilariously, as Mike Gwilym's angry Antipholus, sputtering in frustration, finally attacked the offending intercom through which Dromio communicated his insults and tore it off the wall; it kept right on talking.

Shakespeare adapts *Menaechmi* to stage an examination of the travelling twin by the eccentric quack, Dr Pinch (4. 4). In Plautus the wife and father confront the Traveller, who pretends to be mad in order to escape them; then the father returns with a doctor, who pompously examines the Citizen, pronounces him mad, and orders slaves to carry him away (899 ff.). Shakespeare combines these two scenes to emphasize the theme of madness. Along with Adriana, Pinch examines the Citizen, declares him mad, and orders him bound and removed. The false madness of Plautus' Traveller, merely a pose adopted for the moment, threatens to become real for Shakespeare's Citizen, as frustration drives him to paranoia and insanity. Pinch gives the madness a supernatural dimension by adding to the arrogance of the Latin doctor the hocus-pocus of an Elizabethan exorcist ('I charge thee, Satan, housed within this man, | To yield possession to my holy prayers', 55–6). Shakespeare also endows Pinch with the pomposity of the pedant, a type popular in Italian comedies. The Citizen responds to Pinch's diagnosis by smacking him on the ear. Adriana confronts her husband (not the other twin) and the sparks fly as each spouse tells the truth but flatly contradicts the other. Climactically, Antipholus calls his wife 'Dissembling harlot' (102), accuses her of conspiring with the others to mock him, and threatens to pluck out her eyes. This moment, unlike anything in Plautus' two scenes, reveals the dark side of the confusions and errors; even if played for laughs, it suggests the lurking danger of violence.

In Plautus the twins finally meet and painstakingly unravel the mystery; they plan to auction off the Citizen's goods and live together. Shakespeare also emphasizes laughter but creates a different conclusion, filled with surprising turns. The action shifts to an abbey. Now herself locked out from her spouse, Adriana re-examines her own behaviour, particularly her jealousy. Stung by the Abbess's reprimand, Adriana admits her fault of jealousy, 'She did betray me to my own reproof' (5. 1. 91). She then reclaims her social identity as wife. In chains Egeon asks his son to bail him out; the Citizen does not recognize him, and the father voices his pain and sense of betrayal. The Traveller and his servant enter the scene and finally face their doubles. The reunion of Citizen and Traveller, however, does not end the play but instigates the reunion of the servant Dromios and that of Egeon, soon to be freed, and the Abbess Emilia, his wife. Fraternal recognition leads to family reunion and the restoration of long-sundered bonds between mother and father, parent and child, Syracusan and Ephesian.

The location of the ending at the abbey, the presence of the Abbess, presumably in habit, and the final invitation to a 'gossips' feast' (408), i.e. a godparents' feast or christening—all suggest a benevolent providential conclusion. Tim Supple's striking production (1996) emphasized the divine ordering by having the Abbess preside over the final conclusions and revelations. This nun, not the standard cartoon but a woman who had suffered and found peace in religious life, extended her hands to various pairs on stage, coupling surprisingly, for example, Adriana and the Courtesan. She physically brought everyone into new relationships based on forgiveness and harmony before they departed into the abbey. Good fortune and good will thus create the reintegrated self, the reunited family, and the recreated city. The darker potentialities of Plautine error, the threats of alienation, dislocation, madness, and murder, mercifully recede.

Shakespeare explores these darker potentialities elsewhere. Plautus' *Menaechmi*, for example, informs his next errors play *Twelfth Night* (1601). Shakespeare transfers Menaechmus' feigned madness from the accused to the accusers, the revellers who pretend that Malvolio is mad. The roistering Sir Toby Belch and company trick Malvolio into foolish behaviour and then punish him for lunacy. Like Antipholus of Ephesus Malvolio suffers imprisonment in a dark house (4. 2). Again, a quack doctor, this time Feste the clown disguised as Sir Topas the curate, struts, pontificates, and misdiagnoses the problem, to the acute frustration of the trapped patient. Again the spectre of demonic possession haunts the scene: Feste says, 'Out, hyperbolical fiend, how vexest thou this man!' (26). Shakespeare also remembers his Plautus generally in the second half of the play, where he imposes the errors plot from *Menaechmi* onto the source tale from Barnabe Riche. Like the travelling twins before him, Sebastian arrives in a strange city and gets mistaken for his resident twin. According to the familiar pattern, he meets a woman, Olivia, who seems to know and love him. Like Antipholus, wandering through all adventures, he becomes bewildered: 'What relish is in this? How runs the stream? | Or I am mad, or else this is a dream' (4. 1. 59–60). Sebastian too becomes involved in street violence and draws his weapon. He too falls in love and gets married. Discomforts and questions hover in the air, however, at the end of this errors play. The engaged couples have only just discovered their true identities; Sir Toby and Sir Andrew have bloody heads; Malvolio leaves in a huff; Feste's melancholy refrain rings in our ears, 'The rain it raineth every day'. The adroitly lightened uncertainties of *The Comedy of Errors* here darken into the shadows of madness, alienation, and resentment.

Shakespeare works a final variation on Plautus' *Menaechmi* in *Hamlet*. Like Plautus' Traveller, Hamlet feigns madness when confronting a woman and her father, Ophelia and Polonius. Furthermore, the note of menace often in his voice recalls the fierce and feigning Menaechmus, rather than the mud-wallowing, cock-crowing Amleth from the source tale in Saxo or Belleforest. Plautus' fake madman spouts fragments from Euripides; Shakespeare's too blusters in tragic idiom, ranting threats from revenge plays. *Hamlet* represents Shakespeare's culminating encounter with Plautus' *Menaechmi*. Like Menaechmus or Antipholus, Hamlet wanders through a strange yet familiar world. He meets friends, family, and lovers but all are not who they claim to be; nor is he himself, being alternately a fellow crawling between heaven and earth, a rogue and peasant slave, and his father's son,

Prince Hamlet the Dane. Hamlet suffers a tragic version of errors-play *aporia*, a deep confusion about himself and the world. The play raises to a higher level Plautine questions about identity and the nature of illusion and the self in the world.

Text: Fiorentino's *Il Pecorone*

The Merchant of Venice. In addition to classical literature, Shakespeare constructed comedies from later prose fiction tales of love and adventure.[6] One of the stories in Ser Giovanni Fiorentino's *Il Pecorone* supplied *The Merchant of Venice* with the essentials of plot: the wooing of a lady in Belmont by means of a test, the friendship between adventurer and benefactor, the loan from a Jewish moneylender, the pound of flesh penalty, the imposture of the lady as a learned doctor, the trial and climactic discomfiture of the Jew, the ring switch and comic conclusion. Shakespeare probably read the Italian original (no translation is recorded), supplementing the trial, perhaps, with details from Sylvain's *Orator*, and modelling the casket scenes on a popular legend available in Boccaccio's *Decameron* and John Gower's *Confessio Amantis*.

As so often in his plays, Shakespeare modifies his source to create opposing localities. He develops Fiorentino's implicit contrast between low-lying Venice and Belmont or 'Beautiful Mountain' with a wealth of detail. In Shakespeare's play Venice bustles with commerce, law, and hard realities. Its citizens, primarily men, work as merchants, lawyers, nobles, and magistrates. City life centres on the marketplace, where investors like Antonio seek great wealth at the risk of ruin, and money-lenders like Shylock prey on the needy. Money matters, and Venetians occupy themselves with getting and spending: even the invented clown, Lancelot Gobbo, complains about being 'famished' (2. 2. 100) in Shylock's service and seeks a better deal. Venice also features the contentious drama of the lawcourt, replete with the Duke, robed judges, wealthy leaders ('Magnificoes'), and learned advocates, all struggling to interpret and abide by complicated codes of law.

Belmont, by contrast, appears as a place of love, music, and the imagination. Situated across the waters, home of women, Portia and Nerissa, Belmont features the fairy-tale casket test. This place hosts the lovers, Bassanio and Graziano, as well as two other travellers from

Venice, the eloping Jessica and Lorenzo, added by Shakespeare to Fiorentino's story. In Belmont the sound of music replaces the noise of the marketplace. Before the musicians play in Act 5, Lorenzo sits with Jessica in the moonlight, looks at the stars, and imagines celestial harmonies:

> Look how the floor of heaven
> Is thick inlaid with patens of bright gold.
> There's not the smallest orb which thou behold'st
> But in his motion like an angel sings,
> Still choiring to the young-eyed cherubins.
> Such harmony is in immortal souls,
> But whilst this muddy vesture of decay
> Doth grossly close it in, we cannot hear it.
>
> (5. 1. 58–65)

In Shakespeare's Belmont lovers can almost transcend their earthly bodies ('this muddy vesture of decay') and hear the music of the spheres, symbol of supernatural harmony and cosmic order.

Shakespeare alters Fiorentino's love test to emphasize the courteous romance of Belmont. In *Il Pecorone* the adventurer who sleeps with and makes love to the beautiful Lady of Belmont wins her as wife and becomes the lord of the country; those who fail the test, having fallen victim to a drugged drink, lose all their possessions. In Shakespeare's Belmont, the suitor must instead choose between gold, silver, and lead caskets, each tagged with an inscription. The one who chooses the casket with Portia's image inside gets her and her wealth; the loser must leave and never marry. Fiorentino's love test tries the wit of the suitor; the casket choice, established by Portia's father to protect his daughter, tests his worth, humility, and love. One suitor, Morocco, chooses the gold casket ('Who chooseth me shall gain what many men desire', 2. 7. 5) and gets for his pains a rebuke, 'All that glisters is not gold' (65). Choosing the silver ('Who chooseth me shall get as much as he deserves', 2. 9. 35), Aragon fails similarly for his presumption. In 3. 2, Bassanio chooses the lead ('Who chooseth me must give and hazard all he hath', 2. 7. 9) and wins Portia. Shakespeare adapts the love test into a choice that measures the character of each suitor and that reveals the true lover, the one who humbly dares risk all for his love.

Like his modifications of Plautus in *The Comedy of Errors*, Shakespeare's adoption of the casket test reveals typical habits of reading and writing. We note again the interest in love and the impulse to fuller characterization. Fiorentino's fortune-hunter Giannetto, twice duped by the lady, demonstrates his ingenuity by achieving sexual intercourse with her. 'Now I have what I have desired so long' (Bullough, i. 470), he says at the moment of triumph. As is his custom, Shakespeare tones down the harsher expressions of sexuality in the source and tells a love story. At first Bassanio simply vows to 'get clear of all the debts' by winning a lady 'richly left' (1. 1. 134, 161). Choosing wisely, praising Portia's beauty, however, he demonstrates his worth and growing affection. After winning her, Bassanio asks for Portia's acceptance of him (a gracious touch) and takes her ring; he speaks like a smitten young lover: 'Madam, you have bereft me of all words. | Only my blood speaks to you in my veins' (3. 2. 175–6).

Shakespeare again expands the women in the source, adapting the shadowy Lady of Belmont into the complex and resourceful Portia. Portia shows vivacity, wit, and a touch of cruelty in the discussion of her suitors: the Neapolitan prince loves his horse too much; the County Palatine, full of 'unmannerly sadness' in youth, will probably be a weeping philosopher in age (1. 2. 49); God made Monsieur Le Bon, 'therefore let him pass for a man' (54–5); the English Falconbridge 'hath neither Latin, French, nor Italian', but has bought his 'doublet in Italy, his round hose in France, his bonnet in Germany, and his behaviour everywhere' (66 ff.). Portia shows racial prejudice in the dismissal of gallant Morocco: 'Let all of his complexion choose me so' (2. 7. 79), despite his earlier plea, 'Mislike me not for my complexion' (2. 1. 1.). Unlike the Lady of Belmont, she openly expresses her joy at the moment of the suitor's success:

> O love, be moderate! Allay thy ecstasy.
> In measure rain thy joy; scant this excess.
> (3. 2. 111–12)

Humbly, honestly, and ardently, Portia offers herself to her new husband:

> You see me, Lord Bassanio, where I stand,
> Such as I am. Though for myself alone

> I would not be ambitious in my wish
> To wish myself much better, yet for you
> I would be trebled twenty times myself,
> A thousand times more fair, ten thousand times more rich.
>
> (3.2.149–54)

The power of such language in a living voice turns the Lady of Belmont into a flesh-and-blood lover.

Typically, Shakespeare multiplies and expands the love interest. Other couples join Fiorentino's pair in procession to the altar. Graziano announces to Bassanio his engagement to Nerissa: 'You saw the mistress, I beheld the maid. | You loved, I loved' (3. 2. 198–9). The enchanted air of this Belmont, apparently, renders courtship unnecessary, as Shakespeare provides here an unexpected echo (concordant or discordant?) of the love music between Bassanio and Portia. In Venice Jessica and Lorenzo elope. But this match disquiets as it amuses: Jessica runs away from Shylock's restrictive house, steals his money and jewels, goes on a spending spree. Her behaviour and her father's angry and aggrieved reaction cloud our perspective on romantic love, which in this case appears commingled with deceit, selfishness, and gratuitous cruelty. Ironically, moreover, the lovers whom Lorenzo and Jessica evoke in moonlit Belmont (5. 1. 1 ff.) all ended miserably: Cressida broke faith with Troilus, Pyramus and Thisbe committed suicide, Aeneas deserted Dido, who then killed herself, Jason betrayed Medea, who revenged herself by killing their children. These mythical tragedies suggest the fragility and artificiality of the romantic comedy.

Elsewhere in the play Lancelot Gobbo illustrates the seamy side of love. Lorenzo needles Gobbo about answering to the commonwealth for 'the getting up of the Negro's belly. The Moor is with child by you, Lancelot' (3. 5. 36–7). Lancelot responds, 'It is much that the Moor should be more than reason, but if she be less than an honest woman, she is indeed more than I took her for' (38–40). Punning foolishly on 'more/Moor', Lancelot says that if the woman is less than perfectly chaste, she is still better than he thought her. Once again, Shakespeare invents a comic character to provide a counterpoint to the principals. But this time, unlike the Dromio who deflates starry-eyed sentiment, Lancelot irritates and disturbs. The juvenile punning, indifference to his coming child, disregard of the commonwealth, and racist insult to his former lover bespeak a callous irresponsibility. What elements of selfishness and cruelty lurk in the other lovers? In a play attuned to the dangers of ethnic stereotyping, broken commitments, and high cultural hypocrisy, Lancelot proves himself a Venetian in the worst senses of that word.

Adding to the amatory complications, Shakespeare alters the relationship between benefactor and adventurer: Fiorentino portrays a loving father figure and young charge, Signor Ansaldo and Giannetto. Shakespeare gives us Antonio and the young man he loves so dearly, Bassanio, and leaves unexplained the nature of the relationship. Is this friendship or, as many lately have decided, a homoerotic attachment? The ardour of Antonio's devotion has seemed to many to justify the latter reading; when the knife threatens, he protests:

> Commend me to your honourable wife.
> Tell her the process of Antonio's end.
> Say how I loved you. Speak me fair in death,
> And when the tale is told, bid her be judge
> Whether Bassanio had not once a love.
>
> (4.1.270–4)

Bill Alexander's 1987 Stratford production portrayed a Bassanio completely frustrated by unfulfilled desire for Antonio. This is a viable but not obligatory interpretation. In a manner entirely typical, Shakespeare includes multiple perspectives on love, unsettling any easy answers, introducing questions, tensions, and ambivalences.

This appreciation of complexity, of the mingled good and evil in human life, appears clearly in one of Shakespeare's most striking creations, Shylock. Amplifying the evil of Fiorentino's unnamed, unexplored, and largely unmotivated Jew, Shakespeare portrays Shylock as greedy miser and moneylender. In his family he plays the classical *senex iratus* (angry old man), locking his daughter in the house, opposing her love. When he hears of Jessica's elopement and theft, he rages: 'I would my daughter were dead at my foot and the jewels in her ear! Would she were hearsed at my foot and the ducats in her coffin!' (3. 1. 82–4). Like Marlowe's Barabas in *The Jew of Malta* and other stage Jews, Shylock plots against Christians. In the trial scene he whets the knife for his helpless victim.

But Shakespeare also makes Shylock a more sympathetic figure than Fiorentino's one-dimensional character. Shylock has his own distinctive speech patterns, replete with repetition, biblical allusion, and cautious logic. He lives with hypocritical Christians who condemn usury and then borrow money, who call him names, spit upon his Jewish gaberdine, and kick him like a dog (1. 3. 105 ff.). He laments the theft of his ring, traded by his daughter for a monkey: 'Out upon her! Thou torturest me, Tubal. It was my turquoise. I had it of Leah when I was a bachelor. I would not have given it for a wilderness of monkeys' (3. 1. 112–14). For just a moment we glimpse Shylock as young lover. Moreover, he reasons movingly:

I am a Jew. Hath not a Jew eyes? Hath not a Jew hands, organs, dimensions, senses, affections, passions; fed with the same food, hurt with the same weapons, subject to the same diseases, healed by the same means, warmed and cooled by the same winter and summer as a Christian is? If you prick us do we not bleed? If you tickle us do we not laugh? If you poison us do we not die? And if you wrong us shall we not revenge?　(3. 1. 54–62)

Asserting a common humanity, these lines argue for equality, even as they pervert the argument into a justification for revenge. Possessed of such a voice, Shylock transcends Fiorentino's Jew, who demands the pound of flesh merely 'in order to be able to say that he had put to death the greatest of the Christian merchants' (Bullough, i. 472). Shakespeare's Shylock can grow into full life and assume radically different identities in different productions. Charles Macklin (1741), for example, portrayed him as a menacing, malevolent, ferocious villain; Edmund Kean (1814), as a suffering, sardonic, intelligent victim; William Poel (1898) as a red-wigged and false-nosed clown. Mindful of Jewish life in Palestine, Aharon Meskin endowed Shylock with courage, dignity, and heroic pathos.[7]

The playwright's transforming hand also reveals itself in 4. 1, the trial scene. Here Shakespeare compresses several separate incidents— the merchants' offer of the bond amount many times over, the arrival of the disguised doctor at an inn, the public arbitration of the dispute. He adds other voices and emotional colour to the proceedings. Portia pleads eloquently for mercy:

The quality of mercy is not strained.
It droppeth as the gentle rain from heaven
Upon the place beneath. It is twice blest:
It blesseth him that gives, and him that takes.
(4. 1. 181–4)

'Earthly power doth then show likest God's', she goes on to argue, 'when mercy seasons justice' (193–4). The intended victim, Antonio, professes his love for Bassanio; onlookers like Graziano and Bassanio express horror at Shylock's demand for the pound of flesh. Staging the confrontation in an official setting instead of at an inn, Shakespeare transforms Fiorentino's combat of wits into a compelling struggle that raises questions about law, mercy, and justice. The Lady of Belmont's comic ordeal becomes a charged confrontation between good and evil. Portia's triumph is intensely satisfying at first, a reversal that turns Shylock's insistent adherence to the letter of the law against him. But we may justifiably demur at Graziano's subsequent taunting and at the stipulation that Shylock 'presently become a Christian' (4. 1. 384). In Fiorentino's tale, 'the Jew', so called throughout the story, merely loses his investment and tears the bond to pieces in a fury. Laurence Olivier (1970) took the judgements against him as a series of crushing blows; he exited and after a long silence shocked audiences by howling in anguish off-stage. Patrick Stewart (1978) played Shylock as an outsider who used wit and money to thrive in an alien culture; this shrewd survivor agreed to the terms and exited with an ingratiating laugh at the idea of his christening. Carrying his case of smoked cigarette ends, this Shylock would live on.[8]

The source tale in Fiorentino's *Il Pecorone* presents simple conflicts: the Lady outwits the suitors; Giannetto outwits her; the Lady outwits the Jew. Shakespeare enhances the contrast in settings, expands the love interest, and increases the ethical and intellectual depth.

Tradition: A Classical Conflict—Fathers vs. Lovers

Plautus and Terence inspire Shakespeare directly through texts like the *Menaechmi* but indirectly through classical tradition. They present the conflict between fathers and young lovers (the *adulescens*, or young man, and the *virgo*, or young girl). Generally the father is the son's parent and opposes the match (Plautus' *Mostellaria*, Terence's *Andria*, *Adelphoe*) because the girl is a courtesan, slave, or non-Athenian; sometimes he wants the girl for himself (Plautus' *Mercator*, *Casina*). The young man in love, typically passionate and helpless, acts foolishly, and relies on others, usually a clever slave, for help. The young girl in classical comedy largely remains silent and off stage. No mere imitators of formula, Plautus and Terence inventively vary the players and the game: Euclio cares more about money than his daughter's love affair (Plautus' *Aulularia*); Terence's fathers regularly show depth and subtlety. Unlike most young men in New Comedy, Lysiteles seriously reflects on love, money, and marriage and tries to live reasonably (Plautus' *Trinummus*). A young girl appears on stage in Terence's *Heautontimorumenos* and stars in Plautus' *Persa*.

Despite or perhaps because of the possible variations, the tradition featuring a father blocking young lovers became a staple of European drama. Shakespeare knew it directly, through the plays of Plautus and Terence and in their translations, and indirectly, through many later adaptations and revisions. Writers of prose fiction like Boccaccio and Bandello constantly reworked the standard characters and situations as did contemporary playwrights in Italy, France, Spain, and England. By the time Shakespeare came to write comedies, he found at his disposal familiar characters in a familiar conflict, but one that had a rich history of adaptation. He thus had at hand a rich, dense, well-tested, and flexible configuration for the making of plays.

A Midsummer Night's Dream. The classical conflict between blocking father and young lovers motivates the action of *A Midsummer Night's Dream*. Angry Egeus enters the opening scene with his rebellious daughter Hermia and two rivals for her love—his choice, Demetrius, and hers, Lysander:

> Full of vexation come I, with complaint
> Against my child, my daughter Hermia.
> (I. I. 22–3)

Lysander 'hath bewitched the bosom of my child' (27), Egeus charges to Duke Theseus. Father asserts his right to dispose of daughter as he pleases, according to 'the ancient privilege of Athens' (41). Hermia must be given to Demetrius or to her death, 'according to our law |

Immediately provided in that case' (44–5). Theseus fully supports Egeus with a hyperbolic assertion that must have raised eyebrows then as today, 'To you your father should be as a god' (47). He explains that fathers must rule daughters and offers another alternative, that of the cloister. This is the law of Athens, 'which by no means we may extenuate' (120). Hermia resists the considerable paternal and civic forces ranged against her: 'I would my father looked but with my eyes' (56), she says.

Shakespeare manipulates the classical conflict to engage audience sympathy for the lovers. Egeus offers no reason for his preference but tyrannically asserts his paternal authority. He does not consider his daughter's feelings, as does Baptista in *The Taming of the Shrew*, but reduces the conflict to a simple struggle for power: Lysander has 'turned her obedience which is due to me | To stubborn harshness' (1. 1. 37–8). The young men stand on stage, virtually indistinguishable to the audience. Lysander protests that his birth and wealth, standard considerations for arranged marriages, are 'every way as fairly ranked' (101) as Demetrius'. The audience can see no reason to prefer Demetrius to Lysander. Duke, father, and Demetrius quickly exit and Shakespeare leaves the troubled lovers on stage together to plot an escape from Athens. Peter Hall's film version (1969) represented paternal power by portraying this Athens, the father's domain, as a sterile, oppressive, geometrically patterned place of drab greys and blacks; the lovers flee to a lush green forest, dripping, fertile, and fairy-haunted.

The tragic possibilities of the conflict between Egeus and the lovers, so threateningly presented by the angry father and Duke, echo comically in the Pyramus and Thisbe play staged by the rude mechanicals. Paternal opposition to those mythical lovers, the players remind us, leads to error, desperate confusion, and death by double suicide. In Act 1 Quince assigns Snout the role of Pyramus' father and himself that of Thisbe's father (1. 2. 59), but these characters do not appear in the actual performance at the end of the play. Instead, like Egeus, they hover in the background as ghostly blocking figures. These absent fathers drove the mythological lovers to similarly desperate measures—dangerous escapes, secret meetings, forest violence. Pyramus later addresses the wall that stands 'between her father's ground and mine' (5. 1. 172), another reminder of patriarchal possession, power, and opposition. Struggling against their fathers, Pyramus and Thisbe come to ruin.

The confusions in the enchanted wood end more happily by pairing Lysander with Hermia and Demetrius with Helena, a former and faithful lover. The sight of the new couples and the story of their stay in the forest renew Egeus' complaint to the Duke: 'Enough, enough, my lord, you have enough. | I beg the law, the law upon his head' (4. 1. 153–4). This time, however, instead of backing the father and upholding the law which by no means he can extenuate, Theseus abruptly sides with the lovers: 'Egeus, I will overbear your will, | For in the temple by and by with us | These couples shall eternally be knit' (4. 1. 178–80). Love conquers all, or at least, fatherly objection and Athenian restriction. In one swift stroke Theseus the lover replaces Theseus the duke and resolves the conflict. Michael Hoffman's film (1999) has Theseus' betrothed, Hippolyta, motivate this sudden and unexplained change; she takes the Duke aside and wins leniency for the near-naked, muddy lovers, confused after a night of enchantments. In the Quarto version of the play (1600) Egeus disappears after this point; in the Folio version (1623) he becomes more fully integrated into the reconciliation, taking the lines assigned to Philostrate and playing a sort of master of ceremonies. Peter Brook's celebrated 1970 production played the Quarto ending: Egeus stormed off and did not reappear; Elijah Moshinsky's 1981 BBC version, in contrast, concluded 4. 1 with an embrace between Hermia and her father.[9]

Like Plautus and Terence, Shakespeare uses the classical conflict between fathers and young lovers to motivate the plot. The characters in this play run true to form: the father presents an obstacle in the course of true love; the lovers protest, scheme, get lucky, and finally win. At first paternal authority seems tyrannical caprice and paternal objection an insurmountable obstacle; but the end of the play brings a simple and clean resolution to the classical conflict. This resolution characterizes love as magical power, as an irrational force but one that can triumph over contrary fathers. Shakespeare will vary the characters and their struggle to different purposes in other plays.

All's Well That Ends Well. Shakespeare subverts the classical conflict between fathers and young lovers in *All's Well That Ends Well.* Here he varies the traditional formula at every point. The lovers' fathers are dead, present only in memory, inheritance, and substitute figures: Helen's father, Gérard of Narbonne, bequeaths to her his miraculous skill as a physician. Bertram's father lives on in the King, an old friend who formally and legally substitutes for him and arranges the marriage. The living older generation consists also of Bertram's mother (the Countess) and an aged counsellor named Lafeu. Along with the King, these elderly figures do not oppose young love but enthusiastically support the match between the reluctant Bertram, a young noble, and Helen, a poor girl. Recalling her own bygone love pains—'Even so it was with me when I was young' (1. 3. 124)—the Countess sympathetically hears Helen confess her love for Bertram and promises her aid. Later, hearing of Bertram's desertion, she washes his name out of her blood and regards Helen as 'all my child' (3. 2. 68). Lafeu likewise upsets conventional expectations, supporting Helen's maidenly virtue against Bertram's arrogance. He praises her 'wisdom and constancy' (2. 1. 83), and, supposing her dead, recalls her 'dear perfection' (5. 3. 18).

Though this older generation casts him in the familiar role of young lover (*adulescens*), Bertram defiantly refuses to play the part. After Helen cures the King and wins the right to choose Bertram as husband, he rejects her publicly and scornfully: 'A poor physician's daughter, my wife? Disdain | Rather corrupt me ever' (2. 3. 116–17). Expressing contempt instead of love, Bertram exactly reverses the usual pattern. And Shakespeare emphasizes this reversal by making Helen poor not rich, as she is in the source, Boccaccio's *Decameron* as translated by William Painter. Furthermore, he makes Bertram's concern with social class the motive for the rejection. In classical comedy young men fall for every species of the unprivileged—courtesans, flute girls, orphans—and fathers consequently oppose their loves on material, economic, and civil grounds. Rejecting Helen because of her poverty and lack of social standing, Bertram plays the classical father instead of the classical son.

At first the King responds generously: ''Tis only title thou disdain'st in her, the which | I can build up' (2. 3. 117–18). When Bertram stubbornly refuses, he gets angry:

> My honour's at the stake, which to defeat
> I must produce my power. Here, take her hand,
> Proud, scornful boy, unworthy this good gift,

> That dost in vile misprision shackle up
> My love and her desert.
>
> (150–4)

Like Egeus and many irate fathers, the King sees the conflict as a
power struggle and threatens disassociation to punish the reluctant
lover into submission. Here, however, he makes the threat not because
the young man loves a lower-class woman but because he refuses to.
Unlike Hermia and Lysander, Bertram folds under the pressure. He
publicly consents to the match but privately resolves never to bed
Helen. Instead of confiding in a clever slave, he plots with Paroles,
an unscrupulous braggart soon to be exposed as a coward, and runs off
to the wars. There he plays a debased version of the stereotypical
young lover, struck by lust not love for a local widow's daughter, Diana.

Shakespeare's portrait of Helen completes his subversion of the
classical conflict between fathers and young lovers. The usually mute
and absent *virgo* takes centre stage as Helen confesses her love to the
audience in soliloquy (1. 1. 212 ff.) and to the Countess. She laments
Bertram's unsuitably high social status but hopes to win him anyway.
Helen's expression of desires and attitudes usually reserved for male
lovers has disturbed many critics, who have vilified her as lustful,
selfish, and devious. On the contrary, Helen proves herself loving
and self-sacrificing throughout the play. Offering to cure the King of
his fistula, she risks severe penalties for failure—shame, slander, torture, and death (2. 1. 170–4). When Bertram rejects her she backs off in
confusion and dismay. When he callously tells her that she must get
his ring off his finger and show him their child, she does not, like
Giletta in the source, purpose 'to find means to attain the two things
that thereby she might recover her husband' (Bullough, ii. 392).
Instead she plans a pilgrimage. In Florence Helen does plan the
bed-trick, but this plan aims to rescue Diana and defeat 'him that
would unjustly win' (4. 2. 78). She explains this expedient as a product
of free will and providence:

> Doubt not but heaven
> Hath brought me up to be your daughter's dower,
> As it hath fated her to be my motive
> And helper to a husband.
>
> (4. 4. 18–22)

Neither overly active nor passive, Helen, unlike the conventional *virgo*, shows an admirable capacity for independent action and faith in God.

Helen's glance upward is a habitual reflex. Earlier, when she stunned the court with her successful cure of the royal fistula, she also gave credit to a higher power: 'Heaven hath through me restored the King to health' (2. 3. 65). Consistently Shakespeare imbues this transformed *virgo*, now centre stage, with a distinct sanctity. She moves through trial and misfortune with a mysterious faith and grace (a key word in the play). Louise George Clubb has shown that Helen's spiritual qualities derive ultimately from Italian comedy, which contributed to Europe—and to Shakespeare—influential portraits of devoted, wondrous women.[10] Helen shares with these prototypes quasi-magical power, faithfulness, and a remarkable constancy in misfortune. Undertaking a pilgrimage, she exhibits a capacity for sacrifice consistent with many Italian prototypes. Like them, she undergoes a kind of death, a rumoured one, that tests the devotion of her survivors. Ultimately Helen experiences miraculous restoration and strikes wonder in her audience. The King exclaims: 'Is there no exorcist | Beguiles the truer office of mine eyes? | Is't real that I see?' (5. 3. 306–8). Much to the delight, not distress, of the older generation, love wins: Helen comes back to life and reclaims her husband, Bertram.

Helen may triumphantly return to life in this final scene but Bertram, like his friend Paroles, gets trapped in his own lies and endures public humiliation. He receives no punishment, however, but the love of a remarkable woman. Samuel Johnson objected:

I cannot reconcile my heart to Bertram, a man noble without generosity, and young without truth; who marries Helen as a coward and leaves her as a profligate: when she is dead by his unkindness, sneaks home to a second marriage, is accused by a woman whom he has wronged, defends himself by falsehood, and is dismissed to happiness. (Vickers, v. 114)

Generations of theatre-goers and readers have agreed, feeling that Bertram, like many Shakespearian lovers, gets rewarded much better than he deserves. The problem derives from the inadequacy of Bertram's contrition (one half-line, 5. 3. 310) and our own novelistic expectations. But Shakespeare here inherits a character type largely defined by egocentric desire and practical helplessness. Refusing to sentimentalize, to punish severely and moralistically, or to stage a last-minute conversion, Shakespeare instead presents the classical young lover, the *adulescens*, in all his dramatic and moral inadequacy.[11] Shakespeare adds to the source all of Bertram's worst traits—his snobbery, lust, attraction to Paroles, denial and slander of Diana, and cowardice. Helen's strength, to a large degree, supplies Bertram's deficiencies. Her love and forgiveness reward him despite his faults and anticipate the merciful restorations of Shakespeare's romances, *Pericles* and *The Tempest*.

Othello. The classical comic conflict between father and lovers sets in motion tragedy as well as comedy, though here it undergoes stranger transformation still. As we might expect, the father, Brabanzio, opposes the match between his daughter Desdemona and Othello. Outside the 'father's house' (1. 1. 74) Iago and Roderigo sound the alarm:

> Awake, what ho, Brabanzio, thieves, thieves, thieves!
> Look to your house, your daughter, and your bags.
> Thieves, thieves!
>
> (79–81)

The elopement of Desdemona and Othello here appears as an attack on the house, that is, on Brabanzio's home, honour, and family. Iago and Roderigo consider the daughter as one of the father's possessions, named right before his moneybags. In this conception, the lover becomes a thief who robs the house. We recall Egeus charging that Lysander had 'stol'n the impression' (1. 1. 32) of his daughter's fantasy, and also the elopement and gleeful thievery of Lorenzo and Jessica.

Throughout the assault on Brabanzio, Iago and Roderigo consistently frame the loss in terms of paternal possessions, power, and prerogative:

> Your daughter, if you have not given her leave,
> I say again hath made a gross revolt,
>
> (1. 1. 135–6)

These are the terms Brabanzio uses when he later confronts his daughter: 'Do you perceive in all this noble company | Where most you owe obedience?' (1. 3. 178–9.) In the world of the play Desdemona's revolt threatens Brabanzio's authority, local and familial in nature; it also undermines fundamental principles of societal ordering. Fathers command daughters; daughters obey fathers. In this way the commonwealth of Venice arranges the lives of its citizens, the creation of its families and future generations, the disposition of property. The Duke and other senators, Brabanzio reasons, must recognize the threat Desdemona poses to social order:

> For if such actions may have passage free,
> Bondslaves and pagans shall our statesmen be.
>
> (1. 2. 99–100)

The Moor's conquest of Desdemona threatens Venice itself, signalling the collapse of law and civil tradition.

This angry father, true to type, also loves his daughter. Brabanzio's tormentors depict his loss in graphic sexual terms: 'Even now, now, very now, an old black ram | Is tupping your white ewe' (1.1.88–9); 'your daughter and the Moor are now making the beast with two backs' (117–19). The animal imagery confuses and outrages the father, forcing him to see the lover as a beast who has debased his beloved child. 'Your heart is burst, you have lost half your soul' (87), Iago says to him acutely. Shakespeare adds a superbly individualizing touch, as Brabanzio confesses his subconscious fears: 'This accident is not unlike my dream; | Belief of it oppresses me already' (144–5). Discovering her gone, he appears on stage, bereft and anguished:

> It is too true an evil. Gone she is,
> And what's to come of my despisèd time
> Is naught but bitterness.
>
> (162–4)

Such anguish, animated with the ache of betrayal, reformulates the classic comic conflict. Shakespeare turns the comic stereotype inside out and presents us with a serious, tragic *senex*. This father claims some sympathy because he shows genuine grief and love for his daughter and because he is the victim of obvious manipulation.

Shakespeare further deconstructs the usual comic conflict when Brabanzio faces Othello. The father now slips into the usual role:

like Egeus, he angrily denounces the lover for enchanting his daughter with 'foul charms', 'drugs or minerals' (1. 2. 74–5). He too appeals directly to the Duke for justice. No Lysander, the accused lover, a middle-aged, military Moor, does not for one minute look or act like the conventional *adulescens*. Calm and eloquent, Othello answers the charges: at the father's invitation he visited the house, told his adventures, and fell in love. The dignified, powerful, eloquent general contrasts in every possible way with the helpless youths of the tradition. They yearn passionately; he pointedly disavows youthful ardour—'the young affects | In me defunct' (1. 3. 263–4). And in a stunning reversal of the usual formula, he, not his beloved, is objectionable; Brabanzio objects to Desdemona's choice of the 'Moor' over any of the 'wealthy curlèd darlings' (1. 2. 69) of Italy. The issue is not money but social standing and race.

The opening scenes cast Desdemona as the typical innocent *virgo*, 'tender, fair, and happy... opposite to marriage' (1. 2. 67–8), possessed of 'delicate youth' (75). Like her father and husband, however, the woman who appears on stage has a voice, heart, and mind all her own. Acknowledging her duty to father, she nevertheless asserts that she owes more to husband. She defies convention: 'That I did love the Moor to live with him, | My downright violence and storm of fortunes | May trumpet to the world' (1. 3. 248–50). Fearlessly defying father and senators, she insists on her right to choose for herself. When Brabanzio withdraws in defeat, Desdemona goes even further, claiming the 'rites' (257) of love, i.e. the right of sexual relations; she asks to accompany Othello to war. Independent and sexually assertive, Desdemona surprises her father just as she surprises the audience.

Shakespeare invents Brabanzio out of Cinthio's mere mention of familial opposition (Bullough, vii. 242) and adds to the story the opening scene with Iago and Roderigo as well as the scene of accusation and defence before the Senate. He relies on the classical comic conflict to initiate his tragedy. Upsetting expectations at the outset, each of the principals undergoes further transformation during the course of the play. Brabanzio dies off stage of a broken heart, as Graziano later explains:

Poor Desdemon, I am glad thy father's dead.
Thy match was mortal to him, and pure grief
Shore his old thread in twain.

(5. 2. 211–13)

Desdemona meekly endures insult, sings the haunting willow song,
wonders naïvely about infidelity, and dies a victim of Iago's malice and
Othello's jealousy. Othello becomes the violent barbarian whom Brabanzio feared; he even makes much of a love charm, the enchanted
handkerchief he gave to Desdemona, before killing his wife and
himself. The energies of the inscribed comic paradigm, systematically
and consistently thwarted, add to our sense of tragic destruction and
loss.

Shakespeare uses the traditional conflict between father and lovers
in other comedies: Baptista has two nubile daughters in *The Taming of
the Shrew*; mothers get into the act in *The Merry Wives of Windsor*,
where Anne Page and Fenton outwit the older generation and some
inept suitors. The pattern recurs poignantly in the tragedies too:
brilliant variations include Capulet–Juliet–Romeo, Polonius–
Ophelia–Hamlet, Lear–Cordelia–Burgundy/France. Humanizing
his characters and drawing them into troubled and ambivalent relationships, Shakespeare reads deeply into and against this inherited
tradition.

5

Tragedies

To create his tragedies, Shakespeare read classical and contemporary history and literature. Plutarch's *The Lives of the Noble Grecians and Romans* provided a fascinating mix of fact and fiction, a storehouse of ancient history and legend.[1] The book so charmed Tom Gilthead of Ben Jonson's play, *The Devil is an Ass*, that he named his son Plutarchus:

> That year, sir,
> That I begot him, I bought Plutarch's *Lives*,
> And fell so in love with the book as I called my son
> By his name, in hope he should be like him.
> (3. 2. 21–4)

Sir Thomas North's vigorous, colloquial translation in folio made Plutarch's Greek stories accessible to Shakespeare and others. Shakespeare also created tragedies from contemporary poetry and drama. An Elizabethan play, *The True Chronicle History of King Leir* (1594? pub. 1605), provided the basic narrative of *King Lear*. Throughout his career Shakespeare organized such materials into tragedy by following the revered example of that ancient dramatist, Seneca, master of rhetorical outrage, passionate character, and dark supernaturalism. Senecan tradition shapes Shakespeare's grim tragedies of revenge, *Titus Andronicus* and *Hamlet*.

Text: Plutarch's *Lives*

Julius Caesar. Dramatizing the story of Julius Caesar, perhaps the best known and most controversial figure of antiquity, Shakespeare takes

on an enormous challenge. To meet it, he turns to Plutarch of Chaer-
onea (AD 50–120), who wrote twenty-three pairs of parallel lives (one
Greek, one Roman), including those of Caesar, Brutus, and Antony.
Plutarch sees history as biography, as parallel lives compared and
contrasted, in other words, as the story of dramatic characters. He
provides the playwright with full portraits of Romans living in the
tense and dynamic present, caught between the force of the Roman
past and the unfolding destiny of its future. The three lives perhaps
suggest the threefold division of dramatic interest in *Julius Caesar*
between Caesar, Brutus, and Antony. Plutarch has a sharp dramatic
eye; he loves the revealing anecdote that cuts through historical docu-
mentation and brings to life the ancients in all their noisy, grand,
greedy, pompous, brave, and passionate glory. He begins the *Life of
Caesar*, for example, not by discussing Caesar's birth and early years or
his historical context. Instead, he immediately tells the story of Caesar's capture by the Cilician pirates, 'the cruellest butchers of the
world'. They ask for a ransom of 20 talents; Caesar laughs 'them to
scorn, as though they knew not what a man they had taken', and
promises 50. Caesar makes 'so little reckoning' of the pirates that he,
wanting to sleep, commands them to make no noise. The Cilicians
treat their captive like a prince. He passes the time by writing verses
and reciting orations to his captors; when they do not understand, he
mocks them as 'blockheads and brute beasts' (*Caesar*, 22). Freed,
Caesar returns to steal the pirates' treasure and put them all in prison.

Though Shakespeare decided not to use this story in *Julius Caesar*,
he may have remembered it for Hamlet's episode with the pirates
much later. Just this sort of vivid, dramatic narration runs throughout
the *Lives*, however, where Plutarch continually observes the strengths
and weaknesses of his characters and the tangled mix of their virtues
and vices. Conflicted individuals, with mixed motivations hidden
under deceptive appearances, create history. Discovering the reason
for Caesar's assassination, for example, Plutarch writes: 'But the chiefest cause that made him mortally hated was the covetous desire he had
to be called king; which first gave the people just cause, and next his
secret enemies honest colour, to bear him ill will' (*Caesar*, 80–1).
Friends and enemies bore Caesar ill will; they had just cause and
honest colour, or a good pretext. Elsewhere Plutarch explains that
Cassius conspired against Caesar for reasons of temperament: Cassius

'from his cradle could not abide any manner of tyrants'; such was his hot, stirring nature (*Brutus*, 109–10). Plutarch's reluctance to over-simplify, his tolerance for contradiction, his willingness to see many sides to an issue or person, contribute a defining perspective to Shakespeare's balanced and ambivalent play. Like *Richard II*, *Julius Caesar* presents a power struggle and assassination along with hard political and ethical questions.

Shakespeare borrows from Plutarch specific words and phrases as well as a general ambivalent perspective. Plutarch reports, for example, that the noblest men in Rome were put to death, 'and among that number Cicero was one' (*Brutus*, 137); Shakespeare's Brutus reports that seventy senators died in the proscriptions, 'Cicero being one' (4. 2. 232). The great orator and politician, a major figure in the Elizabethan grammar-school curriculum, falls in a participial phrase, a linguistic afterthought (a schoolboy's revenge?). Later, using practically identical words, Plutarch's and Shakespeare's Lucilius express faith in Brutus' courage:

I dare assure thee that no enemy hath taken nor shall take Marcus Brutus alive. I beseech God keep him from that fortune. For wheresoever he be found, alive or dead, he will be found like himself. (*Brutus*, 168)

> I dare assure thee that no enemy
> Shall ever take alive the noble Brutus.
> The gods defend him from so great a shame.
> When you do find him, or alive or dead,
> He will be found like Brutus, like himself.
> (5. 4. 21–5)

In moments such as these, Shakespeare finds poetry in North's prose. Sometimes the verbal echoing has larger implications as it evokes the alien Roman world and culture. North's frequent use of the word 'constant' and its forms, for example, becomes in Shakespeare a source of thematic interest and irony. Variations of the word 'constant' appear eight times in the play, more than in any other work of Shakespeare. In both Plutarch and Shakespeare Romans aspire to the virtue of constancy, the ability to live virtuously and reasonably despite the storms of human passion or the changes of fortune. Caesar expands this notion of constancy into a kind of supernatural immutability. Ironically, he boasts that he is 'constant as the Northern star', 'unassailable', 'unshaked of motion', just before the conspirators strike him down in a pool of blood (3. 1. 60, 69–70).

Shakespeare's obvious indebtedness to North's Plutarch throughout *Julius Caesar* disappointed many early critics who thought such reliance excessive and restrictive. Samuel Johnson (1765), for example, opined that Shakespeare's close adherence to 'the real story and to Roman manners seems to have impeded the natural vigour of his genius' (Vickers, v. 146); Paul Stapfer (1879) objected to Shakespeare's 'most surprising humility and submission to Plutarch'. Since the important work of M. W. MacCallum (1910), however, most readers have noted Shakespeare's divergences from his source and emphasized his creative reshaping of Plutarch. They call attention to his purposeful rearrangement of the Plutarchan material, particularly his practices of compression, omission, invention, and contradiction. 'Shakespeare's dependence on Plutarch', one recent editor (1988) has concluded, is, in fact, 'the measure of his independence'.[2]

Shakespeare habitually compresses historical events to gain dramatic intensity and focus. After the murder of Caesar, Plutarch's Brutus makes two speeches in defence of the conspiracy, one in the Capitol and another in the Forum. The people, however, are 'not all contented with the murder'; they revile Cinna for accusing Caesar; Brutus, 'afraid to be besieged' (*Brutus*, 126), withdraws. Several days later Antony speaks and turns the crowd fully against Brutus and the others. Later still, at the funeral of Caesar the people discover Caesar's will and generous bequest.

Shakespeare compresses the notice of Brutus' two speeches into one; he invents a powerful piece of prose, composed of antitheses, rhetorical questions, and balanced clauses:

If then that friend demand why Brutus rose against Caesar, this is my answer: not that I loved Caesar less, but that I loved Rome more. Had you rather Caesar were living, and die all slaves, than that Caesar were dead, to live all free men? As Caesar loved me, I weep for him. As he was fortunate, I rejoice at it. As he was valiant, I honour him. But as he was ambitious, I slew him. (3. 2. 20–7)

The speech thrills the crowd. They shout their approval, call for a triumphal procession, cry out 'Let him be Caesar' (51). 'This Caesar was a tyrant' (70), one says; 'We are blessed that Rome is rid of him' (71), agrees another. Immediately after Brutus' address, not several days later, Antony delivers his speech to the very same audience who have just hailed Brutus and vilified Caesar. Antony begins by saying that he comes to bury Caesar not to praise him.

> He hath brought many captives home to Rome,
> Whose ransoms did the general coffers fill.
> Did this in Caesar seem ambitious?
> When that the poor hath cried, Caesar hath wept.
> Ambition should be made of sterner stuff.
> Yet Brutus says he was ambitious,
> And Brutus is an honourable man.
>
> (89–95)

Antony's sentimental portrait of Caesar as friend of the poor, the direct appeal to the audience's financial interests, and repetition of 'Brutus is an honourable man', ever increasingly ironic, sway the crowd. Antony pauses theatrically, weeps, displays the wounds on Caesar's body, and finally produces Caesar's will, bequeathing them his 'walks, | His private arbours, and new-planted orchards' (240–1). Frenzied, the crowd calls for revenge and the death of Brutus and the conspirators. The abrupt turn-around, magnified by Shakespeare's bold compression of the events, declares the venal instability of the people and the dangerous volatility of Roman political life.

No reader of Plutarch can fail to notice how much Shakespeare omits. He ignores the first three-quarters of the *Life of Julius Caesar*. Unlike French playwrights—Muret, Grévin, Garnier—he does not depict Caesar's exciting rise to power. Shakespeare leaves out that exciting episode with the pirates, various military campaigns and strategies, the struggle against Pompey, the currying of the people's favour, the affair with Cleopatra including her notorious offer of herself, wrapped in a mattress, to the conqueror. (George Bernard Shaw dramatized the incident in *Caesar and Cleopatra*.) Shakespeare likewise passes over the renowned acts of clemency and generosity, the personal stories revealing literary skill, abstemiousness, pride, and ambition. Caesar employed multiple secretaries to record his thoughts; he silently ate a salad with perfume on it instead of oil, so as not to embarrass his host. To depict the central figure in a crucial moment of world history, Shakespeare instead adopts a deliberate strategy of omission. His Caesar appears in only three scenes of seventeen, and once more as a ghost (4. 2). He speaks only 150 lines, far fewer than any other title character in a tragedy.[3] This bold strategy of omission magnifies rather than diminishes Caesar: he commands attention in his few scenes and looms as an imperious presence over the rest of the play. Trevor Nunn's 1972 Royal Shakespeare Company production literalized this ongoing presence with a colossal Caesar statue that dominated the stage throughout the play. So rarely present and speaking so little, Caesar appears throughout the play as a mystery, to be deciphered variously by the various persons on stage and in the audience.

As we have noted in the Forum scene, Shakespeare frequently expands on Plutarch and invents freely. The storm (1. 3) and Calpurnia's remembrance (2. 2. 13 ff.) of it incorporate Plutarch's omens—fires in the sky, spirits running up and down, birds in the marketplace, a slave's burning hand, the sacrificial beast without a heart. But Shakespeare adds to these omens thunder and lightning, an earthquake, a lion, a hundred ghastly women, a lioness whelping in the streets, a war in heaven, a rain of blood on the Capitol, and noises of battle, horses, and dying men. More important, he has different individuals offer different interpretations of the supernatural events. The frightened Casca believes that the portents signify 'civil strife in heaven' (1. 3. 11) or an apocalyptic punishment from the incensed gods. Defiantly, Cassius bares his chest to the 'cross blue lightning' (50), asserting that the monstrous portents warn against Caesar's unnatural rise to power. Brutus sleeps soundly through the night and, waking, reads by the light of 'the exhalations whizzing in the air' (2. 1. 44). Cicero calmly refuses to interpret the signs at all:

> Indeed it is a strange-disposèd time;
> But men may construe things after their fashion,
> Clean from the purpose of the things themselves.
> (1. 3. 33–5)

Shakespeare's reworking of the portents illustrates a central problem in the play, that of construing truly instead of after one's own fashion. Searching for the elusive truth, Romans continually assess, interpret, make judgements, come to different conclusions, err. What does the storm mean? Can individuals ever know the truth or do they all simply construct convenient stories? Is Caesar a tyrant, a just ruler, neither, or both? Is Brutus a republican hero or vain self-deluder? Are these options mutually exclusive? Joining the conspirators, Brutus disturbingly decides to 'fashion' justification for his action:

> And since the quarrel
> Will bear no colour for the thing he is,
> Fashion it thus: that what he is, augmented,
> Would run to these and these extremities;
> And therefore think him as a serpent's egg,
> Which, hatched, would as his kind grow mischievous,
> And kill him in the shell.
>
> (2. 1. 28–34)

Brutus kills Caesar not for what he is but for what he might become. Fashioned argument, not irrefutable proof, thus turns the course of world history. The play does not encourage faith in such argument, nor in the ability of the human intellect to perceive truth. During the course of the action, all the major characters fatally miscalculate and misconstrue: Antony tells Caesar not to fear Cassius, 'he's not dangerous' (1. 2. 197). Caesar ignores the Soothsayer and Calpurnia's warning. Brutus spares Antony, and then lets him speak at the funeral, thinking it 'shall advantage more than do us wrong' (3. 1. 244); dismissing Cassius' fears, he marches on to Philippi. Cassius thinks Caesar an ordinary man and, erroneously believing that Titinius is captured, commits suicide; 'My sight was ever thick' (5. 3. 21), he says. The creation of the storm scene expresses a deep scepticism that runs throughout the play, evident in the unreliability of human senses, the uncertainty of human judgement, the dubious practice of constructing rather than discerning verities.

Shakespeare expands and invents elsewhere as well, particularly in his depiction of the assassination. Plutarch's casual simile—Caesar 'was hacked and mangled among them, as a wild beast taken of hunters' (*Caesar*, 94)—provides only the briefest hint for Shakespeare's depiction. Before the murder, Brutus exhorts the conspirators to perform a ritualistic sacrifice, not a bloody slaughter:

> Let's be sacrificers, but not butchers, Caius.
> We all stand up against the spirit of Caesar,
> And in the spirit of men there is no blood.
> O, that we then could come by Caesar's spirit,
> And not dismember Caesar! But, alas,
> Caesar must bleed for it. And, gentle friends,
> Let's kill him boldly, but not wrathfully.
> Let's carve him as a dish fit for the gods,
> Not hew him as a carcass fit for hounds.
>
> (2. 1. 166–74)

Brutus imagines the assassination as a religious rite, dutifully performed by bold, not wrathful, ministers; Caesar will be an offering to the gods, not a butchered animal.[4] The assassination itself, however, shatters this idyllic vision; surrounded by the conspirators who repeatedly stab him, Caesar falls like a hunted beast. For such scenes Elizabethan actors burst concealed pig bladders filled with blood; in most productions red blood still stains the white toga, dripping on the boards, splashing on the murderers.[5]

Afterwards, Brutus tries again to sacramentalize the murder. He attempts to transform the savage spectacle into sacrifice by staging an impromptu ceremony:

> Stoop, Romans, stoop,
> And let us bathe our hands in Caesar's blood
> Up to the elbows, and besmear our swords;
> Then walk we forth even to the market-place,
> And, waving our red weapons o'er our heads,
> Let's all cry 'peace, freedom, liberty!'
>
> (3. 1. 106–11)

Shakespeare wholly invents this ghastly blood-washing. Plutarch, quite contrarily, notes the accidental, not intentional, bloodying of the conspirators: 'Brutus caught a blow on his hand, because he would make one in murdering of him, and all the rest also were every man of them bloodied' (*Brutus*, 124). Shakespeare's Brutus, however, here casts himself as high priest and master celebrant; he wishes to transubstantiate Caesar's blood into a mystical Eucharist that grants Romans peace and freedom. The audience, however, may see only a savage spectacle, a brutal hunt followed by the ceremony of 'fleshing', i.e. the rewarding of hunting animals with a portion of their prey. Brutus may well be an honourable man, but here he seems at best impractical, at worst deluded.

After the assassination Shakespeare expands Plutarch to portray Brutus with sharp irony and deep sympathy. He stages the quarrel between Brutus and Cassius (4. 2), a tense scene of charge and counter-charge, of spiralling anger and offence. Brutus haughtily dismisses his friend, 'Away, slight man' (92); he reproaches Cassius for not sending him sums of gold, declaring that he is incapable of raising money for himself, 'by vile means' (128); he refers to himself by name, a trick of Caesar's style (136). Such arrogance, inextricably tied to his pride and sense of honour, seems vain and dangerous. Shakespeare adds an emotional reconciliation, wherein both men protest their love and friendship (4. 2. 149 ff.). He transfers notice of Portia's death from the end of Plutarch's *Life of Brutus* to this quarrel scene:

> BRUTUS O Cassius, I am sick of many griefs.
> CASSIUS Of your philosophy you make no use,
>   If you give place to accidental evils.
> BRUTUS No man bears sorrow better. Portia is dead.
>
> (198–201)[6]

Here Brutus' philosophy, a stoicism that seeks to live life by principle, immune to emotional turmoil, struggles with his great grief. Emotions long suppressed beneath that proud Roman façade break out and expose the suffering friend and husband beneath. Soon after, Shakespeare invents the Lucius scene to reveal a kinder, gentler Brutus. Looking for comfort, Brutus asks Lucius for a song; the boy complies but falls asleep. Wishing him good rest, Brutus tenderly removes the instrument (4. 2. 305 ff.). The bloody executioner plays gentle master.

Shakespeare not only compresses, ignores, and expands Plutarch, he sometimes contradicts him outright, especially in his portrayals of Antony and Octavius at the end of the play. Plutarch's Antony is a voluptuary, famous for indulgence in theatre, food, wine, and sex. The people, Plutarch writes, abhor 'his banquets and drunken feasts', 'his extremely wasteful expenses upon vain light huswives' (*Antony*, 183). Aware of the conspiracy beforehand, Antony never makes 'Caesar acquainted with this talk' (*Antony*, 187). After the murder, he shows no grief for the slain dictator but plays peacemaker: he sponsors a pardon for the conspirators, assigns provinces to Brutus and Cassius, and recommends the continuance of Caesar's laws and decrees. Having prevented civil war, he leaves the Senate 'more praised and better esteemed than ever man was' (*Antony*, 188). This praise ignites Antony's hope to 'make himself the chiefest man if he might overcome Brutus' (*Antony*, 188). Speaking at Caesar's funeral, he moves 'the common people to compassion'; encouraged, he frames 'his eloquence to make their hearts yearn the more' (*Brutus*, 129). Evolving personal ambition thus spurs the funeral oration and the following civil war.

Shakespeare portrays a very different Antony, loyal to his friend and leader, Caesar. In his first appearance Antony is submissive and obedient: he responds to Caesar's orders with a general pledge: 'When Caesar says "Do this", it is performed' (1. 2. 12). Later, he mourns the fallen leader as 'the noblest man | That ever livèd in the tide of times' (3. 1. 259–60). After the murder Plutarch's peacemaker becomes Shakespeare's revenger. Feigning reconciliation with the conspirators by shaking their bloody hands, Antony, alone on stage, then begs pardon of Caesar's corpse for being 'meek and gentle with these butchers' (3. 1. 258). More angry than ambitious, he prophesies bloody civil war:

> And Caesar's spirit, ranging for revenge,
> With Ate by his side come hot from hell,
> Shall in these confines with a monarch's voice
> Cry 'havoc!' and let slip the dogs of war.
>
> (273–6)

At this point in Mankiewicz's film version (1953), Marlon Brando emphasized Antony's transformation into stage revenger with a malevolent, sardonic smile. Through his rhetoric in the Forum scene, calculated rather than improvised, Antony brings his own prophecy to pass. And to enhance Antony's role as revenger Shakespeare supplies him with the obligatory ghost of the victim. Caesar's ghost, not Plutarch's 'ill angel' (*Caesar*, 100) or 'monstrous spirit' (*Brutus*, 165), ranges through the play for revenge, appearing once on stage (4. 2), and, Brutus reports, once at Sardis and once at Philippi. This stage convention, effective here, attracted ridicule later in *Julius Caesar Travestie* (1861), wherein Caesar strolls back on stage with Calpurnia on his arm: 'You thought you killed me quite, that was unkind, | But here I am all safe and all alive, Oh!' Antony responds: 'Confound it! My oration in the *Times* | Will seem so premature'.[7]

Shakespeare likewise reads against Plutarch in his portrayal of Octavius Caesar. The repetition of the name 'Caesar' in the dialogue evokes the slain Julius, establishing verbally the link between past and future rulers. At Philippi Plutarch's Octavius falls sick and, consequently, Antony wins the glory (*Antony*, 196). Contrarily, Shakespeare's Octavius, ever the cold, efficient, proud, and lethal commander, fully shares in the victory. Shakespeare emphasizes his ascendence over Antony by transferring a conversation between Brutus and Cassius to Octavius and Antony:

> ANTONY Octavius, lead your battle softly on
>   Upon the left hand of the even field.
> OCTAVIUS Upon the right hand, I; keep thou the left.
> ANTONY Why do you cross me in this exigent?
> OCTAVIUS I do not cross you, but I will do so.
>
>   (5. 1. 16–20)

Octavius calmly defies the senior commander, simply asserting the force of his will. In this he echoes ominously Julius Caesar declining to go to the Senate: 'The cause is in my will; I will not come. | That is enough to satisfy the Senate' (2. 2. 71–2). In the last scene Octavius takes Brutus' former followers to his command, organizes Brutus' funeral 'with all respect and rites of burial' (5. 5. 76), and delivers the closing lines of the play. Plutarch's absent soldier becomes Shakespeare's future emperor. The killing of Caesar only brings out the Caesar in other men.

Shakespeare's portrayal of Octavius and his rise to power completes his vision of Roman history as a Plutarchan succession of rises and falls: the play begins with the fall of Pompey, presents the rises and falls of Julius Caesar, Brutus, and Antony, and finally ends with the rise of Octavius Caesar.[8] Shakespeare moulds Plutarch's intersecting narratives into a sustained and coherent exploration of the instabilities and realities of political power. Different cultures have read this exploration differently, as the rich theatrical history of the play amply demonstrates. The young United States, inflamed with republican passion, viewed Brutus as patriot and Caesar as dictator; in the late eighteenth and early nineteenth centuries American actors like Lewis Hallam, Edwin Booth, and Edwin Forrest played Brutus as strong, noble, and dignified. In late nineteenth-century England, however, Beerbohm Tree's production (1898), following Victoria's Diamond Jubilee (1897), reversed these dramatic and moral polarities: the imperial Caesar commanded the stage as hero; Brutus and the conspirators treacherously struck him down. Modern productions have frequently imagined the play in contemporary political terms: Caesar has often appeared as Adolf Hitler, and also as Benito Mussolini (1937), Charles de Gaulle (1968), Anwar Sadat (1981), Fidel Castro (1986), and even as Margaret Thatcher (1993). These days critical and theatrical interpreters tend not to side with either Brutus or Caesar but to view all the politicians as flawed and deluded. Orson Welles's highly adapted and successful version of the play (1937) began this trend, presenting a Fascist Caesar, a demagogical Antony, and a brutally violent mob. Brutus was certainly no hero either in Welles's scathing assessment, but 'the classical picture of the eternal, impotent, ineffectual, fumbling liberal'; 'He's the bourgeois intellectual, who, under a modern dictatorship would be the first to be put up against a wall and shot.'[9]

North's Plutarch serves Shakespeare throughout his career, from *Titus Andronicus* and the portrayal of Theseus in *A Midsummer Night's Dream*, through the three Roman tragedies—*Julius Caesar, Antony and Cleopatra*, and *Coriolanus*—to the late romance *Cymbeline*.[10] Rivalled only by Holinshed's *Chronicles* as a direct source for the plays, Plutarch's *Lives*, translated by Sir Thomas North, shapes Shakespeare's conceptions of the ancient world and his visions of tragedy and history.

Text: *The True Chronicle History of King Leir*

King Lear. Shakespeare created the maddening, excruciating, gigantic *King Lear*—part fairy-tale and part theatre of cruelty—from a variety of sources, chief among them a relatively conventional anonymous play, *The True Chronicle History of King Leir* (wr. 1594, pub. 1605).[11] The source play provides the main elements of the action: the love test, the division of the kingdom, Lear's abdication, the cruelty of two daughters, the faithfulness of one, Lear's misery, his loyal counsellor, his reconciliation with Cordelia, the final war.

Shakespeare transforms the story and central character. Leir is a 'mirror of mild patience', a meek king who 'Puts up all wrongs, and never gives reply' (755–6). Lachrymose and world-weary, he begs, 'Ah gentle Death . . . end my sorrows with thy fatal dart. [*He weeps*' (862, 865). Later, a very docile Leir piously surrenders to an assassin hired by his daughters:

> Let us submit to the will of God:
> Things past all sense, let us not seek to know;
> It is God's will and therefore must be so.
> My friend, I am preparèd for the stroke:
> Strike when thou wilt, and I forgive thee here.
>
> (1656–60)

Befriended by Perillus, Leir lives to characterize his treacherous daughters, as 'quite devoid of love' (1769). Shakespeare's titanic Lear, by contrast, rages throughout the play. At the outset he angrily disinherits his innocent daughter Cordelia for refusing to flatter him. Later, he curses a wicked daughter, Gonoril, for decreasing his retinue:

> You nimble lightnings, dart your blinding flames
> Into her scornful eyes. Infect her beauty,
> You fen-sucked fogs drawn by the pow'rful sun
> To fall and blast her pride
>
> (7.323–6)

Lear begs the gods to touch him with 'noble anger', in other words, with righteous rather than culpable passion. He rails against the elements and against sinful humanity. Lear's rage survives as a keynote of the play even in so radical a cultural translation as Akiro Kurosawa's *Ran* (1985), a film adaptation of *Lear* set in feudal Japan, where the great Lord Hidetora displays all the burning anger of a dishonoured warrior.

To give Lear's rage full scope and to explore its implications, Shakespeare invents the storm scene from the briefest suggestion in *King Leir*. There Leir warns the evil Messenger that hell gapes wide for him if he murders him and his faithful counsellor, Perillus. Thunder peals and lightning strikes (l.1633 stage direction). While the Messenger hesitates in fear, Perillus begs God for protection and justice:

> Oh just *Jehova*, whose almighty power
> Doth govern all things in this spacious world,
> How canst thou suffer such outrageous acts
> To be committed without just revenge.
>
> (1649–52)

After Perillus reminds the murderer about everlasting torments in hell, the thunder sounds again (1739 s.d.). The Messenger drops his daggers; the victims thank God in heaven for their rescue. Threatening divine retribution, the thunder manifests God's watchful care and power of punishment. It symbolizes cosmic order.

Contrarily, braving the storm, Lear rages against the 'cataracts and hurricanoes', the sulphurous and 'thought-executing fires', the 'all-shaking thunder', all the elements that have joined with 'two pernicious daughters' against his old, white head (9. 2 ff.). Lear exhorts the elements to behave as they do in *King Leir*:

> Let the great gods
> That keep this dreadful pother o'er our heads,
> Find out their enemies now.
>
> (9.49–51)

The fury of the elements, Lear cries, should now expose all hidden crime. The wretch who hides his crimes, 'unwhipped of justice', the perjured and 'simular man of virtue' who is incestuous, and the scheming villain should now all cry mercy to 'these dreadful summoners' (51 ff.). The cry, however, remains only an anguished wish. The thunder and lightning here strike against the innocent and guilty alike. No longer a symbol of cosmic order, the thunder functions as a symbol of cosmic disorder. Cordelia later pities her father's exposure to these violent natural elements:

> Was this a face
> To be exposed against the warring winds,
> To stand against the deep dread-bolted thunder

> In the most terrible and nimble stroke
> Of quick cross-lightning?
>
> (21. 29–33)

Dazed, exhausted, bereft of divine providence and consolation, 'more sinned against than sinning' (9. 60), Lear finally seeks shelter against the cold rain.

Largely Shakespeare's invention, Lear's rage and frustrations mark the distance travelled from the source play. Adding as well the Fool, Shakespeare satirizes and humanizes the angry king. Keeping up a running commentary, the Fool mocks Lear for dividing his kingdom:

> LEAR Dost thou call me fool, boy?
> FOOL All thy other titles thou hast given away. That thou
>   wast born with.
>
> (4. 143–5)

In the topsy-turvy world of the play, the King acts foolishly and the Fool speaks wisely. Accompanying Lear into the storm, the Fool arouses his tenderness and compassion:

> LEAR: [*To Fool*] Come on, my boy. How dost, my boy?
>   Art cold?
> I am cold myself.
>
>   .   .   .   .   .
>
> Poor fool and knave, I have one part of my heart
> That sorrows yet for thee
>
> (9. 69–70, 73–4)

In his production, Grigori Kozintsev brilliantly directed Oleg Dal to play the Fool as a bony boy with a shaved head, touched with insanity.[12] This choice provided just the right strangeness, making comprehensible the Fool's otherworldly second sight and blatant disregard for royal proprieties. It also suggested some of Lear's emotional depth and vulnerability, imaged naturally by his paternal affection.

Shakespeare again dips into another book, one of very different style and texture, to round out his play. He adds to the action of *King Leir* a subplot drawn from Sidney's pastoral *Arcadia*—the story of Gloucester and his sons, Edmund and Edgar. This subplot, featuring the suffering father of evil and good children, runs parallel to the story of Lear and his daughters throughout the play, sounding enriching harmonies and discords. Like Gonoril and Regan, Edmund practises deceit and cruelty. The daughters abandon their father to the storm; the normally talkative Edmund enters the stage in Scene 14, speaks not a word, and exits, abandoning his father to Cornwall and Regan's torture. (He, unlike them, repents before dying.) The good children, Lear's Cordelia and Gloucester's Edgar, suffer misunderstanding and exile but remain faithful and minister to their fathers physically and spiritually: Edgar cures Gloucester of despair; Cordelia forgives Lear. Both fathers, Lear and Gloucester, undertake a painful journey of self-knowledge that ends in death.

As ever, Shakespeare contradicts his source text to sharpen conflicts and move in new directions. Leir's sons-in-law, Cornwall and Cambria, behave similarly throughout the action: they meet as suitors for the daughters, enquire solicitously after their 'father', Leir, during his exile (1430, 1989), stand together against Leir's armed return at the end. Shakespeare switches the husbands (his Cornwall marries Regan not Gonoril) and, more important, polarizes the brothers-in-law, just as he had Edmund and Edgar.[13] The wicked Cornwall exhibits a 'fiery quality' (7. 258) and savagely blinds Gloucester. In contrast to Cornwall and to his prototype in the source play, Albany grows into goodness and becomes an advocate of justice. Early on, Gonoril cuts off his weak protest, 'Come, sir, no more' (4. 307). But later Albany denounces his wife publicly, 'O Gonoril, | You are not worth the dust which the rude wind | Blows in your face'; 'What have you done? | Tigers, not daughters, what have you performed?' (16. 29–31, 38–9). Albany looks upward and prophesies:

> If that the heavens do not their visible spirits
> Send quickly down to tame these vile offences,
> It will come,
> Humanity must perforce prey on itself,
> Like monsters of the deep.
>
> (16. 45–9)

Albany's nightmarish vision of humanity preying on itself like monsters glosses much of the late action—the blinding of Gloucester, the poisoning of Regan, the suicide of Gonoril, the killing of Cordelia.

Against such hideous evil Albany finally stands, struggling to save Gloucester and Lear. He emerges at the end of the play, battered and shaken, to consign rule to Edgar and Kent and speak the last lines.[14]

These contrasts between Edgar and Edmund, and Cornwall and Albany, complement the central opposition between the hateful sisters and loving Cordelia. In the source Cordella appears as a fairy-tale Cinderella and a romance heroine. Youngest and most beautiful of three sisters, she attracts their envy and malice. Speaking honestly in the love test, refusing to flatter like her sisters, Cordella enrages Leir and loses her dowry. She willingly accepts her misfortune and falls in love with the King of Gallia disguised as a pilgrim. Giving daily thanks to God for deliverance, Cordella yearns for reconciliation with her father. Disguised as a country girl, she meets him in exile, succours him with food and drink, reveals her true identity. Reunited, they march against England and triumphantly restore Leir to his throne.

The chronicle play supplies the character of Cordelia and most of her story. But Shakespeare emphasizes Cordella's Christian virtue and places it in a more realistic context. The gentlemen describe Cordelia allegorically: 'Patience and sorrow' strive 'who should express her goodliest' (17. 17–18). When Cordelia weeps, 'holy water' falls from 'her heavenly eyes' (31). Throughout the play Lear's youngest daughter moves in an aura of sanctity and purity, courageously speaking the truth, healing, forgiving, and loving her father. At their reunion Shakespeare compresses the five serio-comic kneelings and risings of the source into a poignant and hard-earned reconciliation. The scene in *King Leir* begins with some jog-trot couplets and hectic stage business (Bullough, viii. 393):

> COR But look, dear father, look, behold, and see
>   Thy loving daughter speaketh unto thee.   [*She kneels.*
> LEIR O, stand thou up, it is my part to kneel,
>   And ask forgiveness for my former faults.   [*He kneels.*
> COR O, if you wish, I should enjoy my breath,
>   Dear father, rise, or I receive my death.   [*He riseth.*
> LEIR Then I will rise to satisfy your mind,
>   But kneel again, till pardon be resigned.   [*He kneels.*

In Shakespeare's play Cordelia kneels to Lear and asks for blessing; he kneels to her and begs forgiveness. 'No cause, no cause' (21. 72), she replies, simply and eloquently. This reunion occurs in a very different world from that of the source, that world of fairy tale and romance. In the world of the play, 'Love cools, friendship falls off, brothers divide; in cities mutinies, in countries discords, palaces treason, the bond cracked between son and father' (2. 106–9). In such a place the presence of real suffering and hatred makes real joy and love count for much more. The play demonstrates how little good there is in the world and how precious that little is, manifest in Cordelia.

Shakespeare makes this point unforgettably in the last scene. In the source play Leir and Cordella win the war and return to their home and throne. In the play, however, Lear and Cordelia lose the war and endure imprisonment. With his last breath, Edmund revokes the order to execute Cordelia, but he is too late. '*Enter King Lear with Queen Cordelia in his arms*' (24. 252 s.d.). The grief-stricken father helplessly cradles his beloved daughter, 'dead as earth' (257): 'Why should a dog, a horse, a rat, have life, | And thou no breath at all. O thou wilt come no more. | Never, never, never' (301–3). The agony of Lear's grief and the gratuitousness of Cordelia's death stupefy the onlookers, presenting a scene of cruel fate and human suffering. Cordelia's mute corpse cancels the satisfactions of romance as well as the delusion of a just and morally ordered world. Lear speaks his last line, 'Break, heart, I prithee, break' (306), and dies. In the final speech of the play, Albany directs all to confront the tragic spectacle fully and honestly, 'The weight of this sad time we must obey, | Speak what we feel, not what we ought to say' (318–19). No consolation can remove this cup of suffering from the onlookers; everyone on stage and in the audience must drink it to the dregs.

Not all onlookers have been willing to do so; many have balked at Shakespeare's painful conclusion to the anonymous source play. In 1765 Samuel Johnson remarked, 'I was many years ago so shocked by Cordelia's death that I know not whether I ever endured again to read the last scenes of the play till I undertook to revise them as an editor' (Vickers, v. 140). Disobeying Albany's final injunction, Nahum Tate restored a happy ending to *King Lear*, wherein Edgar rescues Cordelia and Lear anticipates a happy retirement; this adaptation held the stage from 1681 to 1838. Some modern directors, trying a different kind of conclusion, have ended the play with the apocalypse. Ingmar Bergman (1984) collapsed the set and shone a blinding light in the audience's eyes; Robert Sturua (1987) blew the set apart to the sound of thunder or an explosion.[15] But these doomsday endings are finally evasions of a different sort; the harder task is to bear with unbearable loss and live on.

Shakespeare's use of *The True Chronicle History of King Leir* illustrates his reading of a contemporary play. He expands character, juxtaposes genres (the chronicle history play and pastoral romance), mixes modes (the fairy tale and wrenching realism), creates pairs of contrasting characters, arranges plot and subplot into counterpoint, and deepens the ethical and intellectual dilemmas.

Tradition: Senecan Revenge

Praising the skill and range of a visiting acting company, Polonius in *Hamlet* says 'Seneca cannot be too heavy, nor Plautus too light' (2. 2. 400–1). Though he sounds like a pretentious windbag throughout the play, Polonius identifies correctly the much-imitated models of tragedy and comedy respectively. To imagine the unthinkable, speak the unspeakable, and portray the impossible, European writers of tragedy looked to the ten plays of Lucius Annaeus Seneca.[16] There they admired a swelling, superheated rhetoric for outsized rage and grief as well as rhetorical forms—the soliloquy, *stichomythia* (line by line exchange), *sententia* (wise saying), and choral reflection. There they also found useful stock characters—nurse, tyrant, ghost, and messenger—as well as thrilling protagonists like Phaedra, Hercules, Medea, and Atreus, who acted out forbidden desires and impulses. Seneca especially inspired one popular and lurid kind of Renaissance tragedy, the tragedy of revenge.

Revenge tragedy goes further back, of course, at least to Aeschylus' powerful trilogy, the *Oresteia* (fifth century BC). And never really out of fashion, it forms the basis today of any number of Hollywood action films, especially those starring Sylvester Stallone, Mel Gibson, Charles Bronson, and Clint Eastwood. For later writers and film-makers Seneca's plays, especially *Thyestes*, shaped revenge tragedy into a three-phased action consisting of 1. atrocity; 2. the creation of the revenger; and 3. atrocity. The opening atrocity may happen during or before the action of the play; the victims are generally the revenger's family or himself. In this phase sometimes a ghost or supernatural figure such as Fury or Nemesis spurs the action. Thyestes, for example, has stolen Atreus' wife and kingdom; Tantalus and Fury rise from hell to incite revenge. In the second phase the revenger, usually an ordinary, peaceable man, experiences a transformation; in soliloquy and conversation with a restraining confidant, he rouses himself to revenge, sometimes engaging in a quasi-religious ritual of dedication. Appearing or actually turning mad, the revenger becomes a bloodthirsty killer. Atreus, for example, berates himself in his opening soliloquy:

> *Ignave, iners, enervis et (quod maximum,*
> *probrum tyranno rebus in summis reor)*
> *inulte, post tot scelera, post fratris dolos*
> *fasque omne ruptum questibus vanis agis*
> *iratus Atreus?*
>
> (176–80)

Faint-hearted, inactive, nerveless and—what I think the greatest disgrace to a tyrant in danger—unavenged, do you merely make useless complaints after so many crimes, after a brother's deceits and every law broken? You, a wrathful Atreus?

Rousing his spirits (*Age, anime,* 'Up, soul!', 192), Atreus articulates a principle of vengeance that became a popular saying, recalled by many later dramatic figures: *scelera non ulcisceris, | nisi vincis* ('Crimes you don't avenge, unless you outdo them', 195–6). Banishing all piety (*Excede, Pietas,* 249), surrendering to surging passion (260–2), ignoring the fears and objections of his servant, Atreus resolves to perform some great *nefas*, some crime, literally something 'unspeakable'. This resolution culminates in the third phase, the final atrocity, the achievement of revenge. Atreus kills Thyestes' sons and serves them to him for dinner. Drunk with bloodshed and passion, he thinks even this vengeance paltry (*exiguum,* 1053) for his great rage, a rage that recognizes no sense of limit (*modus,* 1051), and that mocks all thought of vigilant gods.

Titus Andronicus. Quoted directly several times, Seneca and Senecan traditions shape this play, Shakespeare's first revenge tragedy. Instead of a single opening atrocity, Shakespeare stages several. Tamora the Goth, new Empress of Rome, turns loose her sons, Chiron and Demetrius, upon Lavinia, daughter of the great Roman general Titus Andronicus. They kill her new husband Bassianus, throw the body into a pit, and drag her off stage. Shakespeare reveals Lavinia's fate in his most sensational stage direction: '*Enter . . . Lavinia, her hands cut off and her tongue cut out, and ravished*' (2. 4). Not satisfied, Tamora and her lover Aaron the Moor further torment Titus and his family. They blame Bassianus' murder on Titus' sons and demand that Titus sacrifice a hand in order to save their lives. Aaron then chops off Titus' hand on stage, exits, and sends back to him the heads of his executed sons and his own severed hand.

The initial Senecan atrocity here undergoes more change than simple multiplication. The depiction of violence on stage caters to the Elizabethan appetite for blood spectacle. In addition to public executions, cockfighting and bearbaiting drew raucous crowds. Accordingly, *Titus Andronicus* features multiple murders and mutilations. Moreover, no ghost or supernatural spirit spurs this bloodshed. Humans alone originate the evil that runs through the play. As if to underscore this point, Shakespeare reworks the conventional Senecan appearance of ghosts or spirits in 5. 2. Tamora appears to Titus disguised as Revenge; her sons call themselves Rapine and Murder. These supernatural spirits, the scene suggests, really have human faces and human hands. Shakespeare modifies the initial atrocity in one other significant way. He begins the action with Titus as revenger and Tamora as victim. In the first scene of the play, Titus, deaf to pleas for mercy, orders the execution of Alarbus, Tamora's son. Roman honour thus demands barbaric sacrifice and initiates the spiralling cycle of bloodshed and revenge.

Following the familiar pattern, Titus turns himself into a Senecan revenger. He overrides the objections of a restraining confidant:

> MARCUS But yet let reason govern thy lament.
> TITUS If there were reason for these miseries,
> Then into limits could I bind my woes.
> When heaven doth weep, doth not the earth o'erflow?
> If the winds rage, doth not the sea wax mad,
> Threat'ning the welkin with his big swoll'n face?

And wilt thou have a reason for this coil?
I am the sea.

(3. 1. 217–24)

Like Medea or Atreus, Titus here repudiates all sense of limit and identifies himself with great elemental forces. He vows to return the wrongs 'Even in their throats that hath committed them' (3. 1. 273). Titus then draws Marcus, Lavinia, and his son Lucius into a circle and demands that all pledge themselves to vengeance. This quasi-religious ritual unites the victims in the sacrament of revenge, administered by a mad high-priest, Titus. In 3. 2 Titus accuses Marcus of murder for killing a fly and then, recalling the blackness of Aaron the Moor, repeatedly strikes the dead insect with a knife. In 4. 3 he has his family shoot into the sky arrows with attached petitions to the gods.

Shakespeare practises another kind of multiplication in the second phase of Senecan revenge action, the creation of the revenger. He provides us with yet another revenger, Aaron the Moor, who introduces himself as such early in the play:

Vengeance is in my heart, death in my hand,
Blood and revenge are hammering in my head.

(2. 3. 38–9)

Aaron resembles Atreus in his candid self-revelation and his agitated mental state. Both Atreus and Aaron show contempt for the gods, the one ignoring omens (696–706), the other mocking conscience and oaths (5. 1. 73 ff.). Atreus' shocking dissatisfaction with his gory revenge finds an echo in Aaron's last speech:

Ten thousand worse than ever yet I did
Would I perform if I might have my will.

(5. 3. 186–7)

The swelling rage within takes on an eerie, insatiable life of its own. Shakespeare's portrayal of this evil revenger, gleeful, relatively unmotivated, and thoroughly remorseless, enables some pity for the deeply suffering and wronged Titus.

Presenting the third phase of Senecan revenge, the final atrocity, Shakespeare again outdoes his classical models, Seneca and Ovid.[17] Titus slits the throats of Chiron and Demetrius on stage and Lavinia, balancing a basin on her handless arms, catches the blood (5. 2. 164 ff.). (Lavinia's role is not easy to manage; having dropped a stage prop, Vivien Leigh later met Noel Coward and his mock-rebuke, 'Butter-stumps!') In the next scene Titus enters 'like a cook' (5. 3. 25 s.d.), stabs his own daughter, reveals the heads of his victims, 'both bakèd in this pie, | Whereof their mother daintily hath fed' (5. 3. 59–60). He then stabs Tamora and gets stabbed by her husband Saturninus. The quick succession of violent incidents threatens to topple the scene into bathos, to push the audience over the edge of credulity into helpless laughter. Deborah Warner's acclaimed 1987 Royal Shakespeare Company production of the play forestalled this threat by exploiting all the latent comedy in the text and by adding some funny bits, like the merry whistling of the servants as they carried in furniture for the horrid banquet. Black comedy, audiences discovered to their amazement, magnified rather than diminished the tension and the terror.

Hamlet. *Titus Andronicus* largely follows its Senecan models. Shake-speare expands upon the three-phased revenge action and creates Aaron to humanize by contrast his revenger, Titus. In *Hamlet* Shake-speare will try different strategies of expansion and humanization, but this time he will directly challenge his Senecan inheritance at every turn.

On the dark battlements of Elsinore, the ghost of murdered King Hamlet walks. He implores his son, 'If thou didst ever thy dear father love ... Revenge his foul and most unnatural murder' (1. 5. 23, 25). Like Senecan ghosts, this one opens the play by demanding vengeance for an atrocity, here his own murder by a brother. But elder Hamlet differs strikingly from Senecan phantasms like Thyestes (*Agamemnon*) and their descendants on the Elizabethan stage. He speaks nothing in his first appearances. Instead of cataloguing the torments of Hades, he refuses to tell the secrets of his prison-house (1. 5. 13 ff.). This spirit who demands bloodshed sounds strangely moral: he bitterly regrets missing last rites, commands Hamlet, 'Taint not thy mind', exhorts him to leave the punishment of his mother 'to heaven' (76 ff., 85–6). No wonder Hamlet ponders the 'questionable shape' (1. 4. 24) of the ghost, 'spirit of health or goblin damned' (21).

From the beginning, then, Shakespeare exploits and subverts Senecan revenge traditions. He does not depict the initial atrocity in bright purples and reds but shrouds it in mists. We can see nothing clearly—the character of Claudius, the virtue or vice of Gertrude, the veracity of the ghost. Unlike other designated avengers, Hamlet wonders if the initial atrocity ever took place; he worries that the story of murder might be an infernal trap, the ghost really a devil who abuses him only to damn him (2. 2. 599 ff.). Relocated in a Christian context, the classical impulse to revenge entails additional perils that threaten the soul as well as the body. Hamlet resolves to test the ghost and his revelation by means of the mousetrap play, which re-enacts the supposed murder in front of the supposed murderer Claudius. Not until this staging (3. 2) does the ghost's story receive confirmation.

This mousetrap play provides Hamlet and the audience with a clear visual image of King Hamlet's murder. But the image raises new questions and introduces new moral problems. Depicting not only Claudius' actual murder of King Hamlet, the mousetrap play represents as well Hamlet's intended murder of King Claudius. Hamlet identifies the assassin not as the player-king's brother but as 'one Lucianus, nephew to the king' (3. 2. 232). And he identifies the action not as usurpation but as revenge, 'Begin, murderer. Pox, leave thy damnable faces and begin. Come: "the croaking raven doth bellow for revenge"' (240–2). Thus the initial atrocity merges disturbingly with the anticipated one. The killing of King Hamlet looks much like the projected killing of King Claudius. To revenge his father, Hamlet must become the loathed other, his mighty opposite and mortal enemy, Claudius.

Though un-Senecan moral perplexities beset him on all sides, Hamlet follows the conventional pattern and tries to re-create himself as Senecan revenger. He deploys the familiar rhetoric of Senecan self-fashioning, beginning with anguished apostrophe:

> O all you host of heaven! O earth! What else?
> And shall I couple hell? O fie! Hold, hold, my heart.
> (1. 5. 92–3)

He formally dedicates himself to revenge by writing its imperatives in his table (1. 5. 110 s.d.) and by ritualistically swearing Marcellus and

Horatio to silence (160 ff.). Like Atreus he berates himself for cowardice in soliloquy:

> Yet I,
> A dull and muddy-mettled rascal, peak
> Like John-a-dreams, unpregnant of my cause,
> And can say nothing—no, not for a king
> Upon whose property and most dear life
> A damned defeat was made. Am I a coward?
>
> (2. 2. 567–72)

And like many Senecan revengers he overrides the objections of a loyal confidant, Horatio, who warns him about the ghost (1. 4. 44, 50–5), who quietly withstands his passionate tirade (5. 2. 64 ff.), who offers cautious advice regarding the fateful duel: 'If your mind dislike anything, obey it' (163). Hamlet speaks fluently the violent, sanguinary language of Senecan revenge; he threatens to dislocate natural processes: 'Now could I drink hot blood, | And do such bitter business as the day | Would quake to look on' (3. 2. 379–81). At times his deeds match his words and he appears to grow into the part. Refusing to slay Claudius at prayer so that he may damn him later, for example, Hamlet puts into chilling practice Atreus' dictum concerning revenge: *scelera non ulcisceris, | nisi vincis* (literally, 'you don't avenge crimes, unless you outdo them', 195–6). In fits of madness, he stabs Polonius and later leaps into Ophelia's grave, ranting, to challenge Laertes.

But Prince Hamlet is not Atreus or Medea, nor was meant to be. His madness comes and goes, originally put on as an 'antic disposition' (1. 5. 173) to fool the court. Throughout the play, Hamlet alternates between rage and reflective questioning:

> To be, or not to be; that is the question:
> Whether 'tis nobler in the mind to suffer
> The slings and arrows of outrageous fortune,
> Or to take arms against a sea of troubles,
> And, by opposing, end them. To die, to sleep—
> No more, and by a sleep to say we end
> The heartache and the thousand natural shocks
> That flesh is heir to—'tis a consummation
> Devoutly to be wished.
>
> (3. 1. 58–66)

The famous lines reveal an anguished intelligence confronting the fallen world, the 'thousand natural shocks | That flesh is heir to'. The melancholy mood leads to a death wish, to desire for the sleep that ends all troubles. World-weary, aching for respite, Hamlet searches for an honourable course of action, wondering whether patient endurance or active confrontation is nobler. This tormented philosophical questioning displays the workings of an active conscience and distinguishes Hamlet from his Senecan prototypes, drunk with passion. Even at the end of the play after overturning Claudius' plot against his life, he asks,

> Is't not perfect conscience
> To quit him with this arm? And is't not to be damned
> To let this canker of our nature come
> In further evil?
>
> (5. 2. 68–71)

Wishing to act in 'perfect conscience', Hamlet struggles with the ethics of Senecan revenge. Unlike his predecessors and their descendants in the play—Pyrrhus, Laertes, and Fortinbras—Hamlet recognizes that the course of Senecan revenge, beginning in atrocity, must inevitably end in atrocity. The moral dilemma this recognition presents, not cowardice or hypersensitivity, gives him troubled pause.

Despite the pause, the play, like Senecan revenge tragedy, ends in atrocity. Laertes, Gertrude, and Hamlet himself die in the last scene. Hamlet finally stabs Claudius with the envenomed rapier, then pours the poisoned drink down his throat:

> Here, thou incestuous, murd'rous, damnèd Dane,
> Drink off this potion. Is thy union here?
> Follow my mother.
>
> (5. 2. 277–9)

Hamlet here achieves a Senecan revenge, bloody, furious, insatiate. Or so it seems. But throughout the play and especially in its conclusion, Shakespeare consistently contradicts the underlying model of Senecan action and the Senecan revenger. Unlike Medea, Atreus, and their many descendants, Hamlet does not plan the culminating atrocity. Instead, Claudius conceives the treachery, sets up the fateful banquet, and disguises his intention with hypocritical politeness. Hamlet thus assumes the role of victim.

Moreover, in the concluding movement of the play Hamlet never rouses himself to sensational crime, *nefas*, but instead exhibits a new-found calm and trust in Providence. Relating his narrow escape from Claudius' plot, Hamlet praises the 'divinity that shapes our ends, | Rough-hew them how we will' (5. 2. 10–11). He dismisses Horatio's misgivings about the duel:

There's a special providence in the fall of a sparrow. If it be now, 'tis not to come. If it be not to come, it will be now. If it be not now, yet it will come. The readiness is all.   (5. 2. 165–70)

Hamlet here alludes to Matthew 10: 29, the passage that asserts the Creator's care over the least of his creatures, even extending to their deaths. The three balanced conditional clauses, so hypnotically similar in sound and cadence, express Hamlet's recognition of his own mortality and his faith that all will pass just as God and God alone wills. Hamlet aspires not to action but to 'readiness', the practice of patience and humble submission to divine plan. No Senecan avenger ever spoke like this. And none ever died as Hamlet does, exchanging forgiveness with Laertes, begging a survivor to tell his story, receiving a final benediction that hints at heavenly reward: 'Now cracks a noble heart. Good night, sweet prince, | And flights of angels sing thee to thy rest' (312–13).

Seneca pervasively charges action and character in *Hamlet*, even as Shakespeare challenges him. Though long suppressed and ignored, this charge has energized important twentieth-century stagings of the play, including Sir John Gielgud's 1964 production starring Richard Burton.[18] Burton's Hamlet broke decisively with past interpretations, repudiating John Philip Kemble's pale and introspective melancholic (1783–1817), Henry Irving's amorous prince (1864–85), and the sensitive, emotional procrastinator of the nineteenth and early twentieth centuries. Burton's Hamlet was witty, charming, theatrical, and eloquent but also powerful and dangerous. His revenger of passionate rhetoric and action has won the day (and the century?) over Laurence Olivier's Freudian and cerebral prince in the 1948 film, which features voiced-over soliloquies, incestuous clinching with Gertrude, and the introductory intonation, 'This is the tragedy of a man who could not make up his mind.' Following Burton, recent Hamlets like Nicol Williamson, Derek Jacobi, Mel Gibson, and Kenneth Branagh have recovered the fierce energy and violence of the originating Senecan revenger.[19]

6

Romances

Towards the end of his career Shakespeare began to write a different kind of play.[1] *Pericles* (1607), *The Winter's Tale* (1609), *Cymbeline* (1610), *The Tempest* (1611), and *The Two Noble Kinsmen* (1613–14) recount marvellous adventures—voyages, shipwrecks, riddles and prophecies, the loss of spouses or children, supernatural apparitions, magic, and miraculous reunions. Called romances or tragicomedies, these plays usually start with a fatal error, crime, or misfortune, move through purgative suffering and repentance, and conclude with some sort of deliverance and restoration. Ben Jonson sneered at such works, 'tales, tempests, and such like drolleries'. So did George Bernard Shaw, who recalled Morton's ridicule of the standard romance recognition by means of a token or birthmark: 'In Morton's masterpiece, *Box and Cox*, Box asks Cox whether he has a strawberry mark on his left arm. "No," says Cox. "Then you are my long-lost brother," says Box as they fall into one another's arms and end the farce happily.'[2]

But Shakespeare worked hard in this genre of improbabilities, reading a variety of sources to create tales of loss and recovery. Contemporary prose romance, so important to the comedies, provides substance for *The Winter's Tale*. A favourite English poet, the medieval Geoffrey Chaucer, supplies *The Two Noble Kinsmen*, written in collaboration with Shakespeare's exciting heir-apparent, John Fletcher. The pastoral genre, featuring shepherds and the rustic life, exerts a formative, pervasive influence over Shakespeare early and late; its flexible themes, characters, and conventions especially enrich an earlier comedy, *As You Like It*, and Shakespeare's romance, *The Tempest*.

Text: Robert Greene's *Pandosto*

The Winter's Tale. A lively author of plays, romances, and miscellaneous works, Robert Greene wrote also the first literary review of Shakespeare's work (1592):

There is an upstart crow, beautified with our feathers, that with his 'Tiger's heart wrapped in a player's hide', supposes he is as well able to bombast out a blank verse as the best of you; and being an absolute Johannes Fac-totum, is in his own conceit the only Shake-scene in a country.

Greene mocks Shakespeare as a pretentious newcomer ('upstart crow'), who steals from others ('beautified with our feathers'), writes bombastic verse ('O tiger's heart wrapped in a woman's hide', *3 Henry VI*, 1. 4. 137), and thinks himself peerless. This hostile notice had no discernible effect on Shakespeare, who continued imitating contemporary authors and writing blank verse. Several decades later Shakespeare helped himself to some of Greene's own feathers, his *Pandosto*, for *The Winter's Tale*, turning the depressing source story into a poetic romance, resonant with mythic and spiritual significance.

Greene's narrative begins with King Pandosto's jealousy over the supposed infidelity of his wife Bellaria. Greene gives probable cause for Pandosto's suspicion: Bellaria acts imprudently with their guest, King Egistus, 'oftentimes coming herself into his bed chamber, to see that nothing should be amiss to mislike him'. There grows 'such a secret uniting of their affections that one could not well be without the other' (Bullough, viii. 158). Pandosto suffers 'doubtful thoughts a long time smothering in his stomach'; these grow to mistrust and finally to 'flaming jealousy' (159). He imprisons Bellaria, who exclaims against fortune and, 'gushing forth streams of tears', passes the time 'with bitter complaints' (165). At the trial Bellaria begs Pandosto to send men to the oracle at Delphi. The oracle pronounces her chaste and Pandosto jealous; ashamed, the King immediately repents and begs forgiveness.

In the beginning of the play Shakespeare lightens the Queen and darkens the King. He portrays Hermione as blameless; she merely gives her hand to Polixenes in courtesy (1. 2. 109 s.d.). Leontes suddenly erupts in a fit of unmotivated jealousy:

> Too hot, too hot:
> To mingle friendship farre is mingling bloods.
> I have *tremor cordis* on me. My heart dances,
> But not for joy, not joy.
>
> (1. 2. 110–13)

Shakespeare emphasizes the intensity and irrationality of the opening passion. Fantasizing about his wife in vivid animal imagery, Leontes refers to his own 'shoots' (130) or horns, 'his pond fished by his next neighbour' (196); he thinks Hermione a 'hobby-horse' (278), his sheets 'goads, thorns, nettles, tails of wasps' (331). Tortured by diseased imaginings, the King rages against the innocent Queen, who, in contrast with Bellaria, proves a model of patience:

> There's some ill planet reigns.
> I must be patient till the heavens look
> With an aspect more favourable. Good my lords,
> I am not prone to weeping, as our sex
> Commonly are; the want of which vain dew
> Perchance shall dry your pities. But I have
> That honourable grief lodged here which burns
> Worse than tears drown.
>
> (2. 1. 107–14)

Refusing to blubber and moan, Hermione defends herself in quiet self-possession and dignity. She asserts her innocence and stands confidently, though sorrowfully, upon the truth. The battle between husband and wife here opposes destructive passion against calm virtue.

In Shakespeare's retelling, the King not the Queen suggests application to the oracle at Delphi. And instead of repenting immediately at the divine revelation, Leontes, unlike Pandosto, deliberately defies it: 'There is no truth at all i'th' oracle. | The sessions shall proceed. This is mere falsehood' (3. 2. 139–40). Leontes' blasphemy receives quick punishment. A servant enters and announces the death of Prince Mamillius. The King recoils in horror: 'Apollo's angry, and the heavens themselves | Do strike at my injustice' (145–6). The Queen swoons and is reported dead. Overcome with guilt and shame, Leontes vows to perform daily penance. The court of Sicily (Shakespeare reverses

Greene's localities, his rural Sicily and courtly Bohemia) becomes a tragic place of sin, loss, and late repentance.

The future lies across the seas in wild Bohemia, where Leontes has had the infant princess Perdita abandoned, wrongly suspected of being illegitimate. The ship that transported her sinks and the counsellor who left her in the wild, Antigonus, gets chased and eaten by a bear. (Along with Crab, the dog in *The Two Gentlemen of Verona*, the bear represents Shakespeare's contribution to animal parts in drama.) Noting these disasters, a Bohemian shepherd discovers the baby: 'Heavy matters, heavy matters. But look thee here, boy. Now bless thyself. Thou metst with things dying, I with things new-born' (3. 3. 109–11). The wreckage of old-world Sicily recedes from view as the Shepherd turns attention to the new life in Bohemia.

Marking the transition, Time appears as a Chorus in the next scene and slides over sixteen years (4. 1. 6). To underscore the contrast between the two worlds productions have often set Sicily in drab greys, whites, and blacks, and Bohemia in riotous colour. The avant-garde director, Peter Zadek, went further in Hamburg, 1978, covering the stage floor in Bohemia with two tons of plastic green slime to suggest the ooze of life, nature's fecund primal matter and energy. He hardly clothed Perdita with a few forsythia branches and played the action in front of a large, bare-breasted statue of Flora. In 1992 Adrian Noble of the Royal Shakespeare Company tried a different approach, focusing on the thief, Autolycus, a character Shakespeare adds to the story, who sings, scams, cons, capers, pickpockets, and plays master of ceremonies in Bohemia. At the beginning of Act 4, Autolycus, garbed in a plaid jacket, striped trousers, a hat, and scarf, descended on a tree with branches made of coloured balloons. 'It was a bold gesture', recalls Richard McCabe, who played Autolycus, 'that told the audience we were now entering a different world'; 'I remember that when the screen lifted to reveal a sky-blue cyclorama and brightly coloured balloon tree, the feeling of release in the audience was almost palpable. I flew down singing "When daffodils begin to peer".'[3] Sicilian tragedy gives way to Bohemian comedy.

The tone and timbre of Shakespeare's adaptation resounds most clearly in the sheep-shearing scene, 4. 4. Greene reports a meeting of 'all the farmers' daughters in Sicilia, whither Fawnia was also bidden as the mistress of the feast' (Bullough, viii. 177). Attired in her 'best garments', Fawnia and the others disport themselves 'in such homely pastimes as shepherds use' (177–8). A prince, Egistus' son, and Fawnia meet and fall in love. Expanding some of the classical allusions in Greene, Shakespeare endows the corresponding scene with rich verse and mythic resonance: the amorous Prince Florizel calls Perdita, 'no shepherdess, but Flora | Peering in April's front' (2–3); Perdita is the goddess of flowers. Florizel likens his disguise as a countryman to various divine metamorphoses for love—Jupiter to a bull, Neptune to a ram, 'and the fire-robed god, | Golden Apollo, a poor humble swain' (27 ff.). In the second half of the play, then, Apollo appears not as an avenging deity but as a disguised lover, the very image of the charming and amorous Florizel. Perdita distributes posies to the assembled crowd on stage; she wishes for spring flowers:

> O Proserpina,
> For the flowers now that, frighted, thou letst fall
> From Dis's wagon!—daffodils,
> That come before the swallow dares, and take
> The winds of March with beauty; violets, dim,
> But sweeter than the lids of Juno's eyes
> Or Cytherea's breath; pale primroses,
> That die unmarried ere they can behold
> Bright Phoebus in his strength.
>
> (116–24)

This evocative passage associates Perdita with Proserpina, the daughter of Ceres, stolen away by Dis and taken to Hades. Proserpina's annual return to earth after apparent death brings spring and vegetation. Perdita evokes Christian myth too: 'Methinks I play as I have seen them do | In Whitsun pastorals' (133–4). Here she refers to the plays and morris dances performed at Whitsuntide, seven Sundays after Easter. Images of folk festivity celebrating the Resurrection thus coalesce with classical images of earthly renewal and fertility. In Bohemia life begins anew; 'The red blood reigns in the winter's pale' (4. 3. 4), as Autolycus puts it.

Out of Greene's materials Shakespeare assembles a symbolic fable of Sicily and Bohemia, tragedy and comedy, death and rebirth, winter and spring, sin and redemption. But oppositions in Shakespeare, including these, rarely prove absolute. A Sicilian, the good Camillo, originally helped Polixenes escape from Leontes' court; there stern Paulina now presides over the King's penitential reformation. Moreover, exiles to Bohemia first encountered, we recall, not a pastoral paradise but a ship-wrecking storm and a man-eating bear. The idyllic sheep-shearing festival hosts also a thief, Autolycus, a dance of satyrs (half-men, half-horses or goats), and Florizel's father, Polixenes, spying on his son. Unmasking, Polixenes angrily disinherits Florizel and shatters the party. Exactly reversing his former action, Camillo again intervenes, this time helping the younger generation escape from Bohemia to Sicily, 'A course more promising | Than a wild dedication of yourselves | To unpathed waters, undreamed shores' (4. 4. 565–7).

At this point Greene's tale turns sour. Receiving the young exiles, Pandosto imprisons the Prince and, not recognizing his grown daughter Fawnia, desires her: 'although he sought by reason and wisdom to suppress this frantic affection, yet he could take no rest' (Bullough, viii. 193). He tries to 'scale the fort of her chastity' (194) by promises. Soon, 'broiling at the heat of unlawful lust' (195), he threatens rape: 'if in short time she would not be won with reason, he would forget all courtesy and compel her to grant by rigour' (196). Later he turns against Fawnia, accuses her of aspiring to a prince, and sentences her and her father to death. When he discovers that she is his own long-lost daughter, Pandosto falls into a melancholy fit and commits suicide. End of story.

Shakespeare changes pervasively Greene's sad tale of incestuous passion and death. Remorseful Leontes, Cleomenes announces, has for sixteen years performed 'a saint-like sorrow' (5. 1. 2). Reformed, he graciously receives the young lovers, welcome 'as is the spring to th'earth' (151). The father innocently compliments his daughter's beauty, only to receive Paulina's mild and undeserved rebuke, 'Your eye hath too much youth in't' (224). Shakespeare chooses to present the reunion between Leontes and Perdita by report. The Third Gentleman says that the King appears 'ready to leap out of himself for joy of his found daughter' (5. 2. 49–50). The sophisticated courtiers who relate the story express their amazement at the wondrous reunion, 'like an old tale' (61). A deep sorrow for what has been lost, the long intervening years, the lives of Antigonus and Mamillius, alternates with and enhances the deep joy of recognition.

Though the reunion of father and daughter functions as a climax in *Pandosto* and elsewhere, notably in *King Lear* and *Pericles*, Shakespeare deliberately chooses to downplay that moment here. He stages instead the miraculous reunion of husband and wife, not dead after all. Radically rewriting Greene's *Pandosto*, Shakespeare takes inspiration from several other texts, perhaps the ninth book of *Amadis de Gaule* (1542), which features a Florisel and a similar deception with statues, and certainly Ovid's tale of Pygmalion in *Metamorphoses* 10. There Pygmalion falls in love with an ivory statue that he has created; Venus magically turns the cold, marble image into warm flesh and blood. Similarly, Paulina presents Hermione to Leontes as a statue. While music plays, Hermione, having lived hidden away for these many years, descends from the pedestal to her husband. Leontes expiates his sins and gains, at long last, his wife and redemption.

Even though the transformation is contrived rather than real, Hermione's descent amazes the audience on stage and (when performed well) in the theatre. John Philip Kemble's important production (1802), for example, strikingly realized the potential power of the scene. Amidst Corinthian columns, elegantly robed in white muslin, lit from behind by lamps, Sarah Siddons' Hermione appeared as a beautiful Greek statue. Siddons electrified audiences by awakening into life and Leontes' warm embrace; one reviewer commented, 'She rose to divinity in the statue scene'.[4] Shakespeare's revision of Ovid into a *coup de théâtre* takes on a transcendental significance, akin to allegory; it exhibits not Venus' magic but the power of penance, time, and forgiveness.

Shakespeare's adaptation of Greene reveals much about his working methods and habits of reading. The playwright freely follows or contradicts sources as he pleases. Previously, he changed the happy ending of the source play into the dark tragedy of *King Lear*; here he reverses the process, converting Greene's woeful ending into a spiritually charged romance. Again he establishes bold locational contrasts (we recall Venice and Belmont in *The Merchant of Venice*, the court and the tavern in the *Henry IV* plays) and again characters move back and forth between them. Recalling old favourites or recent fashions, he combines disparate texts boldly and unpredictably, grafting the Ovidian tale onto the contemporary prose romance. He will revert to Ovid anew for a climactic moment in *The Tempest*. Greene's *Pandosto* largely supplies *The Winter's Tale*, but Shakespeare, as always, hears too the music of many other texts and traditions.

Text: Chaucer's *The Canterbury Tales (The Knight's Tale)*

The Two Noble Kinsmen. Students in Shakespeare's day did not study English literature at school; they discovered it on their own. For the late romance, *The Two Noble Kinsmen*, Shakespeare and Fletcher read Geoffrey Chaucer, 'of all admired' (Prologue, 13). The Prologue registers the difficulty of imitating so great a poet:

> it were an endless thing
> And too ambitious to aspire to him,
> Weak as we are, and almost breathless swim
> In this deep water.
>
> (22–5)

Shakespeare and Fletcher, nevertheless, adapt into dramatic form *The Knight's Tale*, which Shakespeare used for *A Midsummer Night's Dream* some twenty years earlier.[5] Chaucer's Knight recounts the story of Palamon and Arcite, imprisoned Thebans and close friends, who fall in love with the same woman, Emily, sister-in-law of Theseus, Duke of Athens. They resolve their conflict by a formal combat; Arcite wins but the god Saturn, co-operating with Venus, arranges a fatal accident. Dying, Arcite commends Emily to his friend, Palamon; Theseus rounds off the tale with a meditation on fortune.

Shakespeare and Fletcher compress the time of the events in order to turn the narrative into drama.[6] Arcite's death and the betrothal of Palamon and Emily, for example, originally separated by several years, here play as consecutive actions. Moreover, the playwrights drop narrative pictorial conventions for dramatic characterization. Chaucer's Emily appears in the poem as the generic paramour—noble, beautiful, merciful, out-of-reach. The narrator keeps us at a distance, never allowing a close look at her person. Like Palamon, we can only glimpse Emily from afar:

> Yclothed was she fresh, for to devyse [describe]:
> Her yellow hair was braided in a tress
> Behind her back, a yard long, I guess.

> And in the garden, at the sun upriste,
> She walketh up and down, and as her list [it pleased her];
> She gathereth flowers, partly white and red,
> To make a subtle garland for her head;
> And as an angel heavenishly she sung.
>
> (190–7)

Emily is just like the May morning she celebrates—fresh, colourful, garlanded with spring flowers, musical. No quirks or individual characteristics distinguish her from any other beautiful woman; no consciousness translates her from a conventionally beautiful woman to a breathing human being. Emily barely even has a voice: she obeys Theseus' order to marry Palamon without a word; she only speaks once in the poem, praying to Diana to remain celibate and unwed (1439–72).

Shakespeare, by contrast, endows his Emilia with life and personality. She instantly empathizes with the sorrowing queens in 1. 1, and pledges never to take a husband if Theseus refuses to aid them. She reminisces about Flavina, her childhood playmate:

> but I
> And she I sigh and spoke of were things innocent,
> Loved for we did, and like the elements,
> That know not what, nor why, yet do effect
> Rare issues by their operance, our souls
> Did so to one another.
>
> (1. 3. 59–64)

The nostalgic idyll of innocence and mutual sharing constructs a personal history for Emilia even as it contributes to the overall theme of friendship in the play, as represented by Theseus and Pirithous (expanded from the source), and especially by Palamon and Arcite. Remembering Flavina, Emilia asserts that same-sex friendship may be more intense than heterosexual love: 'true love 'tween maid and maid may be | More than in sex dividual' (81–2). Emilia begs Theseus to spare the knights who love her (3. 6), refuses to choose between them, agrees to accept the outcome of the duel, 'else both miscarry' (301). She prays to Diana not for celibacy but for marriage to the knight who 'best loves' (5. 3. 22). Not thinking of her own happiness, she grieves at the prospect of Palamon's execution and then mourns the fallen Arcite. From Chaucer's pretty paper doll, Shakespeare creates a compassionate woman who thinks, speaks, and acts for herself.

This tendency to create interesting, dynamic women, so evident throughout Shakespeare's comedies, also appears in the most striking innovation of the play—the Jailer's Daughter. Without precedent in the source tale, this character falls in love with Palamon, frees him, and then suffers melancholy decline and madness. Shakespeare and Fletcher endow the Jailer's Daughter with emotional intensity and pathos, brilliantly displayed in Imogen Stubbs' comic, charming and moving performance in the Swan Theatre (1986). In one of the soliloquies attributed to Shakespeare, the Jailer's Daughter expresses her desperation:

> Food took I none these two days,
> Sipped some water. I have not closed mine eyes
> Saved when my lids scoured off their brine. Alas,
> Dissolve, my life; let not my sense unsettle,
> Lest I should drown or stab or hang myself.
>
> (3. 2. 26–30)

To cure the subsequent madness a Wooer impersonates Palamon and treats the Jailer's Daughter kindly. We last see her with the supervising doctor and disguised Wooer, who gently promises to play cards with her, kiss her, and sleep with her. The scene ends poignantly:

> JAILER'S DAUGHTER But you shall not hurt me.
> WOOER I will not, sweet.
> JAILER'S DAUGHTER If you do, love, I'll cry.
>
> (5. 4. 112–14)

Shakespeare and Fletcher, moreover, translate the ceremonious pageantry of the poem into elaborate and symbolic scenic display. Three scenes of formal petition, probably requiring three altars and a trapdoor, begin Act 5. Theseus and his train summon the knights with a flourish of cornets (5. 1. 5 s.d.): Palamon and three knights enter by one door, Arcite and three knights by another (5. 1. 7 s.d.). Theseus and his train leave; Palamon and his train leave; Arcite and his knights kneel and pray to Mars. '*There is heard clanging of armour, with a short thunder, as the burst of a battle, whereupon they all rise and bow to the altar'* (60 s.d.). The portent suggests that Mars will grant Arcite victory in the upcoming battle. After Arcite and his company depart, Palamon and his knights return to kneel and pray to Venus. '*Here music is heard, doves are seen to flutter. They fall again upon their faces, then on their knees*' (5. 2. 61 s.d.). The sign suggests that Venus will grant Palamon her favour. The petitioners rise, bow, depart. Emilia enters, hair loosed, accompanied, amidst flowers and incense, to pray to Diana. The image of a deer vanishes under the altar and a rose tree with one rose on it rises in its place. '*Here is heard a sudden twang of instruments and the rose falls from the tree*' (5. 3. 32 s.d.). This action signals Emilia's imminent change from chaste virgin to wedded wife. The women curtsy and leave. Here repetitive staging, replete with aural and visual special effects, produces ritualistic action. The staging images the upcoming battle between Palamon and Arcite, as well as the deeper conflicts between Mars and Venus, male and female, honour and love.

Shakespeare and Fletcher, then, modify, adapt, and read against Chaucer significantly in this play. They also read with him, however, in the matter of love, which Chaucer portrays as *amor hereos*, 'love-sickness', a malady that makes humans see things that are not there and behave irrationally and destructively.[7] Shakespeare and Fletcher also portray love as a dangerous delusion: the Jailer's Daughter lives with an image of the beloved, not with the real person; Palamon and Arcite threaten to kill each other over a woman they have never met. In both the poem and play depictions of Venus manifest suspicion about love and the miseries it causes. Chaucer's temple of Venus exhibits:

> the broken sleeps and the sikes [sighs] cold,
> The sacred tears and the waymentinge [lamentation],
> The fiery strokes of the desiring
> That love's servants in this life endure.
>
> (1062–5)

Jealousy sits nearby in yellow with a cuckoo in her hand, symbol of cuckoldry. Lovers famous for disaster adorn the walls: Narcissus, who futilely loved the image of himself; Medea, who slew her children in rage at her husband's betrayal; Turnus, who died pursuing Lavinia, destined bride of Aeneas.

Shakespeare too depicts the more destructive aspects of human love, stressing in particular the power of Venus to transform lovers for the worse. In 5. 2 Palamon offers his prayer to Venus, 'that mayst force the king | To be his subject's vassal' (15–16). There follows a grotesque description of Venus' effects on the aged: the 70-year old man croaks out 'young lays of love' (21); the 80-year old man weds a 14–year old bride:

> The agèd cramp
> Had screwed his square foot round,
> The gout had knit his fingers into knots,
> Torturing convulsions from his globy eyes
> Had almost drawn their spheres, that what was life
> In him seemed torture. This anatomy
> Had by his young fair fere [mate] a boy, and I
> Believed it was his, for she swore it was,
> And who would not believe her?
>
> (42–50)

The image of such an old, diseased codger impregnating a young girl provides a repulsive example of Venus' power. Palamon's closing rhetorical question again raises the spectre of infidelity and cuckoldry. Neither Chaucer nor the playwrights focus much on the noble and fruitful aspects of human love. They portray instead its ability to deceive, to make foolish, and to incite violence. According to one critic, the play presents a disturbing vision of amorous humans 'walking into the future as through a fog'.[8]

Shakespeare read Chaucer at other times in his career. He revised him extensively again in *Troilus and Cressida*, which refashions Chaucer's *Troilus and Criseyde*, another medievalized story of antiquity drawn from Boccaccio. Chaucer's powerful story of ill-fated love during the Trojan war presents a sympathetic heroine: traded to the Greeks, Criseyde suffers anguish about the loss of her Trojan lover Troilus, thinks of escape, agonizes about her betrayal with Diomedes. Chaucer calls his tale a tragedy in the envoy, 'Go, little book, go, little mine tragedy' (5. 1786); he exhibits humans trapped by circumstances and defeated by their own weaknesses.

Variously categorized as a comedy, history, and tragedy by its earliest readers and publishers, *Troilus and Cressida* might also be called an anti-romance. Shakespeare presents the Trojan war, not as chivalric exercise or marvellous adventure, but as a fracas about 'a whore and a cuckold' (2. 3. 71), about Helen of Troy, that is, stolen by the Trojan Paris from her husband Menelaus. Correspondingly, Cressida blames the female sex for her betrayal, appearing as either a weak, cowardly victim or as a cynical manipulator. Achilles and his Myrmidons climactically slay the unarmed Hector (5. 9), thus converting the heroic battle of the *Iliad* into a cowardly ambush. At the close of the play the sleazy, leering Pandarus bequeathes to the audience his diseases. Ironically, Geoffrey Chaucer, that capacious, generous, extroverted, and comical genius, supplies Shakespeare with two of his darkest and most discomfiting visions of humans in love and at war, *The Two Noble Kinsmen* and *Troilus and Cressida*.

Tradition: The Pastoral Genre

The pastoral genre treats shepherds and their flocks. Beginning with Theocritus' *Idylls* (third century BC) and continuing in Vergil's *Eclogues* (first century AD) [Fig. 4], this genre generally presents fictionalized shepherds living in harmony with nature, competing in verse, falling in love, and opposing the more corrupt world of town and court. Pastoral shepherds enjoy simple pleasures and pastimes in a green world of *otium* or 'leisure', which often recalls the classical Golden Age, a time of peace and plenty. Throughout its history the pastoral appears in various literary forms: in miscellaneous lyrics; in elegies, or formal verse laments; in plays, as in the hugely influential *Aminta* (Tasso), *Il Pastor Fido* (Guarini), and other Italian experiments; and in romances, those sprawling episodic prose works like Sidney's *Arcadia*, descending ultimately from Greek writers such as Longus and Heliodorus. Pastoral poetry and prose supplies an enormously powerful, flexible repertory of characters, configurations, and conventions. Renaissance writers use the pastoral genre to create adventure stories, to satirize contemporary manners, to explore the contrast between nature and civilization, and to reflect on profound psychological, political, and theological issues. Shakespeare read many pastoral works: Montemayor's pastoral romance, *Diana Enamorada*, inspires

D A P H N I S

SERV. VR non Mopfe,boni qñ conueuimus ambo) In loquuntur duo amici paſtores canere
ad delectationem. Vnde & laudant ſe, & ſi-
bijnuicem cedunt. [Boni) Autem,docti, & ſi
gurare aut,boni ambo. [Tu calamos inſtare
leues, ego dicere verſus Hic corylis mixtas
inter côſe
dimos vim-oJ) Ordo eſt, Cur
non Mopſe hic concedimus in
ter vlmos mixtas. corylis .f vt
canamus.Sane.[Inter)Prapo-
ſitio,quia præ poſita eſt,mura-
uit accentum,ſicut circum. [Si
ur ſub incertas Zephyris moːī
ribus vmbras)Dicit quidem ve
recunde ſe illi obtemperare de
bere, oſtendit tamen, quid ſibi
placeat. Nã ex ipſa laude anteſ
& ex arboſ vituperatione,qua
rum incertas vmbras dicit , o-
ſtendit ſuam ſententiã eſſe me
liorê . incertas aũt vmbræ ſunt
& ex ſolis circuitu, & ex mobi
litate ventorum , quod ipſe ſe
dicit , Zephyris motantibus.
Labruſca [Labruſca) Vis agreſtis, quæ,
quia an terra marginibus na-
ſcitur, labruſca dicta eſt à labris
& extremioribus terra .
ASC. VR non Mo-
pſe boni, &c.)
Inducitur duo
paſtores vt dixi
inter ſe amici
Menalcas ma-
ior, & Mopſus minor decore
erdens, & obſequés maiori, to
ta ecloga act.ua eſt, nam nuaq̃
poëta lo quiur,dicit ergo Menalcas poëta Mopſum obſequ-
tune laudas à peritia canendi
(nam laudari op̃ ante pueri lau
dataq̃. virtus creſcit, & immen
ſum gloria exlcat habet) à Mo
pſe qñ nos periit in muſica côma
uenimus ambo,cur non conſe
dimus.locum cepimus etiam
hic inter el nos mixtas corylis
vtmelius concinamus? Ad q̃
Mopſus.Menalca,inquit,cum
ſit maior tuum eſt pire,& prius
locum capere meum ſequi te ,
quocunque ieris ſiue ſub vmbras, quæ ſi incertas ſunt, ſiue
potius ſub antrum quod tam
amcenum eſt,nam labruſcis ex
ornatur . Ordo eſt . O Mopſe
(inquit Menalcas) quoniã nos
ambo boni .i. docti, & periti ,
tu ſupple bonus , hoc eſt doctus, inſtare calamos leues .i. graci-
les,ego ſupp.bonus, & doctus,dicere, id eſt ad dicendum verſus,

MO.

conuenimus .i. ſimul iam venimus (eſt enim præterriti temporis)
hoc eſt qñ congregati ſumus, cur non conſedimus .i. tam etiam
locum ad ſedendum cepimus.(Eſt enim etiam præteriti tempo-
ra conſedimus,ſiue à conſido,ſiue à conſideo,nam in præſenria
conſido eſſet conſidimus,quomodo verſus ſtat eſt,& ſentenria, &
à conſideo conſedimus, quod meri i ratio damnaª) cur inquam
non conſedimus, aut conſidi-
mus hic inter vlmos mixtas co
rytis.i.ſub vmbram amœnam,
& ita vmbram laudat . Ad q̃
Mopſus.Tu,inquit,ô Menalca
es maior .i. ſenior , & prouec-
ctior, & ideo ô Menalca æquã
eſt me pareretibi. obedire, & obtemperare tibi. Eſt autem mo-
rali ſententia, vnde Iuuenalis
Satyra 1 ſ. de priſcis loquens,
inquit, Credebant hoc grande
nefas,& morte pîandum, Si iu
uenis vetuloq̃ pⁿ aſſurrexerit,
& ſi Barbaro diſcumque , puer
licet ipſe viderer. Plura do mi-
ſarra, & maiores glandis acer-
uos, Tam venerabile erat præ
cedere quatuor annis, & æquã
ergo eſt me parere, id eſt rpi-
rram tibi, ſiue nos ſucredimus
ſub vmbras incertas, id eſt du-
bias,& inſtabiles,Ahoc Zephy
ris .i. venris illis verno têpore
flare ſolitis, motantibus.i.fre-
quenter mouentibus .f. rauaos
arborum quos vmbra ſequitur
ſiue nos ſuccedimus potius .i.
cum maiori commodo antro
.i. ad antrum hoc, aſpice .i. vi-
de,vt .i.qualiter labruſca ſiue.
ſtris .i. vitis incula in labrus.i.
extremitatibus agrorum ſpon
te naſcens inſparſit .i. ſparſim
ornauit antrum racemis raris,
per quod innuit , & amœnum
eſſe ſub antrum concedere , &
triſte ſub vmbras incertas,quia
vmbrarum titubatio , & fre-
quens mutatio memoriæ ca-
nentium officeret, & per abſen-
tium vmbrarum etiam ſol ir-
rueret. Regula eſt . Multa
verba repetita, cum qua con-
quentio perpoſterior,præpoſi
tionis caſum regunt, q̃ non
reperantur,datiuum regant,vt
hic ſuccedimus ſub vmbras, &
antro.iſub antrum. De proleſi
pſi,quæ eſt in principio,non eô
uenimus ambo boni, tu inſtare calamos, ego dicere verſus,
alibi dedimus regulam .

A R G V M E N T V M.

EFFLENT *Amici Paſtores Daphnidis oli*
tum atque eius interim laudes concinunt .
quæ cum eiuſmodi ſint, vt niſi magno alicui
viro accommodari recte nequeant , cui ſcili-
cet diuini debeantur honores,iccirco pro Da-
phnide C. Iulium Cæſarem intelligendum putant .

D A P H N I S.
ECLOGA QVINTA.

MENALCAS, MOPSVS.

VR non Mopſe (boni quoniam
conuenimus ambo,
Tu calamos inflare leues , ego dicere verſus)
Hic corylis mixtas inter conſedi
mus vlmos?
Tu maior : tibi me eſt æquum parere Menalca :

Siue ſub incertas Zephyris motantibus vmbras,
Siue antro potius ſuccedimus , aſpice vt antrum
Siluestris raris ſparſit labruſca racemis.

CONVENIMVS ambo)
dimus legitur omnino corrupte.
VARIA
LECT.

SERV. MOntibus in noſtris) ME.Montibus in noſtris ſolus tibi certat Amyntas .
Ac ſi dicerer, in hoc MO.Quid , ſi idem certet Phœbum ſuperare canendo?
territorio. [Tibi cer- ME. Incipe Mopſe prior , ſi quos aut Phyllidis ignes ,
tar)Vſurpatum eſt nam hodie. Aut Alconis habes laudes , aut iurgia Codri
certo tecum dicimus.[Quid,ſi Incipe : paſcentes ſeruabit Tityrus hœdos.
idem certet Phœbum ſuperare MO.Imò hæc , in viridi nuper quæ cortice fagi
canendo? Offenſus côparatio Carmina deſcripſi , & modulans alterna notaui,
ne iſferioris, hoc dixit,licet no Experiar. tu deinde iubeto certe Amyntas .
amare Menalcas diaeri,Solus MA. Lenta ſalix quantum pallenti cedit oliuæ ;
tibi certet Amyntas . quod ta-
mê quia hic aſpere accepit, ille ME. Lenta ſalix quantum pallenti cedit oliuæ :
paulo poſt curat,dicens, Lenta Puniceis humilis quantum ſaliunca roſetis :
ſalix quanrõ pallenti cedit oli- Iudicio noſtro tantum tibi cedit Amyntas .
uæ . [Phyllidis ignes) Phyllis Sed tu deſine plura puer : ſucceſſimus antro .
egiⁿ · Thracưm fuit. Hæc De

mophontem Theſei filium
regem Athenienſium reduen-
tem de Troiano prœlio dile-
xit, & in coniugium ſuum ro-
gauit . ille aut auæ ſe ordinara
rum re ſuam, & ſic ad eius nu-
ptias reuerſorum . Profectus
itaque cum tardaret , Phyllis,
& amoris impatientia,& dolo
ris impulſu , q̃ ſe ſpretam eſſe
crederat , laqueo victam fini-
uit , & conuerſa eſt in arborem
ſui nominis .i. amygdalum ſi-
ne folijs . Poſtea reuerſus De-
mophoon, cognita ſe eius am
pleuus

4. An example of a classical pastoral work in a Renaissance edition: Vergil, *Uni-
versum Poema* (Venice, 1574), 24ᵛ. This page of the *Eclogues* features only nineteen
lines of text, surrounded by a woodcut illustration, argument, and copious commentary by Servius and Ascensius.

an early comedy, *The Two Gentlemen of Verona*. As we have noted already, Sidney's *Arcadia* contributes a subplot to *King Lear*, Greene's *Pandosto* the main plot to *The Winter's Tale*. Thomas Lodge's *Rosalynde* provides Shakespeare with a text that enables him to reflect on the entire pastoral tradition in *As You Like It*. This reflection culminates in *The Tempest*.

As You Like It. Thomas Lodge's English pastoral, *Rosalynde or Euphues' Golden Legacy* (1590), directly inspires Shakespeare's *As You Like It*. Lodge sets the story in the poetic pastoral world, where green meadows provide leisure for shepherds to fall in love and write sonnets. Unlike Thomas Lodge, Shakespeare subjects the pastoral world to a searching critique and questions the conventions of literary love. On such matters the play is by turns satirical and sceptical, as well as genial and accepting.

Lodge's *Rosalynde* portrays the green world as a place of grazing flocks, oaten flutes, and poetical shepherds. Montanus (Silvius in *As You Like It*) writes sonnets to his Phebe; he sings an eclogue (a complicated pastoral poem) with another shepherd, Coridon. Shakespeare's shepherds, however, cannot write elegant poems in complicated verse forms: Audrey does not know what 'poetical' is. 'Is it honest in deed and word? Is it a true thing?' she asks (3. 3. 14–15). William admits he is not 'learned' (5. 1. 37–8). Rosalind mocks Silvius for his silly love poetry: 'You, foolish shepherd, wherefore do you follow her | Like foggy south, puffing with wind and rain?' (3. 5. 50–1).

Lodge's Coridon summarizes the shepherd's life in idealistic terms:

Here, Mistress, shall not Fortune thwart you but in mean misfortunes as in the loss of a few sheep, which as it breeds not beggary, so it can be no extreme prejudice; the next year we may mend all with a fresh increase. Envy stirs not us; we covet not to climb; our desires mount not above our degrees, nor our thoughts above our fortunes. Care cannot harbour in our cottages, nor do our homely couches know broken slumbers. As we exceed not in diet, so we have enough to satisfy.   (Bullough, ii. 188–9)

Coridon celebrates the independence, safety, simplicity, tranquillity, and moderation of the pastoral life. Shakespeare's Corin, however, is 'shepherd to another man'; he does not 'shear' the fleeces that he grazes, in other words, gain profit for his labour. The master who owns the land, furthermore, is 'of churlish disposition, | And little recks to find the way to heaven | By doing deeds of hospitality' (2. 4. 74 ff.). Issues of property, labour, and profit here invade the green glades. This place, moreover, suffers 'winter and rough weather' (2. 5. 8). And here, the play insistently reminds us, one must hunt in order to survive. The exiled Duke Senior pities the deer, 'poor dappled fools', who must have their 'haunches gored' (2. 1. 22–5). (Whose deer? Is Duke Senior a poacher?) Jaques moralizes the spectacle of deer-killing (25 ff.) and later requests a song on the subject (4. 2. 5–6).

Shakespeare's courtly clown, Touchstone, pointedly continues the critique of pastoral conventions by focusing on the physical. Duke Senior may rhapsodize about the simple joys of life in the wood, where are books in brooks, sermons in stones, and good in everything (2. 1. 1 ff.); Touchstone, however, gets tired walking about in the green world: 'I care not for my spirits, if my legs were not weary' (2. 4. 2–3). The forest has few comforts: 'Ay, now am I in Ardenne; the more fool I. When I was at home I was in a better place' (14–15). To him the shepherd's life has a seamy side; Touchstone scolds Corin:

> That is another simple sin in you, to bring the ewes and rams together, and to offer to get your living by the copulation of cattle; to be bawd to a bell-wether, and to betray a she-lamb of a twelvemonth to a crooked-pated old cuckoldly ram, out of all reasonable match. If thou beest not damned for this, the devil himself will have no shepherds.   (3. 2. 76–82)

Here Shakespeare's clown wittily punctures the romantic and sentimental pastoral vision by focusing on gross physical realities: a shepherd, after all, gets his living 'by the copulation of cattle'.

Witty as he is, however, Touchstone does not get the last word. Shakespeare's satire cuts both ways, doubling back to expose the vanity of Touchstone's home, the court, and its courtiers. Touchstone marries Audrey purely for sexual pleasure, 'Come, sweet Audrey. | We must be married, or we must live in bawdry' (3. 3. 86–7). He mocks Corin wittily and agilely in conversation, but his shallow talk of sin and damnation shows vanity and arrogance as well. Reprising Coridon's description of the shepherd's life, Corin forthrightly outlines its occupations and virtues: 'Sir, I am a true labourer: I earn that I eat, get that I wear; owe no man hate, envy no man's happiness; glad of other men's good, content with my harm; and the greatest of my pride is to see my ewes graze and my lambs suck' (3. 2. 71–5). The shepherd's life may be rough and unclean, but the courtier lives, we realize, by hand-kissing, flattery, envy, and hypocrisy; and the court, the play makes clear, has the evil Duke Frederick ruling in place of the good and exiled Duke Senior. As usual, Shakespeare introduces contrary perspectives in his work and allows them to engage and qualify each other.

Shakespeare extends his meditation on the green world into a sceptical review of pastoral passion and literary love. Unlike Lodge's heroine, who appreciates her beloved's saccharine verses and inept tributes ('her lips are like two budded roses'; 'her paps are centres of delight', Bullough, ii. 202), Rosalind deplores such stuff. She mocks Orlando's 'tedious homily of love' (3. 2. 152–3) and lame verses: 'I was never so berhymed since Pythagoras' time that I was an Irish rat, which I can hardly remember' (172–4). Lodge's Rosalynde misses Rosader and worries, 'for Love measures every minute and thinks hours to be days and days to be months' (221). Shakespeare's heroine adapts this idea into two teasing rebukes of Orlando, one for not knowing the exact time ('Then there is no true lover in the forest, else sighing every minute and groaning every hour would detect the lazy foot of time as well as a clock', 3. 2. 296–8), the other for arriving late (4. 1. 42–6). Disguised as Ganymede this Rosalind schools her lover with pungent wit and common sense. Orlando looks too healthy to be moaning about the pain of his unrequited longing. He lacks the marks of a lover, Rosalind says, delivering an impromptu inventory: 'A lean cheek, which you have not; a blue eye and sunken, which you have not; an unquestionable spirit, which you have not; a beard neglected, which you have not...your hose should be ungartered, your bonnet unbanded, your sleeve unbuttoned, your shoe untied' (3. 2. 361–4). Orlando swears he will die if his beloved will not have him; she lectures him sharply: 'No, faith; die by attorney. The poor world is almost six thousand years old, and in all this time there was not any man died in his own person, videlicet, in a love-cause' (4. 1. 88–91). Rosalind cynically warns Orlando about the changes marriage can bring about: 'men are April when they woo, December when they wed. Maids are May when they are maids, but the sky changes when they are wives' (4. 1. 139–41). She warns him that marriage unleashes jealousy, clamour, giddiness, moodiness, and even infidelity (4. 1). Sharp realism and comic wit puncture pastoral pretensions.

As You Like It delightfully departs from Lodge's pastoral romance to offer such moments of instructive fun. Rosalind even turns her wit against the pastoral cruel fair, Phoebe, mocking her 'inky brows' and 'bugle eyeballs' (3. 5. 47–8), telling her to thank 'heaven, fasting, for a good man's love!' (59). 'Sell when you can. You are not for all markets' (61), she advises finally. Though Shakespeare gives Rosalind many witty lines, she, like Touchstone, does not get the last word. Rosalind suffers from the same malady of love that she mocks; in private she longs for her 'child's father' (1. 3. 11), i. e. the man who would father her child, a line whose frank expression of female desire caused some editors to emend it to 'father's child', thus rendering the phrase a harmless reference to herself. Rosalind tells Celia that she is 'many fathom deep' in love (4. 1. 196); she asks breathlessly about Orlando; she swoons when she hears of his injury. In Terry Hands' Royal Shakespeare Company production in 1980 she, no less than Orlando, had some serious things to learn. John Bowe, who played Orlando, remembers their conversation in 5. 2, when he is wounded emotionally and physically:

Rosalind is cruel and he counters her curtly. She goads him and teases him about his love until he can bear it no longer: 'I can live no longer by thinking' [48]. We all felt that it was at this point that Rosalind and Orlando learn their greatest lesson. He realises that the dream is no substitute for the reality, and she realises that she has been very wrong to play with Orlando's emotions.[9]

Rosalind's schooling of Orlando has this capacity to double back on her in self-revelation and surprise. The disguise as Ganymede becomes a *coup de théâtre* and the revelation of a different self, or a different aspect of one complex and fluid identity, continually under examination and reformulation. Cultural notions of gender and the construction of sexual identity further complicate the imposture, as the boy actor playing Rosalind plays Ganymede, who in turn plays Rosalind acting out the love charade for Orlando. Some productions have reimagined the gender-bending play for modern times. Declan Donnellan's all-male Cheek by Jowl production (1991) cast a man as Rosalind and achieved with Orlando, according to one reviewer, 'a beautifully comic erotic tension and a sexual ambiguity that's heightened because both players are men'.[10]

The Tempest. Shakespeare's knowing and well-tempered appreciation for the pastoral genre bears rich fruit in a late play, *The Tempest*. Scholars have found no single source for the main plot, which seems to combine elements historical (usurpation, rebellion), tragical (revenge, and regicide), and comical (courtship, love). Italian pastoral scenarios, featuring a controlling magician, shipwrecked buffoons, lusty satyrs, and young lovers, provide the closest analogues for the action. For this play Shakespeare read some specific texts—Montaigne's essays, some travel literature including works by William Strachey and Sylvester Jourdain, and Ovid's *Metamorphoses*. Throughout, he reworks the familiar tradition of the pastoral genre into a sophisticated romance.

The island setting of *The Tempest* constitutes the *locus amoenus*, or 'pleasant place', of the pastoral genre. Somewhere in the Mediterranean, the island has 'fresh springs, brine-pits, barren place and fertile' (1. 2. 341). It abounds in life and vegetation; a half-human native, Caliban, speaks of crabs (either crabs or crabapples), pig-nuts in the ground, a jay's nest, the nimble marmoset, clust'ring filberts, and young scamels/seamews (whatever they are) from the rock (2. 2. 166 ff.). Though the usually pleasant but bland pastoral landscape here takes on concrete, exotic vitality, the island still provides the conventional retreat from civilization and the courtly world. The archetypal movement from court to country, in fact, has already occurred before the beginning of the play, some twelve years earlier, when Prospero, Duke of Milan, and his daughter Miranda suffered usurpation and exile. And, like the exiles in *A Midsummer Night's Dream*, *As You Like It*, and *The Winter's Tale*, Prospero and his daughter cannot stay for ever in the green world. At the end of the play they will return to Milan.

Freed from the pressures of urban routine, characters in Renaissance pastorals habitually dream of a better world, often recalling the classical Golden Age. Shipwrecked on Prospero's isle, Gonzalo, like Duke Senior, has Utopian fantasies: echoing Montaigne's reflections on Brazil, he imagines ruling a commonwealth on the island with no traffic, magistrates, letters, riches, poverty, use of service, contract, property limits, or tillage of soil. Nature would bountifully produce food on its own; people would be virtuous and innocent:

All things in common nature should produce
Without sweat or endeavour. Treason, felony,
Sword, pike, knife, gun, or need of any engine,
Would I not have; but nature should bring forth
Of its own kind, all foison, all abundance,
To feed my innocent people.

(2. 1. 165–70)

Gonzalo concludes by stating that his commonwealth would 'excel the Golden Age' (174). This vision well expresses the pastoral wish for a simpler, better life, lived harmoniously with nature, as well as the deeper pastoral yearning for the Golden Age and for the Garden of Eden, for prelapsarian innocence. Shakespeare, however, locates Gonzalo's pastoral dream in a qualifying dramatic context. As the storm illustrates, nature on the island can be violent and dangerous. Further trouble lies deep within human beings themselves. Sebastian and Antonio, for example, two villainous auditors, punctuate Gonzalo's vision with mocking commentary:

SEBASTIAN [*to Antonio*] No marrying 'mong his subjects?
ANTONIO None, man, all idle: whores and knaves.

(171–2)

Usurpers and plotters against their own brothers, Sebastian and Antonio prove Gonzalo's dream mere delusion. This pair embodies the greed, ambition, and sinfulness that pervasively colour the human condition. Gonzalo's Utopian longings can never come to pass, not even on Prospero's isle; the world has fallen and we have too.

Traditional pastoral characters assume new identities in this play. The rustic primitives who engage in broad clowning appear as Stefano, the drunken butler, and Trinculo, the shipwrecked court jester. Stefano, who would rule the isle, mimics parodically the aspirations of Gonzalo, Prospero, Caliban, Antonio, and Sebastian. Moreover, the supernatural creatures who usually inhabit the pastoral world—the miscellaneous nymphs, dryads, and others—take on new shapes as Ariel and the other spirits attendant on Prospero. Speaking superbly bright and energetic verse, metamorphosing into different shapes upon command, Ariel serves Prospero but desires freedom. This desire can play more or less seriously. Upon finally gaining independence, for example, Simon Russell Beale's Ariel (Royal Shakespeare Company, 1992) vented long-suppressed anger at his master in a striking gesture: glaring at Prospero he spat in his face and slowly walked off stage. In production the troubled relationship between Ariel and Prospero can reflect on other hierarchical relationships in the play, on that between children and parents, servants and masters, wives and husbands, subjects and rulers, natives and colonizers.

The pastoral satyr appears on Prospero's isle as Caliban. Descending from Greek representations in art and literature, coming to full and varied life in Italian pastorals, the satyr functions as a paradoxical combination of animality, humanity, and divinity. As Robert Henke has well explained, satyrs represent brutish sexual desire but possess the human gifts of speech and song as well as a divine ancestry and vitality.[11] Shakespeare's Caliban clearly embodies all these paradoxes and oppositions. We first meet him as an animal. Prospero calls him 'A freckled whelp, hag-born—not honoured with | A human shape' (1. 2. 285–6); others refer to him as a 'devil', a 'Mooncalf' and a 'monster', a 'debauched fish'. Prospero angrily recalls Caliban's attempted rape of Miranda; Caliban remembers the incident unrepentantly:

> O ho, O ho! Would't had been done!
> Thou didst prevent me; I had peopled else
> This isle with Calibans.
>
> (1. 2. 352–4)

Caliban used only to 'gabble like | A thing most brutish' (359–60) but Prospero taught him language. Now he is glad that he has learned how to curse:

> All the infections that the sun sucks up
> From bogs, fens, flats, on Prosper fall, and make him
> By inch-meal a disease!
>
> (2. 2. 1–3)

Caliban chants a drunken catch with his new-found friends and masters, Stefano and Trinculo (2. 2. 179 ff.). His real music, however, lies in his poetry, particularly in the lyrical evocations of the island's sights and sounds:

Be not afeard. The isle is full of noises,
Sounds, and sweet airs, that give delight and hurt not.
Sometimes a thousand twangling instruments
Will hum about mine ears, and sometime voices
That if I then had waked after long sleep
Will make me sleep again; and then in dreaming
The clouds methought would open and show riches
Ready to drop upon me, that when I waked
I cried to dream again.

(3. 2. 138–46)

Unlike most mortals, with ears closed over by the muddy vesture of decay, as Lorenzo put it (*Merchant of Venice*, 5. 1. 64), Caliban hears celestial music. This speech reveals a supernatural sensitivity to music and a finely tuned poetic imagination, rich in invention, capable of vivid imagery and strong rhythms.

The pastoral satyr called Caliban (perhaps Shakespeare's anagram for one source, Montaigne's essay, 'Of the Cannibals') assumes different life and meaning in different readings of the play. Emphasizing Caliban's bestiality, some see him as representing raw nature in need of Prospero's civilizing art and control. Emphasizing his humanity, others see him as a victim of Prospero's imperial power, a representative of native populations enslaved by European colonizers. Adopting the latter view, David Suchet, the Caliban in Clifford Williams' Royal Shakespeare Company production (1978), recalls his struggle with the role. He thought that Caliban had been misplayed as a fish, a dog with one or several heads, a lizard, a monkey, a snake, a half-ape, half-man with fins for arms, and a tortoise. He decided that Shakespeare drew him as a man, a native who rightfully owned the isle: 'The "monster" was in the eyes of the beholder'.[12] Peter Brook's production (Paris, 1990) deliberately deconstructed this politically correct reading. Brook cast a West African as Prospero, a Japanese actor as Gonzalo, an Indian as Miranda, and another African as Ariel. Playfully and perversely he cast a white actor, David Bennent, as Caliban. The multiracial and multinational casting disabled the contemporary political interpretation (Prospero as colonizer, Caliban as colonized) and, in Dennis Kennedy's words, instead suggested 'the theme of freedom as a universal desire'.

Inhabitants of the pastoral world find various ways to enjoy the *otium* or 'leisure' that characterizes their life. They often fall asleep on grassy banks, Louise Clubb observes, thus facilitating the 'misunderstandings, deceits, and reversals desirable to the plot'.[13] Varying the convention, Prospero puts Miranda to sleep in order to confer with Ariel (1. 1. 186–7). Later Ariel puts to sleep King Alonso, Gonzalo, and others; Antonio and Sebastian then plot to murder the king and his counsellor, whom Ariel awakens with music just in time. The incident reveals the wickedness of the would-be assassins, the vulnerability of the good, and the supervisory control of Ariel. People in the pastoral world also fall in love; they court, yearn, compete, suffer, lose, and win. Italian lovers like Aminta and Silvia (Tasso's *Aminta*) and Amarilli and Mirtillo (Guarini's *Il Pastor Fido*) prepare the way for Shakespeare's lovely Ferdinand and Miranda. Unlike Caliban, Ferdinand endures hardship for Miranda and practises restraint until Prospero finally gives his blessing. The pastoral union has serious political implications, namely the uniting of two kingdoms, Milan and Naples.

The pastoral world also regularly features music and theatrical shows. Literary shepherds compete in songs and entertainments, sometimes staging various pageants. Prospero's island, as Caliban observed, is 'full of noises, | Sounds and sweet airs'. Ariel plays music and sings throughout the play: we have already noted his musical rescue of the king; at another time he offers the shipwrecked and grieving Ferdinand dubious musical comfort:

> Full fathom five thy father lies.
> Of his bones are coral made;
> Those are pearls that were his eyes;
> Nothing of him that doth fade
> But doth suffer a sea-change
> Into something rich and strange.
> Sea-nymphs hourly ring his knell.
> (1. 2. 400–6)

Ariel's song lies to Ferdinand about his father's drowning but hints at some kind of afterlife, thus preparing for the joy of reunion. This haunting, justly celebrated music sounds a keynote in the play, that of transformation into 'something rich and strange'. In 4. 1 music plays again as Prospero stages a wedding masque for Ferdinand and Miranda.

In this scence, difficult to translate to modern stage conventions, various classical deities make grand entrances and chant verse blessings on the young lovers. Remembering the 'foul conspiracy' (139) against his life, Prospero suddenly breaks the spell and shatters the illusion. The spirits of the pageant vanish '*To a strange, hollow, and confused noise*' (143 s. d.). The discordant ending images meanings central to the play: even in the pastoral world musical order and harmony must confront the forces of chaos. The ideal vision of harmonious interaction with gods must always include the reality of Caliban lurking in the brush. Humans cannot return to Eden but must live in the fallen world.

So it is that Prospero at the end of the play finally gives up his magic and returns to Milan. Since antiquity, of course, the pastoral world has always featured magic prominently (see Theocritus, *Idylls* 2, for example). Prospero's magic creates the opening tempest, charms the inhabitants of the isle, brings his enemies, especially his usurping brother Antonio, into his reach. Prospero proudly recalls his magical feats just before he renounces his power forever.

> I have bedimmed
> The noontide sun, called forth the mutinous winds,
> And 'twixt the green sea and azured vault
> Set roaring war—to the dread rattling thunder
> Have I given fire, and rifted Jove's stout oak
> With his own bolt; the strong-based promontory
> Have I made shake, and by the spurs plucked up
> The pine and cedar; graves at my command
> Have waked their sleepers, oped, and let 'em forth
> By my so potent art. But this rough magic
> I here abjure.
>
> (5. 1. 41–51)

This striking evocation owes to Medea's celebration of magic in Ovid's *Metamorphoses*. But unlike Medea, Prospero renounces such spells, abjures this 'rough magic'. He returns to Milan, to the corrupt, non-pastoral world of frenetic business and mortality, where 'Every third thought shall be my grave' (5. 1. 315). The final pastoral movement, from country to court, mixes contrasting moods—anticipation and resignation, hope and despair, joy and sorrow.

Shakespeare uses pastoral traditions in *The Tempest* to explore the tensions between nature and civilization. These tensions manifest themselves in political struggle, just as they do in Vergil's *Eclogues*, a master-text of pastoral literature for Shakespeare and his contemporaries. In unclassical fashion, however, Shakespeare here tilts the pastoral idyll into romance, into a story of purgative suffering, forgiveness, and restoration. At the climax of the action Ariel says that he would pity the prisoners if he were human. Prospero responds:

> Hast thou, which art but air, a touch, a feeling
> Of their afflictions, and shall not myself,
> One of their kind, that relish all as sharply
> Passion as they, be kindlier moved than thou art?
> Though with their high wrongs I am struck to th' quick,
> Yet with my nobler reason 'gainst my fury
> Do I take part. The rarer action is
> In virtue than in vengeance. They being penitent,
> The sole drift of my purpose doth extend
> Not a frown further.
>
> (5. 1. 21–30)

Pitying the suffering of his prisoners, recognizing their common humanity, Prospero puts aside anger and chooses forgiveness. Shakespeare's play, however, does not provide precisely the conclusion that Prospero here anticipates. Alonso repents, but not Sebastian and Antonio. Prospero forgives them anyway and this suggests that he has finally given up his magic, his need to control others, to impose order and prescribe conditions. 'Their senses I'll restore, | And they shall be themselves' (31–2), he says. The conventional pastoral restoration of identity here becomes charged with moral significance as characters variously become themselves, for better or for worse. Breaking his staff and drowning his book, Prospero the magician becomes man, 'sometime Duke of Milan'. Alonso comments appropriately: in one voyage,

> Ferdinand ... found a wife,
> Where he himself was lost; Prospero his dukedom

In a poor isle; and all of us ourselves,
When no man was his own.

(5. 1. 213–16)

Shakespeare's pastoral romance plays finally as a drama of finding, all the more affecting for its clear-eyed portrayal of loss.

Throughout his career Shakespeare continuously adverts to pastoral characters, themes, and situations. Tormented by the horrors of civil war, King Henry VI dreams of the simple, carefree life of a shepherd tending his flock (*3 Henry VI*, 2. 5. 21 ff.). Edgar prefaces the trial scene in Quarto *King Lear* with a shepherd's song (13. 36–40). This play's exploration of nature as creative and destructive, as life-giving and red in tooth and claw, constitutes a powerful anti-pastoral. Other plays embody what Sukanta Chaudhuri has called the 'cyclic structure' of pastoral romance, namely, the movement from the court to the country and then back to the court again.[14] *A Midsummer Night's Dream* opposes the forest outside Athens, a green world of magic and love, to the court world of law and restriction. Similarly, Bohemian meadows in *The Winter's Tale* contrast with the tragic Sicilian court, providing a place for respite, regeneration, and rebirth. As this play and *The Tempest* illustrate, Shakespeare's engagement with the pastoral genre bears particularly rich fruit in his romances.

7

Shakespeare as Reader

Habits of Reading

An early critic, Charlotte Lennox (1753–4), acerbically surveyed Shakespeare and his habits of reading. In her opinion, Shakespeare introduced improbabilities and inconsistencies and usually changed his sources for the worse; witness, for example, her hostile account of *Much Ado About Nothing*:

This fable, absurd and ridiculous as it is, was drawn from the foregoing story of Ginevra in Ariosto's *Orlando Furioso*, a fiction which, as it is managed by the epic poet, is neither improbable nor unnatural, but by Shakespeare mangled and defaced, full of inconsistencies, contradictions, and blunders.... Shakespeare, by changing the persons, altering some of the circumstances and inventing others, has made the whole an improbable contrivance, borrowed just enough to show his poverty of invention, and added enough to show his want of judgment. (Vickers, iv. 140)

Virtually no one today agrees with Lennox's sweeping negative judgements, refreshing though they may be in an age of bardolatry. Instead, modern critics tend to praise Shakespeare's dramatic language and creative transformations; they also look for recurrent patterns in his reading and writing. As we have noted, Shakespeare reads as a man of his time, actively and analogically, alert to parallels and analogues, sensitive to moral and political meanings. And as we have also observed, specifically in the discussion of *Julius Caesar*, he habitually practises compression, omission, innovation, and contradiction. In addition, Shakespeare exhibits specific habits of reading, and reading against a text.[1]

1. *Shakespeare reads competitively.* Shakespeare contests his authors, seeking to make old books new, to outdo model texts. He greatly expands Ovid in *Venus and Adonis* and *The Rape of Lucrece*. He doubles the number of identical twins (two sets instead of Plautus' one) in *The Comedy of Errors* to increase exponentially the confusions. The same competitive impulse appears in an early tragedy, *Titus Andronicus*, where the lead character vows to surpass the gory revenge of the mythological archetype, Procne (5. 2. 193–4). Combining Senecan and Ovidian antecedents, Titus arranges for several murders and serves up several corpses. Competition does not always take the form of mere multiplication. Sometimes Shakespeare engages in a running battle of wits with a tradition or source book. *All's Well That Ends Well* subverts the usual comic formula that opposes parents and young lovers. Here the older generation actively fosters the match between Helen and Bertram; and here the young lover, instead of being rash, impractical, infatuate, objects to the lady's poor social standing.

Shakespeare pointedly contends with Holinshed's *Chronicles* throughout *Macbeth*. He gives us a King Duncan who rules graciously and competently rather than ineffectually; his Banquo, unlike Holinshed's, remains virtuous, refusing to sully his hands with conspiracy and regicide. Holinshed's Macbeth rules liberally and well for ten years; Shakespeare's usurper acts the brutal tyrant immediately and never enjoys a single night of peace. Cumulatively, these changes portray Macbeth's assassination of Duncan as a sinful murder, as the study of a good man who gives his 'eternal jewel', his soul, to the devil (3. 1. 69). And yet, Shakespeare endows Macbeth with eloquence and moral sensitivity. He invents for the killer anguished reflections and a soul-sick weariness:

> Tomorrow, and tomorrow, and tomorrow
> Creeps in this petty pace from day to day
> To the last syllable of recorded time,
> And all our yesterdays have lighted fools
> The way to dusty death.
>
> (5. 5. 18–22)

All Macbeth's daring and ambition lead to this exhausted nihilism, to a sense that life merely creeps along meaninglessly towards death. These changes convey the enormity of Macbeth's king-killing and his own horror at what he has become. Here and throughout his work Shakespeare actively competes with his source texts, consciously shouldering the burden of the past, yet just as consciously proclaiming his own artistic independence.

2. *Shakespeare reads eclectically.*   Shakespeare conjoins separate texts and traditions freely and unpredictably. *A Midsummer Night's Dream*, for example, probably draws on sources ancient (Ovid, Plutarch, and Seneca), medieval (Chaucer and *Huon of Bordeaux*), and contemporary (Reginald Scot and Thomas Nashe), and a host of other texts. *The Winter's Tale* departs from Greene's *Pandosto* to borrow the idea of a statue coming to life from Ovid's *Metamorphoses*. *The Tempest*, similarly, lifts Medea's speech from Ovid to supply Prospero's renunciation of magic. Sometimes Shakespeare wanders far afield; he lifts a subplot from Sidney's pastoral romance, *Arcadia*, for his historical tragedy, *King Lear*.

To create *King Lear* Shakespeare ranges even further in his reading, to a sensational anti-Catholic diatribe, Samuel Harsnett's *A Declaration of Egregious Popish Impostures* (1603). Harsnett's exposure of fraudulent exorcisms suggests the storm, some features of Edgar's pretended madness, and the concern with devils. Edgar names Harsnett's specific devils—Flibbertigibbet, Modo, Mahu, Frateretto, Hoppedance; he hears voices: 'Frateretto calls me, and tells me Nero is an angler in the lake of darkness. Pray, innocent; beware the foul fiend' (13. 6–8). Summoned by Satan, Edgar imagines hell and tells the listeners to pray and to beware the evil one in their midst. On the one hand, Edgar, like Harsnett's Catholics, merely invents these demons, feigning madness, pretending possession in order to hide his identity. On the other, Edgar's warnings about devils running amok in the world ring strangely true in the play, where humans prey on each other like 'monsters of the deep' (16. 49). Harsnett's sensational tale fires Shakespeare's imagination, enabling him to widen the scope of the chronicle history and to portray an evil which is dark, mysterious, and profound.

3. *Shakespeare focuses on dramatic character in his reading.*   Since moderns have largely defined themselves by reacting against the character-analysis school of criticism, recent scholars have not much discussed Shakespeare's characterizations. But comparisons of sources

and the plays repeatedly show Shakespeare creating dominant characters who command the stage. In the history plays and tragedies, all named after individuals, a single figure (or several in series) focuses the shapeless sequence of events and provides dramatic interest. (Shakespeare learned well the method of Plutarch's *Lives*.) The playwright gives dramatic voice to his characters: Richard II speaks moving, elegiac poetry; Henry V orates grandly, converses privately, and speaks in soliloquy. Drawing on the traditions of Vice, Richard III is a glib, swaggering trickster, whose impudence and rhetorical verve distinguish him from Holinshed's relatively staid figure. Multiple dramatic traditions and sources bring to full life the figures of Shylock and Falstaff.

In *Othello* Shakespeare creates from Giraldi Cinthio's dull, unnamed Moor a courageous and eloquent protagonist. He invents Othello's opening defence against the charge of witchcraft. Demonstrating poise and rhetorical power, Othello tells his own life story before the Senate, a tale of 'disastrous chances, | Of moving accidents by flood and field, | Of hair-breadth scapes i' th'imminent deadly breach' (1. 3. 133–5). He movingly protests his love for Desdemona; even in his rage we hear what Wilson Knight called the '*Othello* music', the accent of the exotic voyager:[2]

> Like to the Pontic Sea,
> Whose icy current and compulsive course
> Ne'er knows retiring ebb, but keeps due on
> To the Propontic and the Hellespont,
> Even so my bloody thoughts with violent pace
> Shall ne'er look back.
>
> (3. 4. 456–61)

Unlike Giraldi Cinthio, Shakespeare makes Othello general of an army against the Turkish menace in order to emphasize his nobility and military character. He also endows the general with deep insecurities: Othello frets about his race, roughness, and age: 'Haply for I am black, | And have not those soft parts of conversation | That chamberers have; or for I am declined | Into the vale of years—' (3. 3. 267–70). Believing his wife unfaithful, Othello loses his eloquence, dignity, and self-possession: he strikes Desdemona, raves disjointedly in front of the Venetian embassy, falls into an epileptic fit. Othello kills

Desdemona in anguished delusion, then awakens to the truth. How unlike Giraldi Cinthio's mutely complicitous Moor, who has someone else do the killing, never recognizes his error, never laments his incomparable loss, denies the murder, and finally gets killed by Desdemona's kinsmen. Othello turns the sword of justice against himself and dies with a kiss. From the sketch in the source Shakespeare creates a tragic figure.

4. *Shakespeare expands the roles of the women from his sources.* In his works Shakespeare frequently develops the female characters of his sources into fuller individuals who lead demanding and troubled lives. Unlike Plautus' *matrona*, Adriana struggles with her sister, her husband, and her own jealousy in *The Comedy of Errors*. Unlike the Lady of Belmont, Portia shows cruel wit in *The Merchant of Venice*, privately mocking her suitors; she also rises higher than the prototype in the love scene with Bassanio and in her performance as learned doctor at the trial. Unlike Emily in Chaucer's tale, Emilia in *The Two Noble Kinsmen* has a distinct past, including a childhood friend Flavina, a compassionate nature, and a comico-tragic double in the Jailer's Daughter. The women in the history plays (from Mistress Quickly in *1 Henry IV* to Queen Margaret in *Richard III*) actively comment on unfolding events, register the impact on private life and families, and even oppose the movements of history. So do some women in the Roman tragedies: Lavinia (*Titus Andronicus*), Portia (*Julius Caesar*), and Cleopatra (*Antony and Cleopatra*). Shakespeare, moreover, gives heroines like Viola and Rosalind centre stage. Sometimes he endows women—Helen (*All's Well That Ends Well*), Isabella (*Measure for Measure*), and Cordelia (*King Lear*)—with a supernatural goodness and holiness, a halo of sanctity that can partially transform the fallen worlds in which they live.

Beatrice in *Much Ado About Nothing* also illustrates Shakespeare's habit of expansive reading. Shakespeare adds the Beatrice–Benedick plot to the main story of Claudio and Hero, drawn from Ariosto through Bandello. Beatrice sparkles in her combats of wit with Benedick, twitting, teasing, and mocking him. The soldier returned from wars, Benedick greets her as Lady Disdain and asks if she is yet living; she retorts, 'Is it possible disdain should die while she hath such meet food to feed it as Signor Benedick? Courtesy itself must convert to disdain if you come in her presence' (1. 1. 114–17). Beatrice vows never to take a husband; there will be no romantic claptrap, no amorous swoons or moonlight delusions for this lady: 'I have a good eye, uncle', she says to Leonato, 'I can see a church by daylight' (2. 1. 74–5). The comic plotters in the play work to make a marriage for her just as the tragic ones work to break the marriage of her cousin Hero. Both plots succeed in the remarkable 4. 1, where slander shatters the wedding ceremony of Hero and Claudio; in the aftermath, Beatrice and Benedick finally reveal their love for each other:

> BEATRICE You have stayed me in a happy hour. I was
>   about to protest I loved you.
> BENEDICK And do it with all thy heart.
> BEATRICE I love you with so much of my heart that none
>   is left to protest.
>
> (284–8)

The lovely, lyrical moment is hard-won but short-lived, as Beatrice immediately asks Benedick to prove his new love by killing Claudio. Both lovers have to work at their relationship amidst the painful realities of their families, desires, and situations. Precedented perhaps by the witty wooers of *Love's Labour's Lost* and *The Taming of the Shrew*, Shakespeare's invented Beatrice captivates viewers of the play, as many actresses have demonstrated, including Emma Thompson throughout her witty and nuanced portrayal in Branagh's film (1993).

5. *Shakespeare romanticizes* eros *and focuses on love*. Plautus' *Menaechmi* portrays the pleasures of illicit sex with the courtesan Erotium; the citizen twin argues with his nagging wife and finally sells her. *The Comedy of Errors* softens the hard edges of Plautine lust: the Courtesan takes a less prominent role, the travelling twin falls in love, the citizen and his wife work towards an uneasy reconciliation. Shakespeare multiplies the various permutations of desire and love in *A Midsummer Night's Dream*. He also expands the heroine's amorous schooling in *As You Like It*. Elsewhere Shakespeare tends to revise sources when they get explicitly or unpleasantly erotic. He replaces Giletta's repeated sexual encounters with Helen's bed-trick and exchange of rings in *All's Well*. He eliminates the King's incestuous desire for his long-lost daughter in *The Winter's Tale*.

Twelfth Night well illustrates Shakespeare's general tendencies regarding *eros* and love. The main source, Barnabe Riche's *Farewell to Military Profession* (1581), tells a lurid tale of lust and betrayal. Having drunk from 'the poisoned cup' (Bullough, ii. 345) of error, the lovers fall prey to their appetites. Shakespeare drops Silla's original infatuation and desertion by her beloved and substitutes happenstance: Viola has not met Orsino before her shipwreck. A ship captain attempts rape in Riche's tale; he becomes a courteous gentleman in Shakespeare's retelling. Julina's sexual encounter and pregnancy become Olivia's courtship and marriage. Unlike his prototype, Sebastian never deserts his beloved. And unlike her prototype, Silla, Viola shows love, patience, and devotion to her beloved Orsino. Viola's revelation of identity, often a magical moment of recognition in the theatre, does not require Silla's stripping and the exposure of her breasts. Viola and Orsino grow to a mutual understanding. Shakespeare certainly can dramatize desire and even attempted rape (witness Sonnet 129 and *The Two Gentlemen of Verona*) but he usually chooses to explore the dynamics of love, courtship, and marriage.

6. *Shakespeare increases the ethical and intellectual complexity of his sources.* The Rape of Lucrece exhibits the collision of Christian and classical values regarding honour, sin, and suicide. The histories dramatize great debates about the origins of sovereignty, law, kingship, usurpation, and regicide. In the *Henry IV* plays, Gaunt and others articulate Tudor orthodoxy about the divine right of kings while Bolingbroke steals the crown. Contrary to Holinshed's account, *Henry V* presents a heroic and anti-heroic view of history at the same time. *Richard II* and *Julius Caesar* stage the contemporary tyrannicide debate in the settings of England and ancient Rome respectively. What right have the conspirators to kill the leader? What, finally, does the assassination achieve?

Even the comedies raise hard questions. *Measure for Measure* poses a difficult ethical dilemma: Claudio's sister, Isabella, a novice, can save her brother, condemned for fornication, only if she herself yields sexually to the corrupt magistrate Angelo. The two confrontations between Isabella and Angelo (2.2, 2.4), largely invented by Shakespeare, feature brilliant debate. Isabella begs mercy for a sin she abhors, and Angelo resolves to punish a crime he desperately wants to commit. Possessed by lust, Angelo poses a devastating question: 'Might there not be a charity in sin | To save this brother's life?' (2. 4. 63–4). Isabella answers, 'Better it were a brother died at once | Than that a sister, by redeeming him, | Should die for ever' (2. 4. 107–9). She later retorts: 'Ignominy in ransom and free pardon | Are of two houses; lawful mercy | Is nothing kin to foul redemption' (112–14).

These confrontations leave us with no easy answers. Angelo's initial response to Isabella's plea for pity carries conviction, 'I show it most of all when I show justice' (2. 2. 102). And Isabella's conclusion, reached in a fury of self-righteousness, must give us pause: 'Then Isabel live chaste, and brother die: | More than our brother is our chastity' (2. 4. 184–5). That doesn't sound like anything in Matthew, Mark, Luke, or John. Isabella's certainty that sexual intercourse with Angelo will damn her to hell, despite the circumstances, makes God another Angelo, intent only on harshly punishing sexual activity, insistent only on the letter, not the spirit, of the law. And we do not wish to see Claudio die. On the other hand, right is right and wrong is wrong, some Catholic doctrine teaches, and Isabella wants to be a nun. Pope John Paul II's encyclical, *Veritatis Splendor* (1993), 'The Splendour of Truth', restates traditional Catholic principles and provides a basis for ethical judgement: an act that debases human dignity is intrinsically evil (*intrinsece malum*) and as such can never be ordered to God; it is not licit to do such evil (e.g. murder, prostitution, and slavery) that good may come of it. Traditional Catholic teaching supports the audience's instinctive repugnance at what is, after all, rape and extortion by other names. We loathe the lusty, hypocritical Angelo and pity the outraged Isabella. We do not want to see him possess her. Here Shakespeare transforms the source materials into an engaging meditation on crime and punishment, justice and mercy, charity and self-love, virtue and vice, and on the sometimes sliding line between these apparent opposites. Unlike many of his source texts which preach and harry the reader into submission, Shakespeare's plays dramatize opposing views and ideas. They tend to see and present both sides, to delight in the debate rather than the resolution.

7. *Shakespeare adds to sources comic characters and subplots.* An additional pair of identical twins, the Dromios, increases Plautine con-

fusions in *The Comedy of Errors*. Shakespeare often injects a clown into his plots: Lancelot in *The Merchant of Venice*, Feste in *Twelfth Night*, Dogberry in *Much Ado About Nothing*, Pistol in *All's Well That Ends Well*, the Fool in *King Lear*, Autolycus in *The Winter's Tale*. The hungover Barnardine in *Measure for Measure* refuses to be executed and imperiously dismisses his captors; Shakespeare spares him by inventing a gratuitous plot-twist. These very different figures range from buffoons like Dogberry to witty commentators like Feste. Comic characters such as these variously illuminate the main characters and action, often affording comic deflation or satirical perspective. Falstaff and the tavern crew bring into serious question the honour and ethics of their supposed betters, the nobles at court.

Sometimes Shakespeare imports not comic character but comic plot. Reading analogically, imagining always parallels and doubles, he adds to the Amleth story of Saxo and Belleforest the story of Polonius, Ophelia, and Hamlet. These characters enact the familiar configuration of blocking father (*senex*), maiden (*virgo*), and young lover (*adulescens*). Like the prototypical Plautine father, Polonius is meddlesome, self-important, and foolish; he commands Ophelia to break off the relationship. Like a submissive *virgo*, Ophelia obeys. But instead of presenting young love triumphant, Shakespeare shatters the inscribed comic pattern. Hamlet refuses to play the importunate lover, spurning the girl himself in woman-hating rage; brutally he stabs the father eavesdropping behind a curtain. The meddlesome Polonius does not look so laughable as his bloody corpse gets hauled away by a callous killer: 'I'll lug the guts into the neighbour room' (3. 4. 186). And the obedient *virgo* Ophelia reappears mad, her ravings revealing grief, rage, betrayal, and repressed sexuality: 'Young men will do't if they come to't, | By Cock, they are to blame' (4. 5. 60–1). Here the shattered comic configuration augments the tragic sense of frustration and suffering.

8. *Shakespeare emphasizes contrasts in locality.* Shakespeare typically creates a conflict between First and Second places: the First is a court or city, a daylight place of getting and spending, of dukes, merchants, and laws. The Second is a wood or fantasy kingdom, a night-time place of dreaming and loving, of spirits, poetry, and freedom. Restrictive Athens of *A Midsummer Night's Dream*, for example, opposes the

magical wood. The city in *The Merchant of Venice* hosts Shylock and the bond plot; Belmont has the casket test and lovers in the moonlight. Shakespeare heightens the polarity of Venice and Cyprus in *Othello*, transferring the action from the city senatorial chambers to Cyprus, a lonely outpost of civilization threatened by Turks from without and Iago from within. First and Second places do not oppose each other absolutely. Love blossoms in Athens and Venice too; the wood outside Athens is the home of quarrelling fairies, and Belmont's casket test fulfils the command of Portia's dead father. The barbarism in *Othello* begins in Venice with Iago's malignity and racial prejudice.

Shakespeare amplifies Plutarch's contrasts between Rome and Egypt in *Antony and Cleopatra*. The play shuttles back and forth between Rome and Cleopatra's luxurious palace at Alexandria in Egypt, moving to other locations in the Mediterranean as well. Rome is a place of soldiers, business, and military honour, the domain of Octavius, a sober and efficient military commander. Egypt is a place of 'lascivious wassails [carousals]' (1. 4. 56), the fertile playground of Cleopatra, indolent and sensual queen. The Roman Antony, who used to 'drink | The stale of horses' (1. 4. 61–2), in Egypt 'fishes, drinks, and wastes | The lamps of night in revel' (1. 4. 4–5). The contrast in localities images other contrasts in the play, the opposition between honour and love, duty and pleasure, male and female, reason and the imagination, tragedy and comedy. But these opposed settings mirror each other in the course of the action. Roman honour begins to look like another kind of self-indulgent fantasy. And Cleopatra dies with a grandly stoic Roman gesture: she commits suicide to avoid disgrace. Like the contrasts in other plays, those in *Antony and Cleopatra* appear finally not as mutually exclusive antitheses but as interconnected alternatives.

9. *Shakespeare reads retentively and reminiscently.* Past sources and Shakespeare's own past work productively furnish present imaginings. He does not forget much and seems to have enjoyed rereading. Sometimes a word or phrase will bubble up in memory: the portents describing the death of Caesar recur in *Hamlet* (Additional Passages, A). Sometimes a character returns for a second engagement: Chaucer's Theseus appears in an early comedy, *A Midsummer Night's Dream*, and in a late romance, *The Two Noble Kinsmen*. Shakespeare has a vivid

memory for theatrical scenes and plays: the comically jealous Thorello of Jonson's *Every Man in His Humour* (1598), a play that opened with Shakespeare and his company as the cast, reappears as Othello years later. Plautus' *Menaechmi* shapes the confusion and resolution of *The Comedy of Errors* as well as those of *Twelfth Night*. The Bible, North's Plutarch, Golding's Ovid, and Holinshed's *Chronicles* surface again and again throughout the canon.

In *Pericles* Shakespeare returns to one source of *The Comedy of Errors*, namely the tale of 'Apollonius of Tyre', as told by John Gower and others. This tale contributed to *Errors* the frame plot of Egeon's shipwreck, separation from his wife, and their eventual reunion. The story of loss and recovery more substantially supplies the episodic plot of *Pericles*, including the incest of Antiochus, the wanderings of Pericles, his marriage, his daughter's forced sojourn in a brothel, and the final family reunion. At the end Shakespeare creates from the source tale a musical, magical recognition scene between father and daughter. Marina heals Pericles and restores him to life; he salutes her, 'Thou that begett'st him that did thee beget' (21. 183). (T. S. Eliot celebrated this moment in his lovely poem, 'Marina': 'What seas what shores what granite islands towards my timbers | And woodthrush calling through the fog | My daughter'). The play then stages again the climactic reunion of husband and wife, this time, however, expressing the joy and wonder pointedly muted in the earlier meeting of Egeon and Emilia. Recognizing his wife Thaisa, long presumed dead, Pericles exclaims:

> This, this! No more, you gods! Your present kindness
> Makes my past miseries sports; you shall do well
> That on the touching of her lips I may
> Melt, and no more be seen.—O come, be buried
> A second time in my arms.
>
> (22. 62–6)

The story of Apollonius here culminates in romance redemption, as human patience and heavenly powers turn past sorrow into present joy.

10. *Shakespeare reads experimentally and defiantly.*   As we have continually noted, Shakespeare reads across and against literary types and

genres. Sonnets and lyric traditions ignite love scenes in drama. The Ovidian tale of Pyramus and Thisbe plays as burlesque in *A Midsummer Night's Dream* and as tragedy in the deep structure and imagery of *Romeo and Juliet*. Comic figures like the braggart soldier appear in histories and tragedies, notably transformed and enlarged in the persons of Falstaff, Hotspur, and Henry V. A perennial object of scorn and laughter, the cuckold, becomes a serious tragic figure in Othello.[3] The ancient and venerable story of the Trojan War in *Troilus and Cressida* shows humanity at its worst, irrational, brutish, and self-destructive. Shakespeare never rests content with received texts and traditions; he always revises them, reworks their context, combines them with other elements, turns them inside out or upside down. He converts the happy ending of *King Leir* into tragedy, the incest and suicide of Greene's *Pandosto* into wondrous romance.

In *Timon of Athens* Shakespeare reworks a passage he came across in North's Plutarch, specifically, the story of a misanthrope, Timon of Athens. Plutarch relates Timon's anger at fellow Athenians and his withdrawal from human society to gloss Antony's bitter withdrawal after his defeat at Actium. In *Timon of Athens* Shakespeare builds a tragedy from Plutarch's anecdote and from other sources that ridiculed Timon's misanthropy. Thus Shakespeare casts a minor and traditionally comic figure—self-important, inflexible, anti-festive—into the role of tragic hero. Confronted with human greed and selfishness, his Timon retreats and curses Athens: 'Plagues incident to men, | Your potent and infectious fevers heap | On Athens, ripe for stroke!' (4. 1. 21–3). Unlike the classical tragic hero in Sophocles, say, whose isolation results from some divine curse or firmly held principle, Timon's isolation is an enormous fit of pique that expands to full-blown hatred of all that is human. Shakespeare seems also to experiment here with the classical notion of *anagnorisis*, or 'recognition'. Aristotle defined *anagnorisis* as the discovery of a friend in one thought to be an enemy or of an enemy in one thought to be a friend. Timon misperceives both friends and enemies alike. First he wrongly assumes that all Athenians are his loving comrades, generous and charitable. Then, rudely disillusioned, he thinks everyone false, venal, self-interested. He never recognizes anyone truly. Here we see on a grand scale the restless experimentalism that characterizes Shakespeare's often defiant reading of texts and traditions throughout his career.

Shakespeare gets many a good laugh at the expense of readers and book learning. The pedants in his plays, notably Holofernes and Nathaniel in *Love's Labour's Lost*, display enough arrogance and ignorance to give later critics, especially those reading his reading, ample reason for caution. The history of scholarly enquiry as represented here has done its best with available materials. We cannot confuse probabilities with certainties, however, and must always remember that many important texts—Shakespeare's own plays like *Cardenio* and *Love's Labour's Won*, published pamphlets and books, plays he saw and acted in—remain lost. Still, as always, readers may continue to trace Shakespeare's reading in his work and dream of the sum total, Shakespeare's library.

The Dream of Shakespeare's Library

Peter Greenaway's surrealistic film adaptation of *The Tempest*, *Prospero's Books*, envisions the playwright as a magician, conjuring the fantastic story and its characters into existence through the act of reading. People have long dreamt of Shakespeare in the same way. And many, consequently, have tried to imagine the entire collection of manuscripts, broadsides, pamphlets, and books that Shakespeare read over the course of his life, though we cannot confidently identify a single volume as belonging to him. Which did he own, beg, or borrow? Which did he hear recited or see performed? Which did he skim, pore over, mark up? What does the total library of his reading, broadly conceived, look like?

There can be no definitive answers to such questions, of course. But four centuries of scholarship have witnessed interesting attempts to place real books and authors on the imaginary shelves. The earliest commentators occasionally noted specific texts behind the works. A spectator at the first performance of *The Comedy of Errors* at Gray's Inn (1594–5) saw its similarity to Plautus' *Menaechmi*. Identifying a chief source for the early poetry, Francis Meres proclaimed in 1598 that 'the sweet, witty soul of Ovid lives in mellifluous and honey-tongued William Shakespeare'. John Manningham (1601/2) observed the resemblance of *Twelfth Night* to Plautus and to Italian drama, specifically *Gl'Ingannati*.[4] Attempting a comprehensive list of Shakespeare's reading in 1691, Gerard Langbaine identified a number of sources, including English chronicles (Grafton, Holinshed, Stow) and Italian collections (Giraldi Cinthio, Bandello) (Vickers, i. 418–23). Later writers greatly expanded the collection with classical texts.

In 1767 Richard Farmer removed the Latin and Greek tomes from Shakespeare's shelves and replaced them with translations from the classics and contemporary works.[5] Scornfully attacking the notion of Shakespeare's learning, Farmer demonstrated Shakespeare's reliance on North's Plutarch for the Roman plays, Golding's Ovid for *The Tempest*, Lydgate's *Troy Book* for *Troilus and Cressida*, and Gascoigne's *Supposes* for *The Taming of the Shrew*. He identified certain foreign phrases in Shakespeare's work as commonplaces and some quotations as deriving from misremembered schoolbooks rather than original texts. Arrogant and full of himself (he hoped with one admirer that the question of Shakespeare's learning was 'now forever decided', Vickers, v. 261), Farmer usefully corrected and supplemented the record of Shakespeare's reading. In his eagerness to deny all classical learning to Shakespeare, he overstated the case, however. Demonstrating that Shakespeare read the standard grammar-school books, T. W. Baldwin, *William Shakespere's Small Latine and Lesse Greek* (1944), restocked Shakespeare's shelves with Greek and Latin authors: Aesop, Psalms, New Testament, Terence, Mantuan, Palingenius, Cicero, Quintilian, Susenbrotus, Erasmus, Vergil, Horace, Juvenal, Persius, Seneca, Ovid, Sallust, Caesar, and Livy.

Learned eighteenth- and nineteenth-century scholars directly and indirectly added texts to Shakespeare's imaginary library. Adducing verbal parallels, providing contemporary glosses, Edward Capell, George Steevens, the great Edmond Malone and others widened the scope of Shakespeare's reading, particularly in contemporary poetry and drama. Later, Victorian scholars catalogued Shakespeare's references to the Bible.[6] The microscopic notice of possible echoes and analogues eventually gave rise to organized collections of important source texts. J. P. Collier gathered known sources together under the title *Shakespeare's Library* (two volumes, 1843). W. C. Hazlitt added much material and reissued *Shakespeare's Library* in six volumes (1874–6). At the beginning of the twentieth century Israel Gollancz served as general editor for a series of reprints entitled *The Shakespeare Library* (about ten volumes published). Henry R. D. Anders carefully summarized scholarly research in his annotated catalogue, *Shakespeare's Books* (1904).

Renovating the library, the twentieth century has refurbished the collection and added several new wings. We have already noted T. W. Baldwin's work in the grammar-school curricula, later supplemented by Virgil K. Whitaker, *Shakespeare's Use of Learning* (1953). Through several decades Kenneth Muir weighed evidence judiciously and concisely, made new discoveries, and contributed sharp insights into Shakespeare's creative processes; much of his work appears in *The Sources of Shakespeare's Plays* (1977). Geoffrey Bullough gathered into eight volumes Shakespeare's reading in *Narrative and Dramatic Sources of Shakespeare* (1957–75), along with probable and possible sources and analogues. Some editions of Shakespeare's work, notably the Signet, New Variorum, and Bantam paperbacks edited by David Bevington, reprint selections from acknowledged sources. Taken together these various works constitute Shakespeare's library today. Catalogues to the collection abound; most convenient for quick reference to sources is the tabulation, 'Chronology and Sources', in *The Riverside Shakespeare*, with categories derived from Geoffrey Bullough. Researchers in Shakespeare studies add new titles all the time.[7]

Surveying the state of Shakespeare's library as currently conceived, we can hazard some general observations. Though Elizabethan schools emphasized the study of Greek, no Greek text has appeared behind Shakespeare's works. Nor should we be much surprised, as Greek was difficult to learn; Clenardus' standard textbook, for example, with italic Greek on a crowded page and explanations in Latin, could intimidate the most eager student. Moreover, Tudor England, encouraged by Latin writers and St Paul, associated Greeks with licentiousness and perfidy. This view received confirmation by the Tudor myth that traced British ancestry through Brut to that famous enemy of the Greeks, the formerly Trojan and later Roman Aeneas. At the grammar school, however, Shakespeare acquired reasonable competence in Latin, the universal language of educated discourse [Fig. 5]. Shakespeare returns to Ovid throughout his career, especially to the *Metamorphoses*, and also to Horace, Seneca, Vergil, and Cicero. He quotes Latin texts sporadically throughout his works and coins words of Latin origin—abruption, circummured, conflux, exsufflicate, and

5. The opening illustration of Alexander Nowell's *Catechismus Parvus Primum Latine Qui Ediscatur* (London, 1573). Young boys such as Shakespeare first learned Latin in settings like this one, where a pupil gives recitation to a stern-looking teacher. Shakespeare may have taken his revenge in comic portrayals of schooling and schoolmasters throughout his career.

tortive, for example.[8] In *The Merry Wives of Windsor* he even stages a comical Latin lesson featuring a reluctant pupil named (appropriately?) William:

> EVANS What is your genitive case plural, William?
> WILLIAM Genitive case?
> EVANS Ay.
> WILLIAM *Genitivo: 'horum, harum, horum'*.

MISTRESS QUICKLY Vengeance of Jenny's case! Fie on her!
Never name her, child, if she be a whore.

(4. 1. 52–7)

Shakespeare's library certainly contained books in French and Italian, as well as those in Latin. The poet read Eliot's *Ortho-Epia Gallica*, a French conversation manual, and perhaps works by Boaistuau and Belleforest. He wrote some amusing French scenes in *Henry V*. Since the Italian language enjoyed a vogue in Elizabethan London, those with training in Latin could acquire the rudiments with little difficulty. Shakespeare probably read Ariosto, Giraldi Cinthio, Bandello, Fiorentino, Florio's conversation manuals, and some plays in Italian.[9] And he read translations of works in ancient and modern languages. In addition to North's Plutarch and Golding's Ovid, Shakespeare turned to Holland's Pliny, Chapman's Homer, Florio's Montaigne, Googe's Palingenius, and Adlington's Apuleius.

The majority of Shakespeare's books were English. As we have seen in the previous chapters, Shakespeare read the chronicles of Holinshed and Hall, and also those of Grafton, Fabyan, Stow, and Foxe. He certainly knew the poetry of Chaucer, Gower, Lydgate, Spenser, Sidney (and the *Arcadia*), Drayton, Daniel, and *The Mirror for Magistrates*. He read much from the dashing and controversial Robert Greene, particularly from his novels, *Menaphon* and *Pandosto*, conycatching pamphlets, and plays. He learned to write sophisticated, musical, rhetorical prose from the courtly and urbane John Lyly. And as a working playwright in a volatile and difficult trade, Shakespeare knew about the old medieval morality and mystery plays as well as the current works of his competitors—Thomas Kyd, Christopher Marlowe, Ben Jonson, Thomas Middleton, John Fletcher, and many others. Play quartos may have been unwelcome at Oxford's Bodleian Library, but they constituted an important part of Shakespeare's reading.

The term 'reading', of course, covers a wide variety of interactions. As a working man of the theatre, Shakespeare must have read, consulted, written, doctored, revised, watched, rehearsed, and acted in hundreds of scenes and plays. He worked alone and with other writers and actors; he knew well the repertory of his own company as well as those of the competition. As we might expect, he always kept an especially sharp look-out for usable material, sometimes imitating current crowd-pleasers from rival theatres, sometimes reworking an old standby that was perhaps gathering dust in the company archives. A lost revenge thriller contributed materially to *Hamlet*. Outdated romantic plays like *Sir Clyomon and Sir Clamydes* (1570) and *The Rare Triumphs of Love and Fortune* (1582) furnished *Cymbeline* (1610). Shakespeare read plays in print as well as those being performed on the stages of the inns, courtyards, court, private theatres, and public playhouses that constituted his working world.

The new millennium will doubtless bring many changes to our current dream of Shakespeare's library. We now look not only at books but at traditions, inherited sets of expectations, reflexes, and conventions that cannot be traced to specific readings of specific texts. Observing traditions, readers can now account for structural, thematic, ideational, imagistic, and generic linkages; they can see beyond the narrow range of texts indicated by the evidence of verbal echo. Moreover, scholars are now reimagining the creative process, reevaluating the role of print, and redefining literature. They are dreaming other dreams entirely. Recent critical theory has decentred the author; in other words, it has shifted attention from the individual creative mind to the complex mix of factors—social, economic, political, and cultural—that go into the making of a text. The old model of creativity was vertical and hierarchical with the author in the middle: Shakespeare read books and transformed them into works of art; subtexts lay beneath the texts of his work. The new model is horizontal and associative: texts all exist in complicated cultural relations to each other. According to some critics these days, there are no source texts, only an endless and bewitching array of intertexts. Contemporary pamphlets about domestic relations, witches, or the Spanish invasion can reveal much about Shakespeare's plays, whether he ever read them or not. Today scholars look more for these intertexts (often called contexts) rather than for source texts (subtexts). In the new millennium scholars may still dream of Shakespeare's library, but they will envision the collection differently. Stacks of books privately owned and read will share space with literary and cultural databases, infinitely flexible, accessible, and expandable.

I. ELIZABETHAN READING

1. S. Schoenbaum has ably separated fact from fancy, *William Shakespeare: A Documentary Life* (New York: Oxford Univ. Press, 1975).

2. Shaw as quoted by Stanley Wells, *Shakespeare: The Poet and His Plays* (London: Methuen, 1997), 64. The standard studies of Shakespeare and his sources are Kenneth Muir, *The Sources of Shakespeare's Plays* (London: Methuen, 1978); Bullough.

3. See Thomas M. Greene, *The Light in Troy: Imitation and Discovery in Renaissance Poetry* (New Haven: Yale Univ. Press, 1982). One can sample Renaissance writers on the subject in Bernard Weinberg, *A History of Literary Criticism in the Italian Renaissance*, 2 vols. (Univ. of Chicago Press, 1961); *Elizabethan Critical Essays*, ed. G. Gregory Smith, 2 vols. (Oxford: Clarendon Press, 1904, repr. 1971).

4. On literacy rates in the period see David Cressy, *Literacy and the Social Order: Reading and Writing in Tudor and Stuart England* (Cambridge: Cambridge Univ. Press, 1980). Keith Thomas distinguishes between different kinds of literacies (partial vs. whole, reading vs. writing, numeracy vs. literacy) in 'The Meaning of Literacy in Early Modern England', in Gerd Baumann (ed.), *The Written Word: Literacy in Transition* (Oxford: Clarendon Press, 1986), 97–131.

5. See T. W. Baldwin, *William Shakspere's Petty School* (Urbana, Ill.: Univ. of Illinois Press, 1943); also, his *William Shakspere's Small Latine and Lesse Greek*, 2 vols. (Urbana, Ill: Univ. of Illinois Press, 1944); Anthony Grafton and Lisa Jardine, *From Humanism to the Humanities: Education and the Liberal Arts in Fifteenth- and Sixteenth-Century Europe* (Cambridge, Mass.: Harvard Univ. Press, 1986); Anthony Grafton, *Commerce with the Classics: Ancient Books and Renaissance Readers* (Ann Arbor: Univ. of Michigan Press, 1997).

6. See Robert Kilburn Root, *Classical Mythology in Shakespeare* (1903; repr. New York: Gordian Press, 1965); Naseeb Shaheen has gathered his earlier work on Scriptural allusion into *Biblical References in Shakespeare's Plays* (Newark, Del.: Univ. of Delaware Press, 1999).

7. Richard Farmer, *An Essay on the Learning of Shakespeare* (Cambridge, 1767); see also J. A. K. Thomson, *Shakespeare and the Classics* (1952; repr. London: George Allen and Unwin, 1966).

8. Some were published; see Ann Moss, *Printed Commonplace-Books and the Structuring of Renaissance Thought* (Oxford: Clarendon Press, 1996).

9. Emrys Jones, *The Origins of Shakespeare* (Oxford: Clarendon Press, 1977), 16.

10. William H. Sherman, 'The Evidence of the Margin', a handout distributed to the 'Habits of Reading in Early Modern England' seminar, Folger Shakespeare Library, 14 July 1997.

11. For analysis see Sir Edward Maunde Thompson, *Shakespeare's Handwriting* (Oxford: Clarendon Press, 1916).

12. See Mark Bland, 'The London Book-Trade in 1600', in David Kastan (ed.), *A Companion to Shakespeare* (Oxford: Blackwell, 1999), 450–63, from which I draw this paragraph.

13. Peter W. M. Blayney, *The First Folio of Shakespeare* (Washington, DC: Folger Library Publications, 1991), 25–32; see also his *The Bookshops in Paul's Cross Churchyard* (London: The Bibliographical Society, 1990); and 'The Publication of Playbooks', in John D. Cox and David Scott Kastan (eds.), *A New History of Early English Drama* (New York: Columbia Univ. Press, 1997), 383–422.

14. Laurie E. Maguire provides a clear explanation of the process, 'The Craft of Printing (1600)', in *A Companion to Shakespeare*, 434–49.

15. *Elizabethan Critical Essays*, ed. Smith, ii. 177.

16. Alfred Harbage, *As They Liked It: An Essay on Shakespeare and Morality* (New York: Macmillan, 1947), 6.

17. In this paragraph I follow Heidi Brayman Hackel, '"Rowme" of Its Own: Printed Drama in Early Modern Libraries', *A New History of Early English Drama*, 113–30 (114–19); the statistic below about English books in the Bodleian comes from Thomas, 'The Meaning of Literacy', 101.

18. For a probing discussion see Peter Holland, 'Theseus' Shadows in *A Midsummer Night's Dream*', *Shakespeare Survey*, 47 (1994), 139–51.

19. I do not treat the Bible here, important though it is as a text and as a tradition, because it has a volume of its own in this series.

2. POEMS

1. The sonnets appeared in print with a narrative poem, 'A Lover's Complaint', in 1609. Shakespeare wrote some miscellaneous verses, including 'The Phoenix and the Turtle' (1601), and possibly some poems in William Jaggard's collection, *The Passionate Pilgrim* (1599).

2. These include Narcissus' un-Ovidian death by drowning (161–2; cf. *Hero and Leander*, 74–6), the jennet breaking her reins (260–4; cf. *HL* 625–30), the kiss restoring consciousness (473–4; cf. *HL* 485–8), and the prophetic

conclusion—Venus' grim forecast about human love (1135 ff.) paralleling the prediction that learning and poverty will always go together (*HL* 465–70); I cite *Hero and Leander* from *The Complete Works of Christopher Marlowe*, i. *Translations*, ed. Roma Gill (Oxford: Clarendon Press, 1987).

3. G. Blakemore Evans *et al.* (eds.), *The Riverside Shakespeare*, 2nd edn. (Boston: Houghton Mifflin, 1997), 1961, 1965, 1962.

4. I quote Ovid from the Loeb Classical Library editions, *Metamorphoses with an English Translation by Frank Justus Miller*, 2 vols., 3rd edn., rev. G. P. Goold (1977); *Fasti with an English Translation by Sir James George Frazer*, 2nd edn., rev. G. P. Goold (1989). As always, other texts and traditions add to the mix: Shakespeare's own sonnets (1–17) echo in Venus' arguments about seizing the day and preserving beauty through procreation (129–74); Vergil's *Georgics* 3. 75–94, in the description of breeding jennet (289–322); Neoplatonic traditions, in the allegorical imagery and in the treatment of beauty and love.

5. *Fabularum Ovidii Interpretatio, Ethica, Physica, et Historica* (Cambridge, 1584), 150; *Ovid's Metamorphosis Englished, Mythologized, and Represented in Figures* (Oxford, 1632), 160. On allegorized and moralized Ovid see Douglas Bush, *Mythology and the Renaissance Tradition in English Poetry*, 2nd edn. (New York: Norton, 1963), 11–16; Jonathan Bate, *Shakespeare and Ovid* (Oxford: Clarendon Press, 1993), 25–31.

6. Anthony Burgess, *Nothing Like the Sun: A Story of Shakespeare's Love-Life* (New York: Norton, 1964), 171. In this section I quote Golding's translation from W. H. D. Rouse (ed.), *Shakespeare's Ovid* (London: Centaur Press, 1961).

7. Blakemore Evans *et al.* (eds.), *The Riverside Shakespeare*, 1970.

8. He uses also Livy's *Ab Urbe Condita* (1. 57–60), and Vergil's *Aeneid* 1 and 2 for the description of Troy (1366 ff.). Shakespeare incorporates in *Lucrece* features of the popular complaint poem, *A Mirrour for Magistrates* (1559), and Samuel Daniel's *The Complaint of Rosamond* (1592), for example, both featuring first-person narration, lamentation, and moralization.

9. St Augustine, *The City of God*, tr. George E. McCracken *et al.*, The Loeb Classical Library, 7 vols. (1957–72), i. 88–9.

10. All but three of Shakespeare's sonnets take the standard English form: 99 (fifteen lines long), 126 (six couplets), 145 (tetrameters).

11. There were precursors, but in Dante's *Purgatorio* (24. 57) Bonagiunta uses the phrase *dolce stil novo* to characterize Dante's poetic innovation; he (24. 51) refers to Dante's *La Vita Nuova*, 19, *Donne ch'avete intelletto d'amore*, 'Ladies, whose understanding is of love', the great canzone that celebrates Beatrice as a new creation, the incarnation of divine love and beauty on

earth. I cite Dante from *The Divine Comedy*, ed. Charles Singleton, 3 vols. (Princeton: Princeton Univ. Press, 1982–8).

12. I cite Petrarch and translations from *The Canzoniere*, trans. Mark Musa (Bloomington, Ind.: Indiana Univ. Press, 1996). References are to poems not pages.

13. Sir Thomas Wyatt, *Collected Poems*, ed. Joost Daalder (London: Oxford Univ. Press, 1975), 25.

3. HISTORIES

1. Recent editors have added to the Folio list of ten plays *Edward III* and also *Sir Thomas More*, both of which Shakespeare at least had a hand in. The term 'history' also had the more generalized meaning of 'story'. Several plays from other genres carry the word 'history' in their titles: *The Merchant of Venice* (Quarto version, 1600) appears as a 'Comical History'; *King Lear* (Quarto version, 1608) similarly appears as 'Chronicle History'. Both the Quarto and Folio title-pages of *Richard III* advertise the play as a tragedy. A number of the Roman plays—such as *Julius Caesar* and *Antony and Cleopatra*—also qualify as histories, as does a tragedy like *King Lear* and a romance like *Cymbeline*, both also indebted to Holinshed.

2. For a lucid general guide to this reshaping see Peter Saccio, *Shakespeare's English Kings: History, Chronicle, and Drama* (New York: Oxford Univ. Press, 1977). Incorporating other accounts—those of Protestants like William Harrison and Abraham Fleming and Catholics like Richard Stanyhurst and Edmund Campion, for example—Holinshed's history features a polyphony of voices.

3. On the women in these plays see Phyllis Rackin and Jean E. Howard, *Engendering a Nation: A Feminist Account of Shakespeare's English Histories* (London: Routledge, 1997).

4. *Holinshed's Chronicles: Richard II (1398–1400), Henry IV and Henry V*, ed. R. S. Wallace and Alma Hansen (Oxford: Clarendon Press, 1923), 47. I have used this edition, hereafter cited parenthetically in the text, for passages not included by Bullough.

5. See the discussion by Robert Smallwood, in Jonathan Bate and Russell Jackson (eds.), *Shakespeare: An Illustrated Stage History* (Oxford: Oxford Univ. Press, 1996), 182–6.

6. See *King Henry V*, ed. T. W. Craik (London: Routledge, 1995), 84 and facing illustration.

7. Quoted by James N. Loehlin, *Shakespeare in Performance: Henry V* (Manchester: Manchester Univ. Press, 1996), 71.

8. Noting that the stage direction for 4. 6. specifies Henry's entrance with prisoners, Gary Taylor indicates that the prisoners be killed on stage here, thus demonstrating Henry's cold-blooded heroism (*Henry V*, ed. Taylor (Oxford: Clarendon Press, 1982), 32–4).

9. Saints plays re-enacted the spiritual struggles and triumphs of God's virtuous heroes. The cycle or miracle plays collectively dramatized biblical stories and salvation history from creation to the life of Christ and the Last Judgement.

10. Peter J. Houle lists the plays and provides pertinent references, *The English Morality and Related Drama: A Bibliographical Survey* (Hamden, Conn.: Archon Books, 1972).

11. Arguing that Shakespeare was forced to change names, the Oxford editors have adopted the original Oldcastle for Falstaff in *1 Henry IV*. See Wells and Taylor, *A Textual Companion*, 330–1. I have chosen to retain the name Falstaff throughout this discussion.

12. David Bevington (ed.), *Medieval Drama* (Boston: Houghton Mifflin, 1975), 647–9.

13. Bernard Spivack, *Shakespeare and the Allegory of Evil: The History of a Metaphor in Relation to His Major Villains* (New York: Columbia Univ. Press, 1958), 168–70; see also 388–407. Subsequent references are cited parenthetically in the text. See also *King Richard III*, ed. Antony Hammond (London: Methuen, 1981), 99–102.

14. See *Henry V*, 2. 3. 16–17. The reading incorporates Lewis Theobald's famous emendation, 'babbled' for the Folio's 'table'.

15. On this and related points see *Henry IV, Part I*, ed. David Bevington (Oxford: Clarendon Press, 1987), 24–34; *The First Part of King Henry IV*, ed. Herbert Weil and Judith Weil (Cambridge: Cambridge Univ. Press, 1997), 9–12, 27–40.

4. COMEDIES

1. Below I quote Plautus from the Loeb Classical Library edition, *Plautus with an English Translation by Paul Nixon*, 5 vols. (1916–38). For further discussion of topics treated in this chapter, especially *The Comedy of Errors* and *All's Well That Ends Well*, see my *Shakespeare and Classical Comedy: The Influence of Plautus and Terence* (Oxford: Clarendon Press, 1994, repr., 1997).

2. Perhaps he knew the fanciful, episodic, influential Greek romances so admired by his contemporaries—Chariton's *Chaereas and Callirhoe*, for example, or Heliodorus' *Aethiopica*. He certainly read their descendants, as well as the Roman prose fiction of Apuleius, *The Golden Ass* (translated by

Adlington), the tale of Apollonius of Tyre, and Elizabethan narratives such as Sir Philip Sidney's *Arcadia*.

3. Shakespeare knew also the traditions, and perhaps the texts, of Italian comedy, both *commedia erudita*, the innovative, neo-classical plays of writers like Ariosto and Della Porta, as well as *commedia dell'arte*, the exuberant practice of dramatic improvisation. English antecedents and contemporaries offered local inspiration: John Lyly wrote influential romantic comedies which blended sophisticated wit, pert pages, and low comic types; Ben Jonson offered satiric portraits of 'humourous' characters, figures dominated by some special affectation or folly.

4. *Pascal's Pensées*, trans. H. F. Stewart (New York: Pantheon, 1950), 55.

5. The first is Paul Nixon's rendering in the Loeb Classical Library edition; the second belongs to Erich Segal, *Plautus: Three Comedies* (New York: Harper Row, 1969); Segal records the others, 148 n.

6. Fiorentino's collection may influence *The Merry Wives of Windsor*, especially Falstaff's unsuccessful attempts to seduce the wives, and Master Ford's jealousy. Three other Shakespearian comedies derive from Italian collections, either in the original language or in translation: *Much Ado About Nothing* (Bandello's *Novelle*), *Measure for Measure* (Cinthio's *Hecatommithi* as represented in Whetstone's play, *Promos and Cassandra*), and *All's Well That Ends Well* (Boccaccio's *Decameron*, as translated by Painter, *The Palace of Pleasure*). Leo Salingar points out (*Shakespeare and the Traditions of Comedy* (Cambridge: Cambridge Univ. Press, 1974), 301–3), that the plays based on Italian *novelle* share certain characteristics: a seriousness in tone, a decrease in revelry scenes, an immoral blocking character—Shylock, Don John, Bertram, Angelo, the recourse to law culminating in trials, a de-emphasis on magic, green worlds, and woodlands, and the presence of broken or deferred nuptials.

7. See Toby Lelyveld, *Shylock on the Stage* (Cleveland: Western Reserve Univ., 1960); *The Merchant of Venice*, ed. M. M. Mahood (Cambridge: Cambridge Univ. Press, 1987), 42–53; Avraham Oz, '*The Merchant of Venice* in Israel', in Dennis Kennedy (ed.), *Foreign Shakespeare: Contemporary Performance* (Cambridge: Cambridge Univ. Press, 1993), 56–75 (63–4).

8. See Patrick Stewart's account of the role in Philip Brockbank (ed.), *Players of Shakespeare: Essays in Shakespearian Performance by Twelve Players with the Royal Shakespeare Company* (Cambridge: Cambridge Univ. Press, 1985), 11–28.

9. See Gary Jay Williams, *Our Moonlight Revels: A Midsummer Night's Dream in the Theater* (Iowa City: Univ. of Iowa Press, 1997), 35, 229–30; *A Midsummer Night's Dream*, ed. Peter Holland (Oxford: Clarendon Press, 1994), 265–8.

10. Louise George Clubb, *Italian Drama in Shakespeare's Time* (New Haven: Yale Univ. Press, 1989), 65–89, discusses such plays as Bibbiena's *La Calandria*, Piccolomini's *L'amor costante*, Borghini's *La Donna costante*, Bargagli's *La pellegrina*, and Della Porta's *Gli duoi fratelli rivali* in this connection.

11. Other male lovers in Shakespeare display callousness, selfishness, stupidity, and worse, and seem to be rewarded beyond their deserts: Proteus in *The Two Gentlemen of Verona* threatens rape but ends up with the love of the good and faithful Julia. Claudio's callous treatment of the innocent Hero in *Much Ado About Nothing* appears to be insufficently repented and excessively forgiven. Angelo's attempts at rape and betrayal in *Measure for Measure* win for him the love of a good woman, his former fiancée Mariana; the Duke's lies and disguises in that play entitle him, it seems, to propose to Isabella.

5. TRAGEDIES

1. I cite Plutarch from *Shakespeare's Plutarch*, ed. T. J. B. Spencer (Harmondsworth: Penguin, 1964).

2. Paul Stapfer, *Shakespeare and Classical Antiquity*, trans. Emily J. Carey (London: C. Kegan Paul, 1880), 8 (originally published in French, 1879); M. W. MacCallum, *Shakespeare's Roman Plays and Their Background* (London: Macmillan, 1910, repr. 1967); Marvin Spevack (ed.), *Julius Caesar* (Cambridge: Cambridge Univ. Press, 1988), 13.

3. Marvin Spevack (ed.), *A Complete and Systematic Concordance to the Works of Shakespeare*, 9 vols. (Hildesheim: Georg Olms, 1968–80), iii. 607 ff. Caesar's ghost speaks three additional lines; Antony speaks 328 lines, Cassius, 505, and Brutus, 720.

4. On the imagery of hunting and ritual see Brents Stirling, '"Or Else This Were a Savage Spectacle"', *Publications of the Modern Language Association*, 66 (1951), 765–74; Naomi Liebler, '"Thou bleeding piece of earth": The Ritual Ground of *Julius Caesar*', *Shakespeare Studies*, 14 (1981), 175–96. Gail Paster argues that the conspirators feminize Caesar by making him bleed; she analyses the blood as it relates to gender in the play, *The Body Embarrassed: Drama and the Disciplines of Shame in Early Modern England* (Ithaca, NY: Cornell Univ. Press, 1993), 99–112.

5. For some gory details see John Ripley, *Julius Caesar on Stage in England and America 1599–1973* (Cambridge: Cambridge Univ. Press, 1980), 252, 266–7, 271–2; Peter Holland, *English Shakespeares: Shakespeare on the English Stage in the 1990s* (Cambridge: Cambridge Univ. Press, 1997), 80, 232–3.

6. There is another revelation of Portia's death at 4. 2. 198–211; see Wells and Taylor, *A Textual Companion*, 387.

7. *Nineteenth-Century Shakespeare Burlesques*, ed. Stanley Wells, 5 vols. (London: Diploma Press, 1977–8), iv. 49.

8. See John W. Velz, 'Undular Structure in *Julius Caesar*', *Modern Language Review*, 66 (1971), 21–30.

9. Welles as quoted by Dennis Kennedy, *Looking at Shakespeare: A Visual History of Twentieth-Century Performance* (Cambridge: Cambridge Univ. Press, 1993), 148; on the stage history see Ripley, *Julius Caesar on Stage*; *Julius Caesar*, ed. David Daniell (London: Thomas Nelson and Sons, 1998), 99–121.

10. The *Life of Antony* joins with the *Life of Alcibiades* to furnish *Timon of Athens*. Recollections of Plutarch appear elsewhere in the canon: Bassanio praises Portia as 'nothing undervalued | To Cato's daughter, Brutus' Portia' (*Merchant of Venice*, 1. 1. 165–6). Unwittingly parodying Plutarch's methods in the *Lives*, Fluellen compares Henry V to Alexander the Pig (*Henry V*, 4. 7. 12–13).

11. I cite *King Leir* from Bullough's reprint, vii. 337–402. Two versions of Shakespeare's play exist, the Quarto and the Folio. On these two texts see the discussion and references provided by Wells and Taylor, *A Textual Companion*, 510 ff. I cite the Quarto in this discussion.

12. Grigori Kozintsev, *King Lear: The Space of Tragedy*, trans. Mary Mackintosh (London: Heinemann, 1977), 72: 'He is the boy from Auschwitz whom they forced to play the violin in an orchestra of dead men; and beat him so that he should play merry tunes. He has childlike, tormented eyes'.

13. Edmund and Edgar, and Cornwall and Albany join other contrasting fraternal pairs: Don John and Don Pedro (*Much Ado About Nothing*), Orlando and Oliver (*As You Like It*), King Hamlet and Claudius, Antonio and Prospero (*Tempest*).

14. These lines are assigned to Edgar in the Folio; see Michael J. Warren, 'Quarto and Folio *King Lear* and the Interpretation of Albany and Edgar', in David Bevington and Jay L. Halio (eds.), *Shakespeare: Pattern of Excelling Nature* (Newark, Del.: Univ. of Delaware Press, 1978), 95–107.

15. On these recent productions see Kennedy, *Looking at Shakespeare*, 304.

16. *Octavia* is spurious but was considered Senecan; this section on Senecan revenge owes to my earlier study, *Shakespeare and Classical Tragedy: The Influence of Seneca* (Oxford: Clarendon Press, 1992, repr. 1997), esp. 11–67. I quote Seneca from the Loeb Classical Library edition, *Tragedies*, trans. Frank Justus Miller, 2 vols. (1917, repr. 1979).

17. The play recalls Ovid's Philomela (*Met.* 6. 438–674), a woman, like Lavinia, raped, mutilated, and revenged; witness Titus: 'For worse than Phi-

lomel you used my daughter, | And worse than Progne I will be revenged'
(5. 2. 193–4).

18. See Richard L. Sterne, *John Gielgud Directs Richard Burton in Hamlet: A Journal of Rehearsals* (New York: Random House, 1967); also David Bevington's succinct summary of the production history of the play, *Hamlet*, ed. Bevington (New York: Bantam, 1988), pp. xxx–xxxix; Anthony B. Dawson, *Shakespeare in Performance: Hamlet* (Manchester: Manchester Univ. Press, 1995).

19. Seneca's portraits of swelling passion and the will to power inspire Shakespeare's tyrant tragedies, *Richard III* and *Macbeth*. His *Hercules Furens* depicts a murderous madness and awakening that supplies the climactic moments of *Othello* and *King Lear*. Senecan traditions provide material for parody in the Pyramus and Thisbe play of *A Midsummer Night's Dream* and for transformation in the late romances.

6.   ROMANCES

1. In 1608 Shakespeare's company, the King's Men, leased Blackfriars Theatre, an intimate, artificially lit playing space that catered to courtly audiences. Though Shakespeare's romances played elsewhere, in the public theatre and at court, their emotional climaxes and special effects well suited the new venue.

2. Edwin Wilson (ed.), *Shaw on Shakespeare* (New York: Dutton, 1961), 64; I quote Jonson above and Greene below from G. Blakemore Evans *et al.* (eds.), *The Riverside Shakespeare*, 2nd edn. (Boston: Houghton Mifflin, 1997), 1969, 1959.

3. On Zadek's production see Dennis Kennedy, *Looking at Shakespeare: A Visual History of Twentieth-Century Performance* (Cambridge: Cambridge Univ. Press, 1993), 272–4; on Noble's, Robert Smallwood (ed.), *Players of Shakespeare 4* (Cambridge: Cambridge Univ. Press, 1998), 60–70 (63).

4. For the quotation and an account of Kemble's production, see Dennis Bartholomeusz, *The Winter's Tale in Performance in England and America* (Cambridge: Cambridge Univ. Press, 1982), 42–63 (61).

5. For references I cite *The Knight's Tale*, ed. A. C. Spearing (Cambridge: Cambridge Univ. Press, 1966, rev. 1995). For the reference to *Troilus and Criseyde* below, I use *Chaucer's Major Poetry*, ed. Albert C. Baugh (New York: Appleton-Century Crofts, 1963).

6. Stylistic studies usually assign to Shakespeare Act 1; Act 2, scene 1; Act 3, scenes 1, 2; Act 5 (except for scene 4); Fletcher seems to have written the middle scenes, which show the rivalry of Palamon and Arcite, and the subplots—the love of the Jailer's Daughter for Palamon and the rustics' entertainment for Theseus. Wells and Taylor, *A Textual Companion*, 625.

7. For discussion see *The Knight's Tale*, ed. Spearing, 18–22.
8. Philip Edwards, 'On the Design of *The Two Noble Kinsmen*', *Review of English Literature*, 5 (1964), 89–105 (104).
9. Philip Brockbank (ed.), *Players of Shakespeare: Essays in Shakespearian Performance by Twelve Players with the Royal Shakespeare Company* (Cambridge: Cambridge Univ. Press, 1985), 74.
10. Paul Taylor in Stanley Wells (ed.), *Shakespeare in the Theatre: An Anthology of Criticism* (Oxford: Clarendon Press, 1997), 317.
11. Robert Henke, *Pastoral Transformations: Italian Tragicomedy and Shakespeare's Late Plays* (Newark, Del.: Univ. of Delaware Press, 1997), 107–19.
12. Brockbank (ed.), *Players of Shakespeare*, 172. For the production and quotation below, see Kennedy, *Looking at Shakespeare*, 283–5 (285).
13. *Italian Drama in Shakespeare's Time* (New Haven: Yale Univ. Press, 1989), 116.
14. Sukanta Chaudhuri, *Renaissance Pastoral and its English Developments* (Oxford: Clarendon Press, 1989), 251–9.

7. SHAKESPEARE AS READER

1. See Kenneth Muir, *The Sources of Shakespeare's Plays* (London: Methuen, 1978), 1–13; Bullough, viii. 341–405; Russ McDonald, *The Bedford Companion to Shakespeare* (Boston: Bedford Books, 1996), 100–17.
2. G. Wilson Knight, *The Wheel of Fire*, 4th edn. (London: Methuen, 1949 repr. 1970), 97–119.
3. Shakespeare often builds tragedies from comic structures; see Susan Snyder, *The Comic Matrix of Shakespeare's Tragedies* (Princeton: Princeton Univ. Press, 1979).
4. See G. Blakemore Evans *et al.* (eds.), *The Riverside Shakespeare*, 2nd edn. (Boston: Houghton Mifflin, 1997), 1963, 1970, 1966.
5. Richard Farmer, *An Essay on Shakespeare's Learning* (Cambridge, 1767).
6. See e.g. Thomas Ray Eaton, *Shakespeare and the Bible* (1860); James Rees, *Shakespeare and the Bible* (1876); Charles Bullock, *Shakespeare's Debt to the Bible* (1879?); James Buchan Brown, *Bible Truths with Shakespearian Parallels* (1886).
7. The Garland annotated bibliographies of individual plays provide a guide to modern findings; more recent discoveries are recorded in the annual bibliographies of *Shakespeare Quarterly*.
8. Stanley Wells, *Shakespeare: The Poet and His Plays* (London: Methuen, 1997), 13.
9. Naseeb Shaheen, 'Shakespeare's Knowledge of Italian', *Shakespeare Survey*, 47 (1994), 161–9.

Further Reading

ELIZABETHAN PRINTING AND READING

Elizabeth L. Eisenstein explores the origins of book-making and the impact of print in *The Printing Press as an Agent of Change: Communications and Cultural Transformations in Early-Modern Europe*, 2 vols. (Cambridge: Cambridge Univ. Press, 1979). Harold Love, *Scribal Publication in Seventeenth-Century England* (Oxford: Clarendon Press, 1993), bears witness to the continuing vitality and importance of manuscripts. Peter W. M. Blayney illuminates Elizabethan printing and the book trade in *The First Folio of Shakespeare* (Washington, DC: Folger Library Publications, 1991), and 'The Publication of Playbooks', in John D. Cox and David Scott Kastan (eds.), *A New History of Early English Drama* (New York: Columbia Univ. Press, 1997), 383–422. William E. Slights, 'The Edifying Margins of Renaissance English Books', *Renaissance Quarterly*, 42 (1989), 682–716, discusses the widespread Renaissance practice of annotation, as does Evelyn Byrd Tribble, *Margins and Marginality: The Printed Page in Early Modern England* (Charlottesville, Va.: Univ. Press of Virginia, 1993). Tessa Watt, *Cheap Print and Popular Piety, 1550–1640* (Cambridge: Cambridge Univ. Press, 1991), analyses the outpouring of religious and devotional writing; Alexandra Halasz, the more secular side of the popular market in *The Marketplace of Print: Pamphlets and the Public Sphere in Early Modern England* (Cambridge: Cambridge Univ. Press, 1997). Two studies of brilliant and flamboyant early modern readers shed light on general reading practices in the period: Anthony Grafton and Lisa Jardine, ' "Studied for Action": How Gabriel Harvey Read His Livy', *Past and Present*, 129 (1990), 30–78; William H. Sherman, *John Dee: The Politics of Reading and Writing in the English Renaissance* (Amherst, Mass.: Univ. of Massachusetts Press, 1995).

SHAKESPEARE'S READING

T. W. Baldwin studies Shakespeare's relation to the Elizabethan grammar-school curriculum in his ponderously learned *William Shakspere's Small Latine and Lesse Greek*, 2 vols. (Urbana, Ill.: University of Illinois Press, 1944). F. P. Wilson contributes a brief, perceptive discussion of the evidence and problems, 'Shakespeare's Reading', *Shakespeare Studies*, 3 (1950), 14–21. Virgil K. Whitaker attempts a synthetic overview, *Shakespeare's Use of Learning: An Inquiry into the Growth of his Mind and Art* (San Marino, Calif.: The

Huntington Library, 1953). Geoffrey Bullough reprints sources, definite, probable, and possible, as well as analogues in *Narrative and Dramatic Sources of Shakespeare*, 8 vols. (London: Routledge and Kegan Paul, 1957–75); he reflects on larger patterns of reading in volume viii. Kenneth Muir analyses the evidence of Shakespeare's reading for each play in *The Sources of Shakespeare's Plays* (London: Methuen, 1977), a gem of clarity and concision.

Full discussion of sources and Shakespeare's use of them appears in editions of his individual plays and poems, notably those in the Oxford, Cambridge, and New Arden series. On Shakespeare's classical reading, see John W. Velz's exhaustive annotated bibliography, *Shakespeare and the Classical Tradition: A Critical Guide to Commentary, 1660–1960* (Minneapolis: Univ. of Minnesota Press, 1968, now being updated); Reuben A. Brower's wide-ranging and literate study, *Hero and Saint: Shakespeare and the Graeco-Roman Heroic Tradition* (New York: Oxford Univ. Press. 1971); Robert S. Miola, *Shakespeare and Classical Tragedy: The Influence of Seneca* (Oxford: Clarendon Press, 1992, repr. 1997); also his *Shakespeare and Classical Comedy: The Influence of Plautus and Terence* (Oxford: Clarendon Press, 1994, repr. 1997); Charles and Michelle Martindale's readable survey, *Shakespeare and the Uses of Antiquity* (London: Routledge, 1990); Jonathan Bate's incisive *Shakespeare and Ovid* (Oxford: Clarendon Press, 1993). Some helpful studies of Shakespeare's medieval reading include Bernard Spivack's treatment of the Vice figure, *Shakespeare and the Allegory of Evil: The History of a Metaphor in Relation to his Major Villains* (New York: Columbia Univ. Press, 1958); two accounts of Shakespeare's use of Chaucer: Ann Thompson, *Shakespeare's Chaucer: A Study in Literary Origins* (New York: Barnes and Noble, 1978), and E. Talbot Donaldson, *The Swan at the Well: Shakespeare Reading Chaucer* (New Haven: Yale Univ. Press, 1985). Howard Felperin discusses medieval traditions as well as texts in *Shakespearean Representation: Mimesis and Modernity in Elizabethan Tragedy* (Princeton: Princeton Univ. Press, 1977); so likewise (though focusing on drama), Alan C. Dessen, *Shakespeare and the Late Moral Plays* (Lincoln, Nebr.: Univ. of Nebraska Press, 1986).

Lucid and comprehensive on individual texts and general backgrounds are Leo Salingar, *Shakespeare and the Traditions of Comedy* (Cambridge: Cambridge Univ. Press, 1974), and Emrys Jones, *The Origins of Shakespeare* (Oxford: Clarendon Press, 1977). Peter Saccio provides a sensible guide to Shakespeare's use of Holinshed and other historical sources, *Shakespeare's English Kings: History, Chronicle, and Drama* (New York: Oxford Univ. Press, 1977). Concerned with Shakespeare's reading of texts as well as his response to literary culture and tradition, Louise George Clubb has ignited interest in Shakespeare's Italian backgrounds, *Italian Drama in Shakespeare's Time* (New Haven: Yale Univ. Press, 1989); following her lead, Robert Henke has fruitfully examined Shakespeare's late plays in the light of Italian poetic theory and practice, *Pastoral Transformations: Italian Tragicomedy and Shakespeare's Late Plays* (Newark, Del.: Univ. of Delaware Press, 1997). Recent studies which discuss Shakespeare's reading include Peter Holland, 'Theseus' Shadows in *A Midsummer Night's Dream*', *Shakespeare Survey*, 47 (1994), 139–51; Martha Tuck Rozett, *Talking Back to Shakespeare* (Newark, Del.: Univ. of Delaware Press, 1994); Stephen J. Lynch, *Shakespearean Intertextuality: Studies in Selected Sources and Plays* (Westport, Conn.: Greenwood Press, 1998); and five essays under the rubric 'Reading' in David Scott Kastan (ed.), *A Companion to Shakespeare* (Oxford: Blackwell, 1999), 139–222.